Oh My Goddess!

ああっ女神さまっ

24

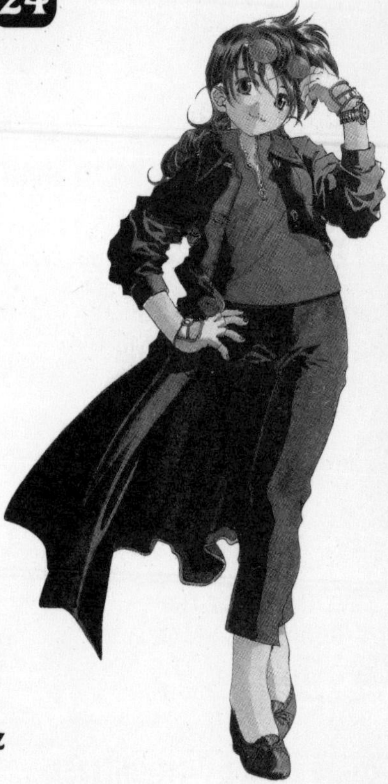

STORY AND ART BY
Kosuke Fujishima

TRANSLATION BY
Dana Lewis AND Lea Hernandez

LETTERING AND TOUCH-UP BY
Tom Orzechowski

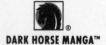

DARK HORSE MANGA™

CHAPTER 149

Running Dialogue

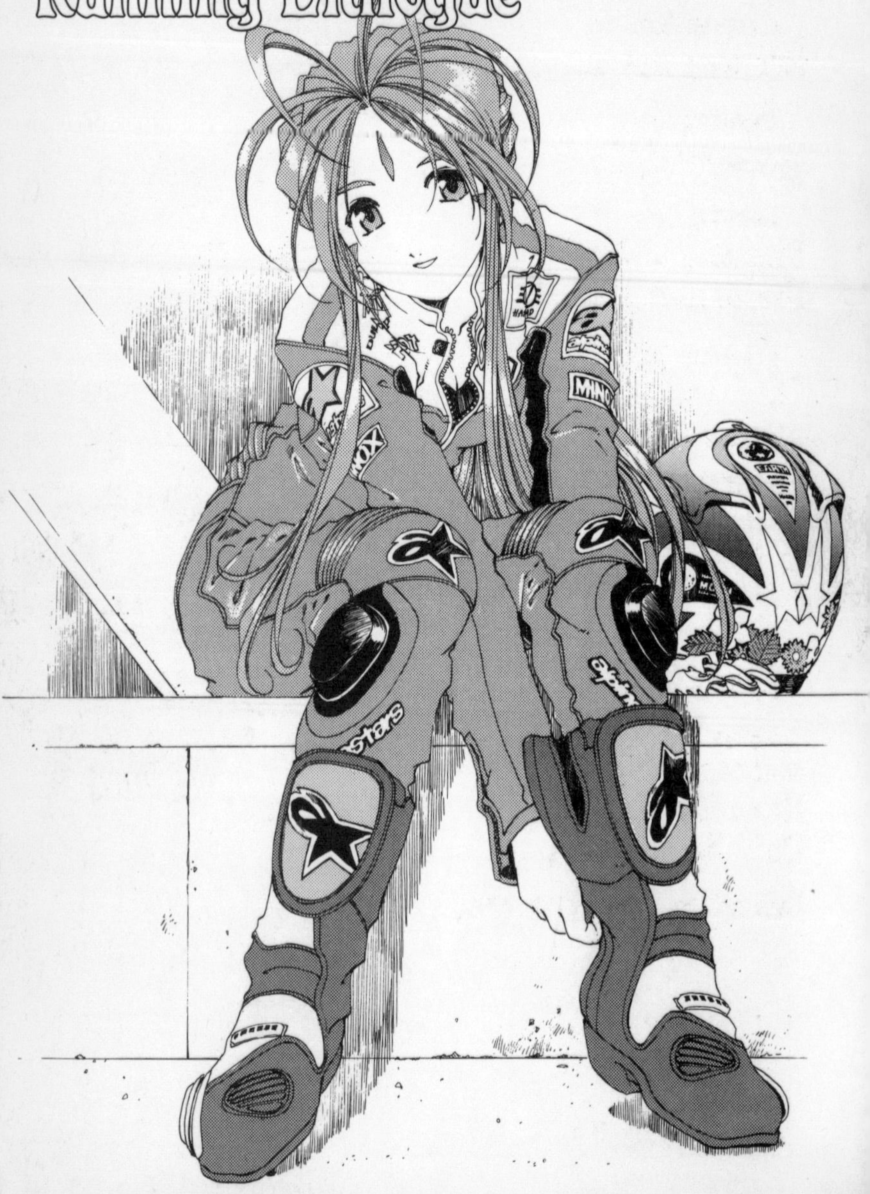

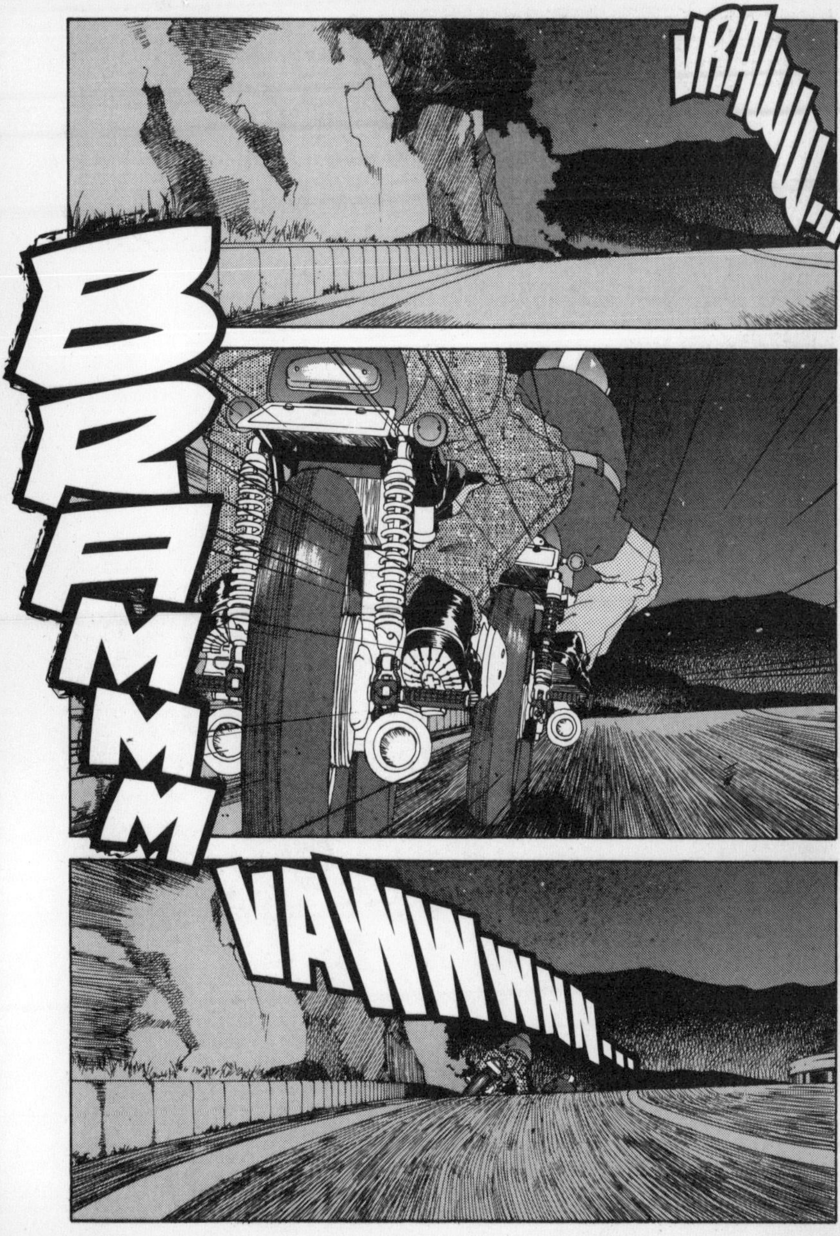
VRAWWW...
BRAMMMM
VAWWWNNN...

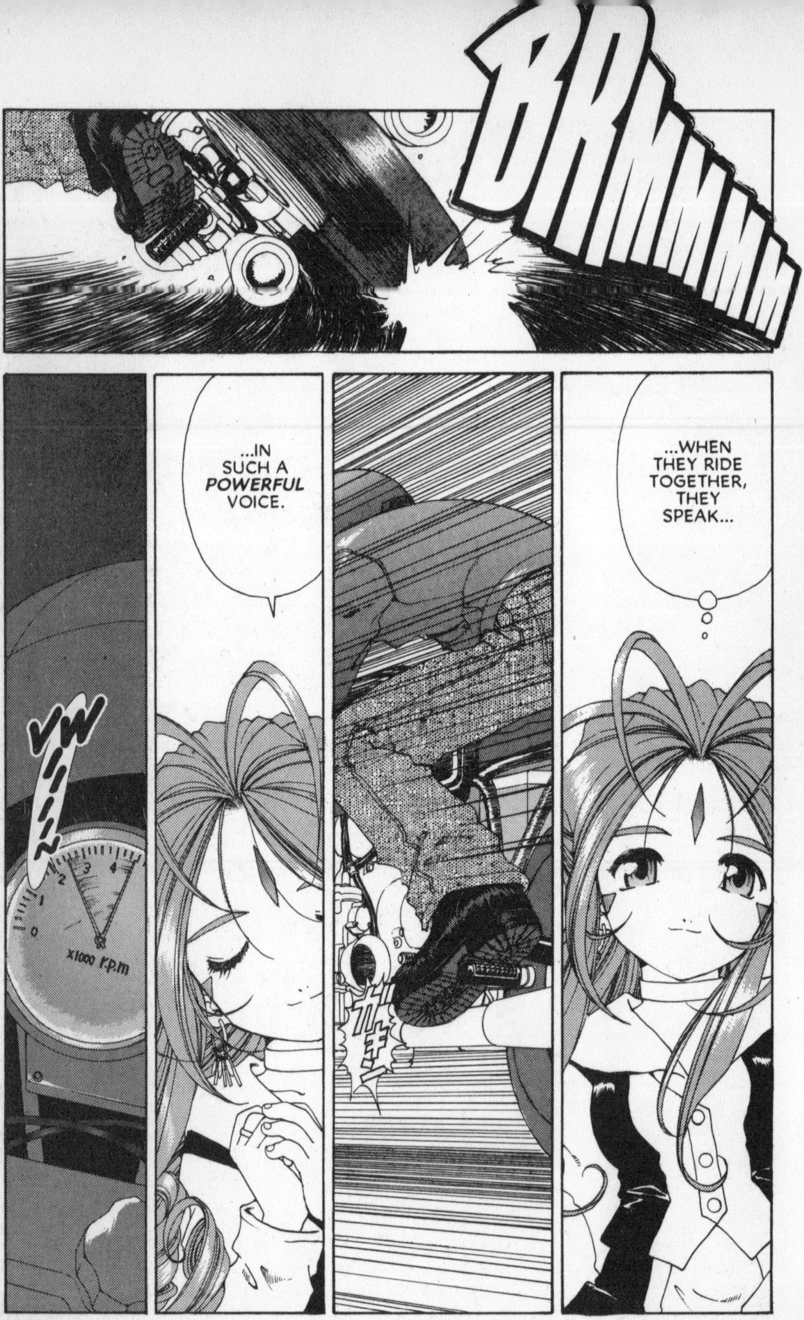
BRMMMMM
...WHEN THEY RIDE TOGETHER, THEY SPEAK...
...IN SUCH A *POWERFUL* VOICE.
VWIIIIN
x1000 r.p.m

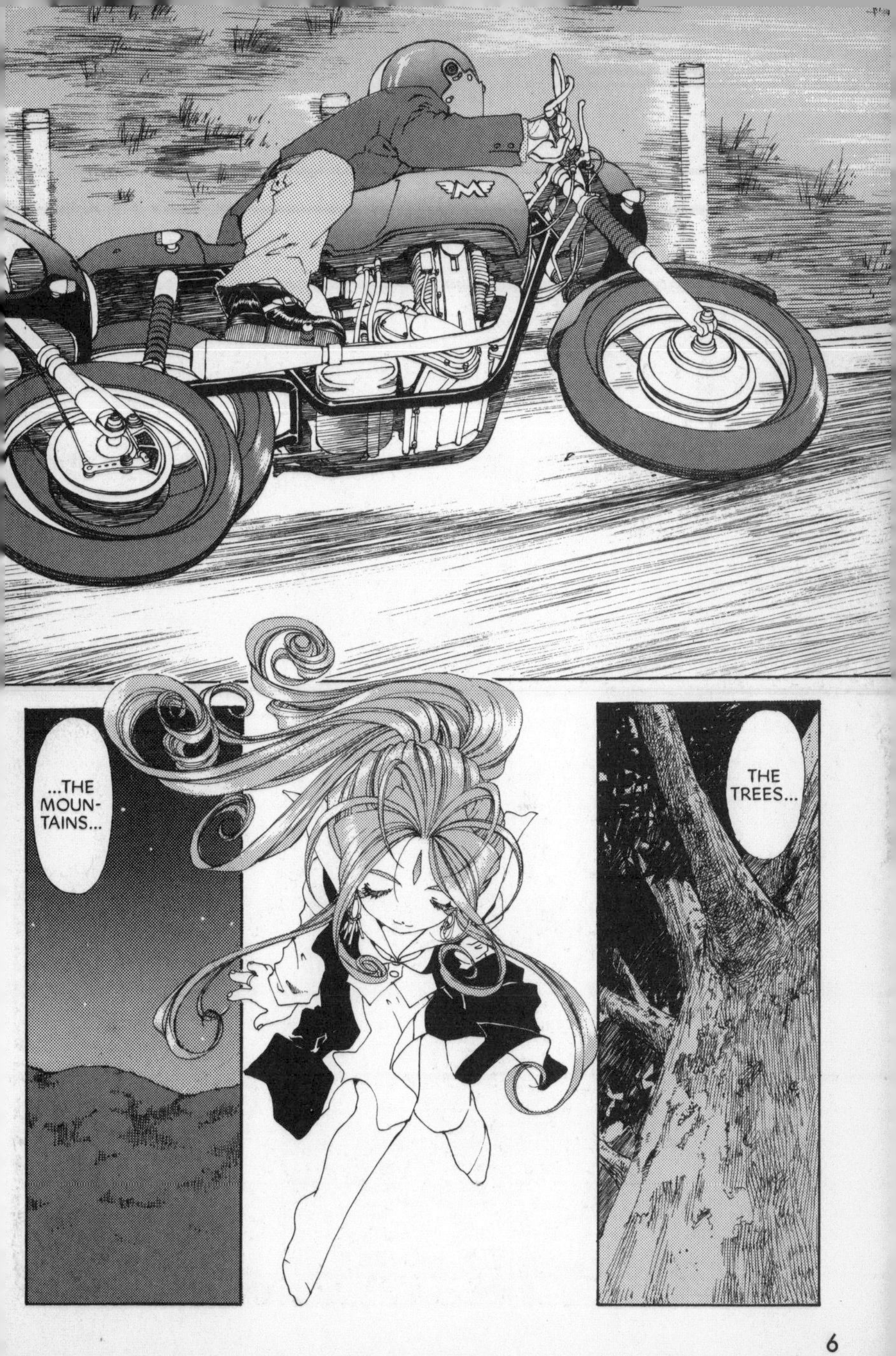
THE TREES...
...THE MOUNTAINS...

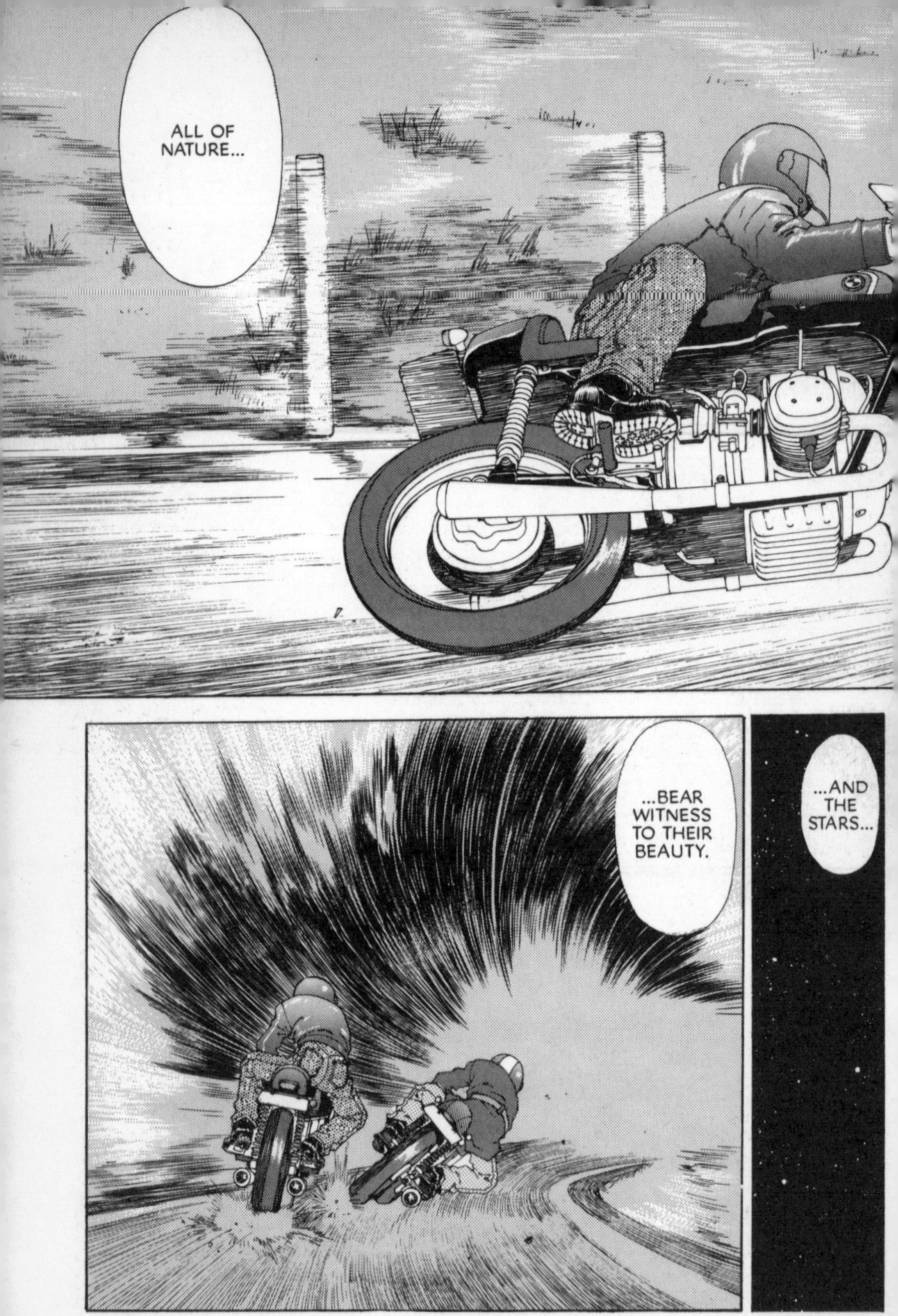
ALL OF NATURE...
...AND THE STARS...
...BEAR WITNESS TO THEIR BEAUTY.

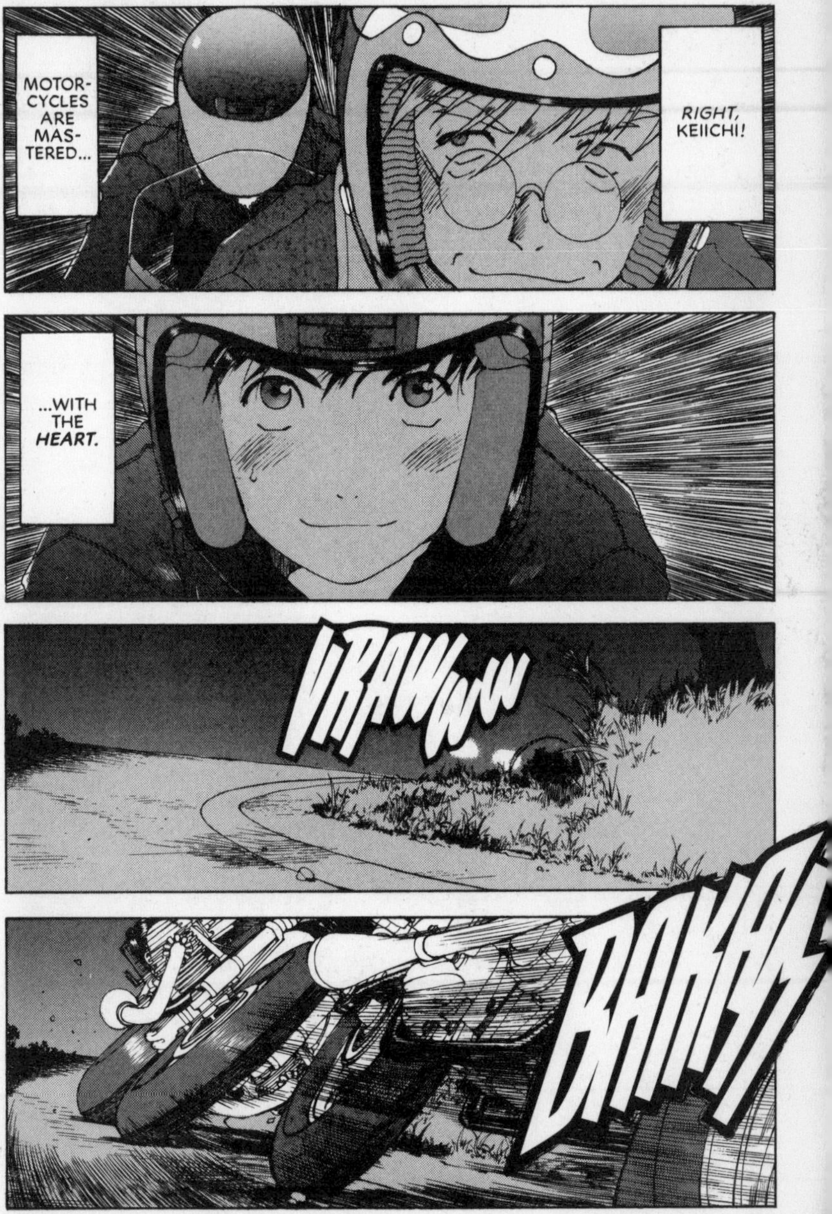
RIGHT, KEIICHI!
MOTOR-CYCLES ARE MAS-TERED...
...WITH THE *HEART.*
VRAWWWW

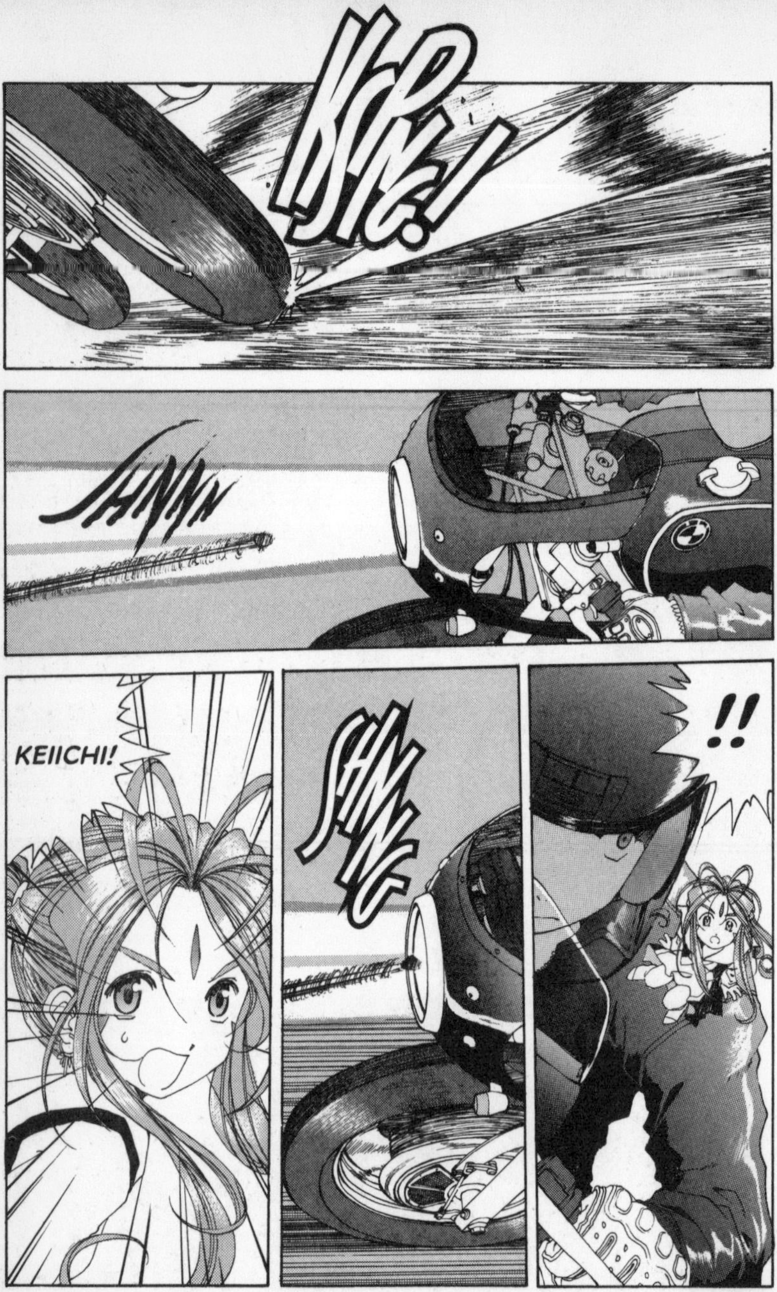
!!
KEIICHI!

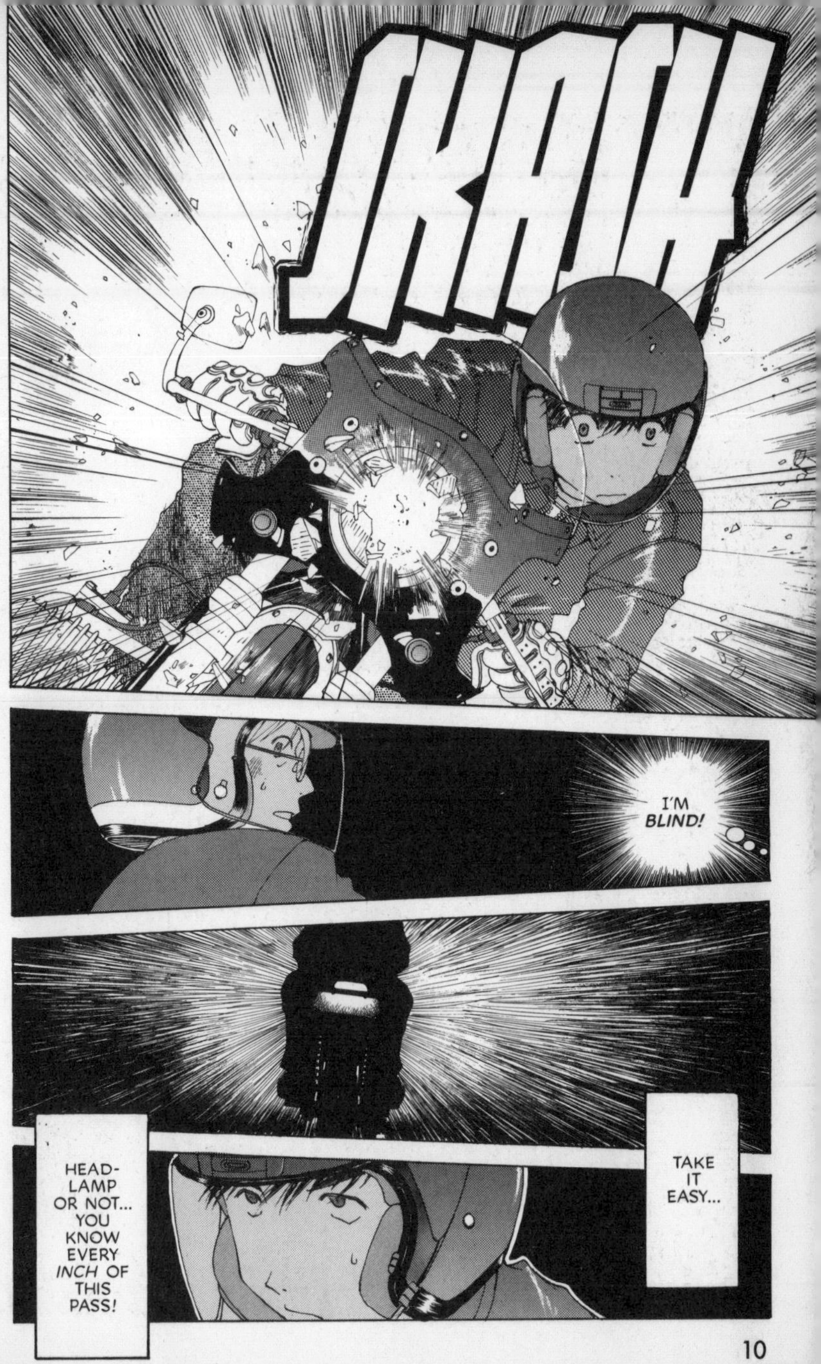
SKRAK!
I'M *BLIND!*
TAKE IT EASY...
HEAD-LAMP OR NOT... YOU KNOW EVERY *INCH* OF THIS PASS!

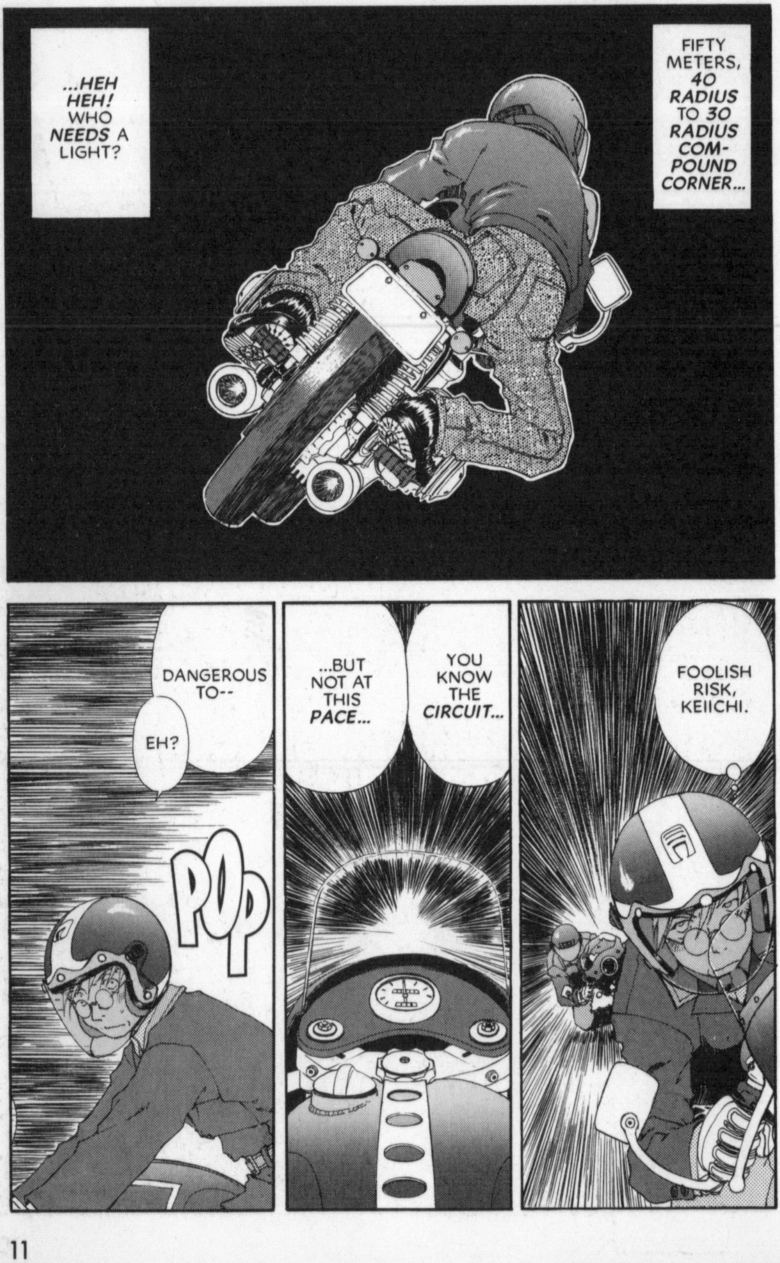
FIFTY METERS, *40* RADIUS TO *30* RADIUS COMPOUND CORNER...
...HEH HEH! WHO *NEEDS* A LIGHT?
FOOLISH RISK, KEIICHI.
YOU KNOW THE *CIRCUIT*...
...BUT NOT AT THIS *PACE*...
DANGEROUS TO--
EH?
POP

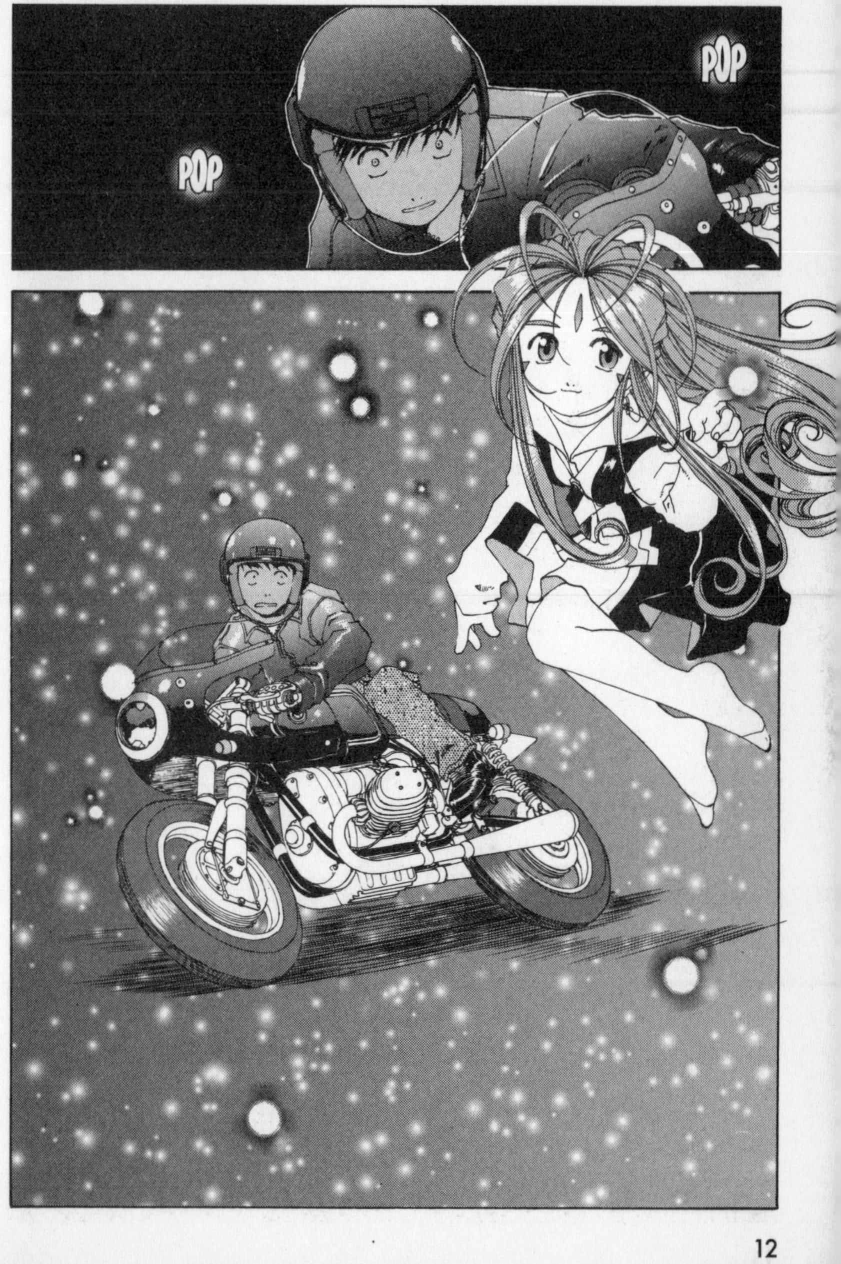
POP
POP

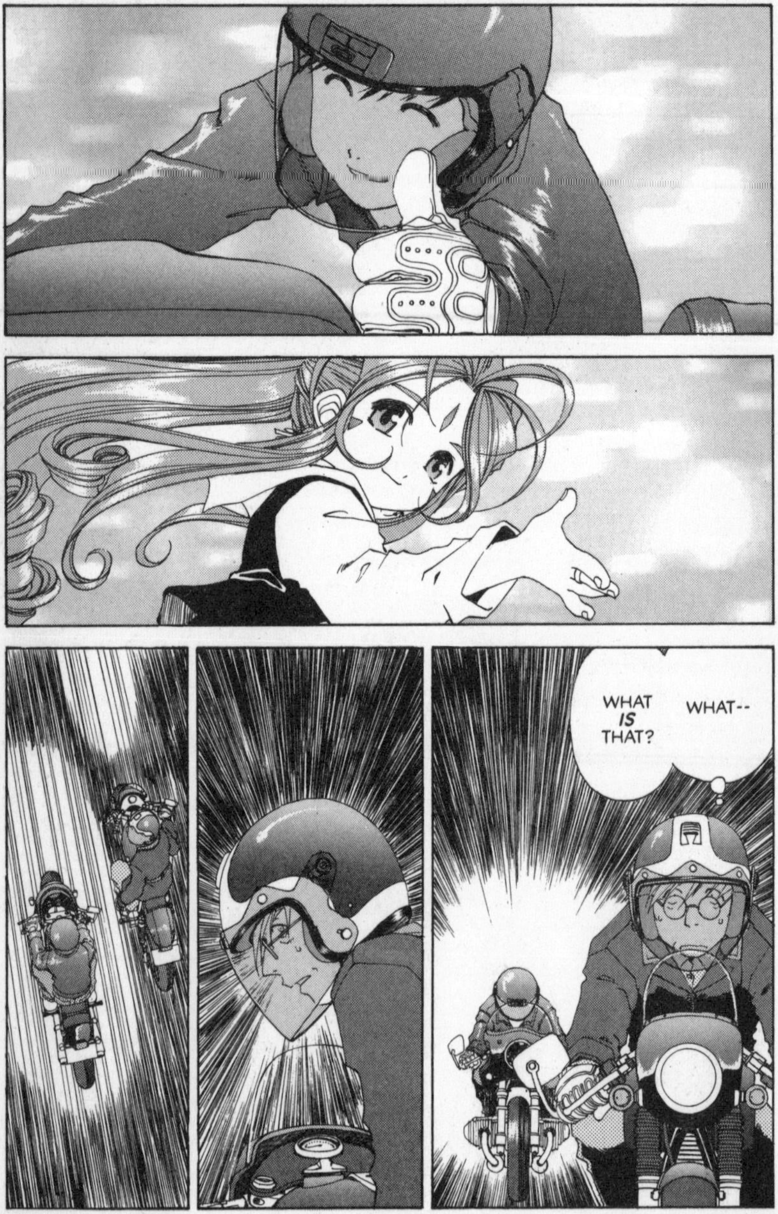
WHAT--
WHAT *IS* THAT?

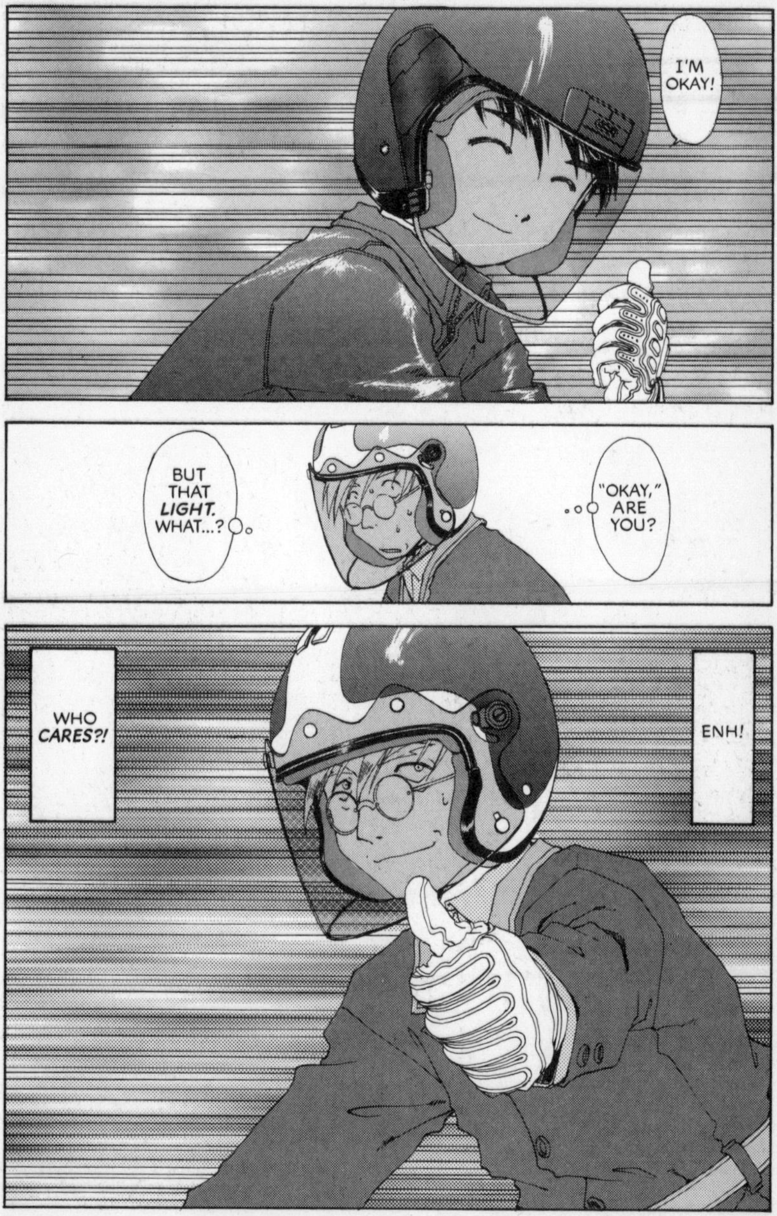
I'M OKAY!
"OKAY," ARE YOU?
BUT THAT *LIGHT.* WHAT...?
ENH!
WHO *CARES?!*

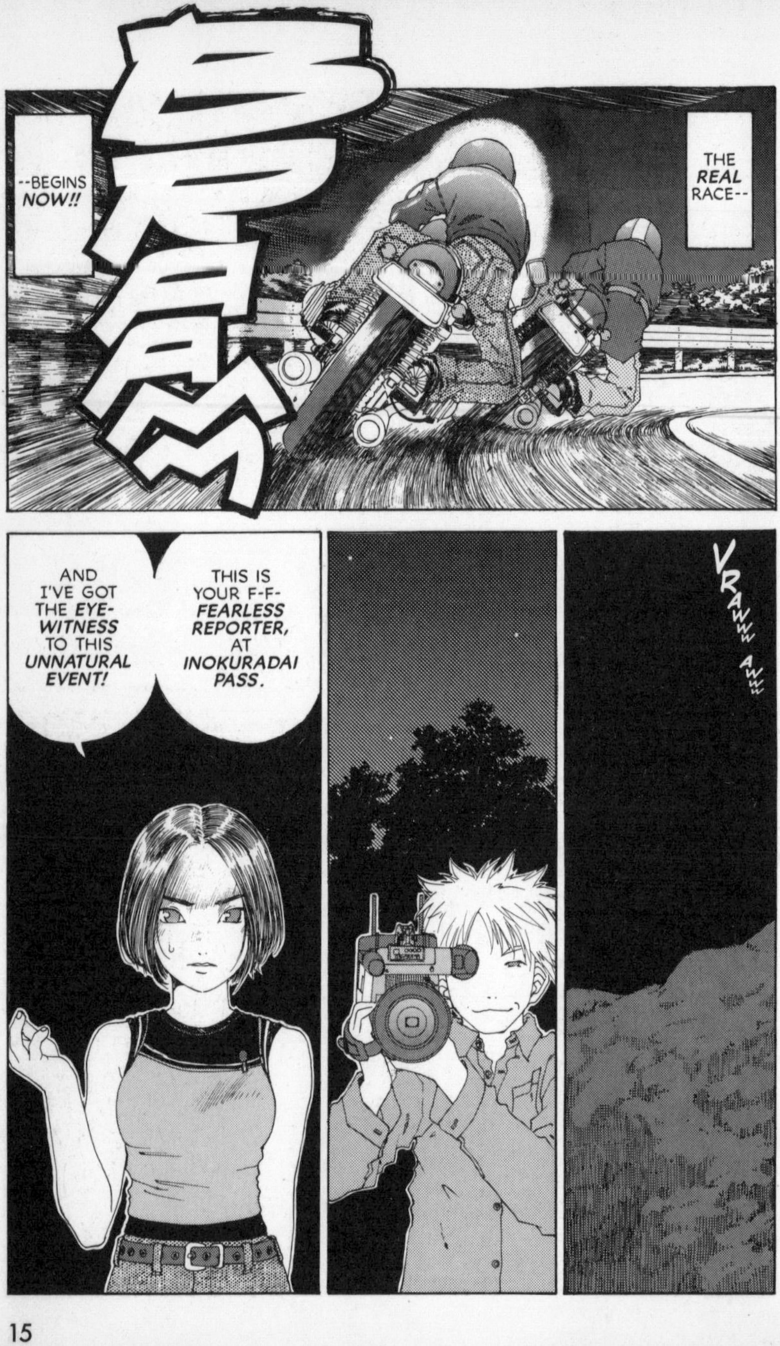
THE *REAL* RACE--
--BEGINS *NOW!!*
BRAAM
VRAWWW AWWW
THIS IS YOUR F-F- *FEARLESS REPORTER,* AT *INOKURADAI PASS*.
AND I'VE GOT THE *EYE-WITNESS* TO THIS *UNNATURAL EVENT!*

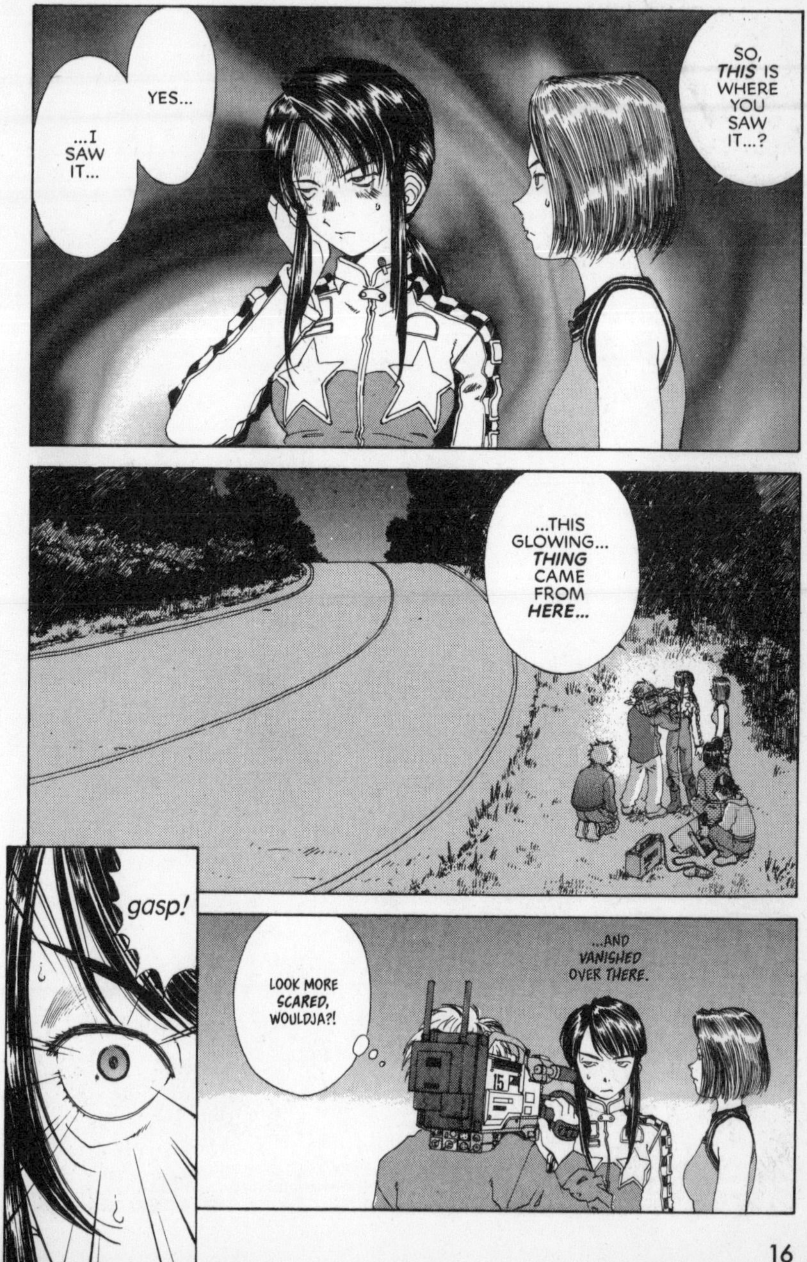
SO, THIS IS WHERE YOU SAW IT...?
YES...
...I SAW IT...
...THIS GLOWING... THING CAME FROM HERE...
...AND VANISHED OVER THERE.
LOOK MORE SCARED, WOULDJA?!
gasp!

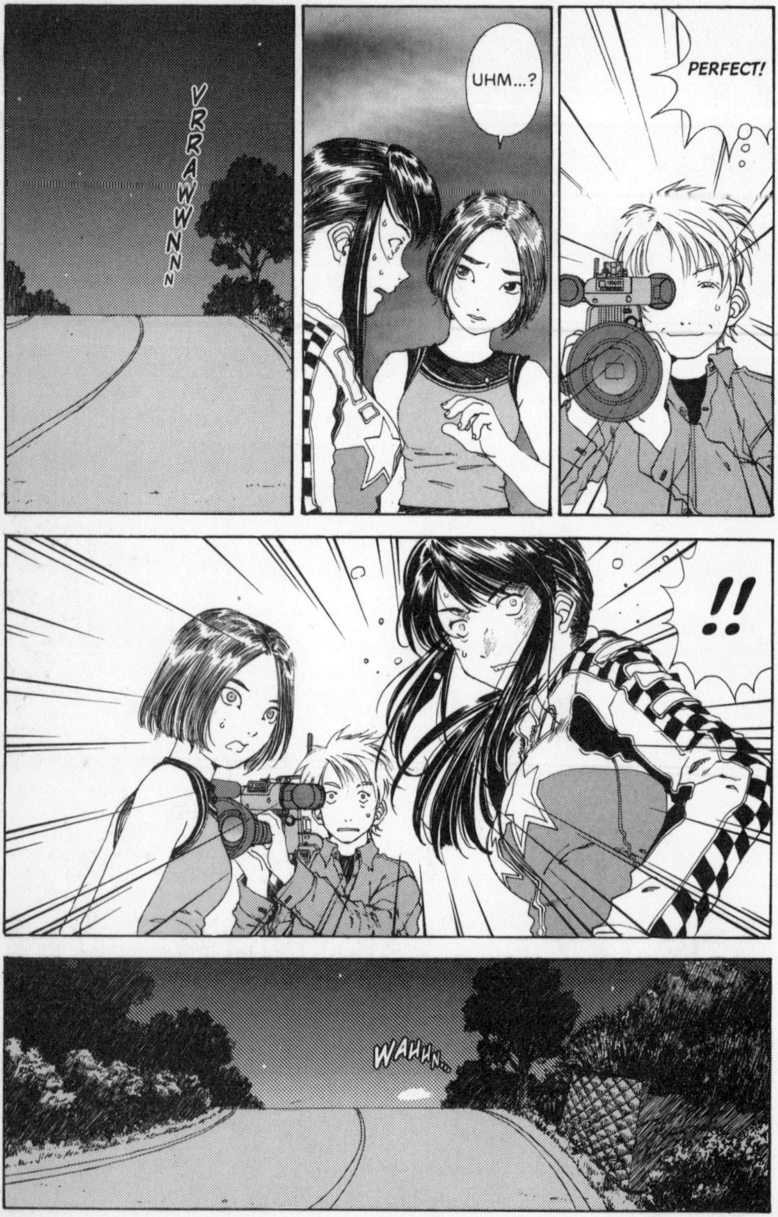
PERFECT!
UHM...?
VRRAWWNNN
!!
WAHHN...

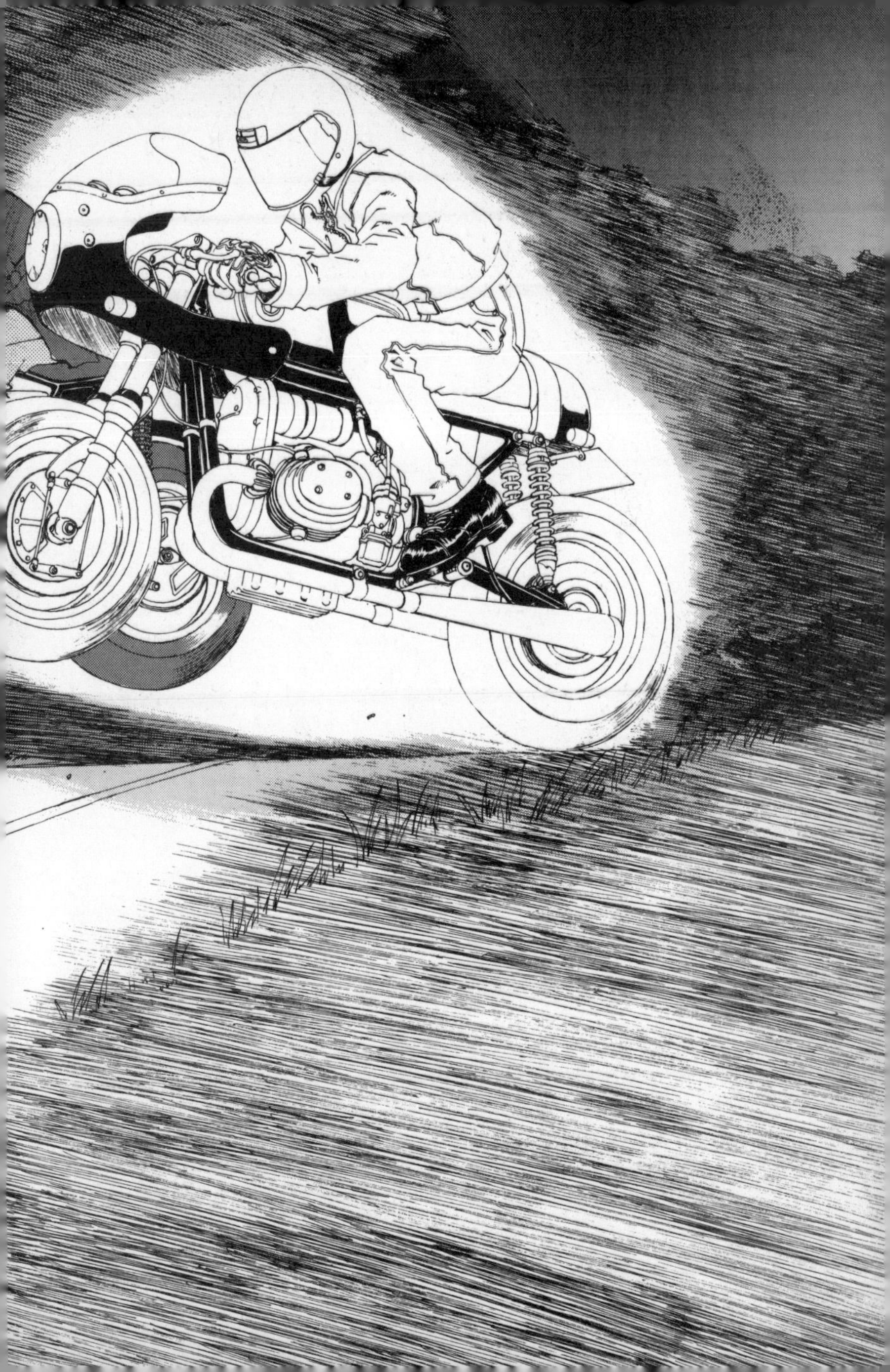

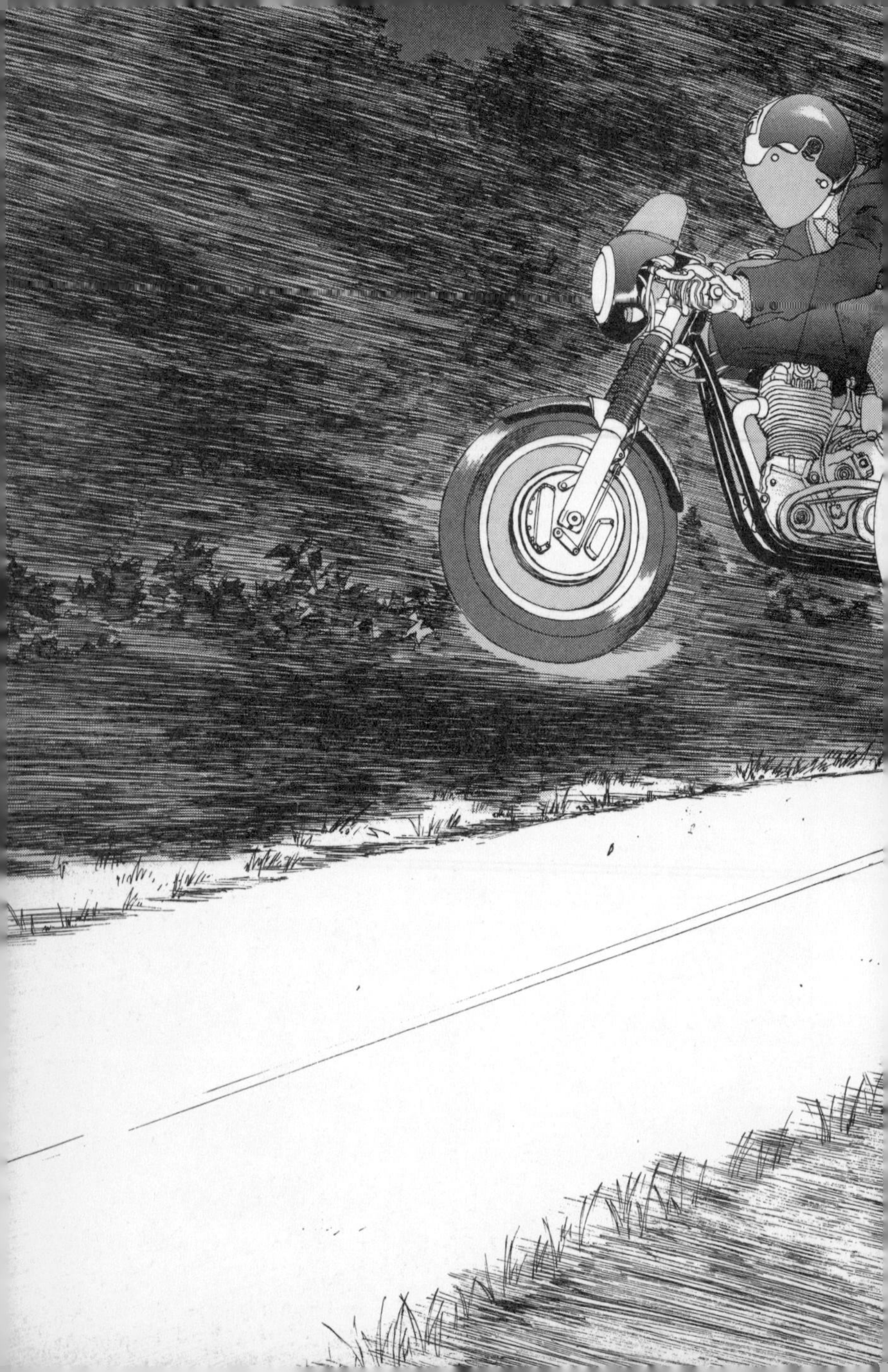

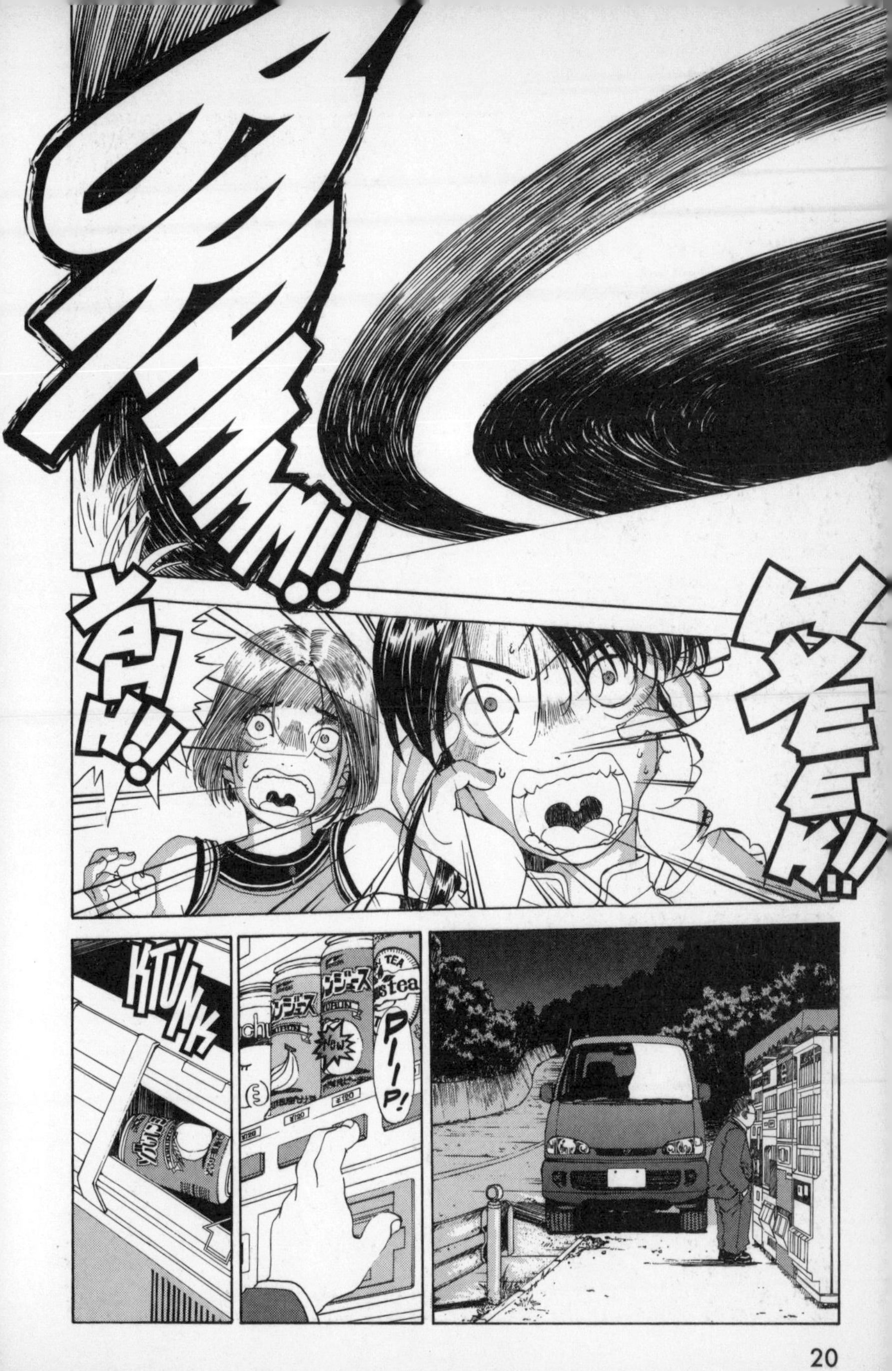
SLAMM!!
YEEEK!!
YAAH!!
P--P!
KTUNK

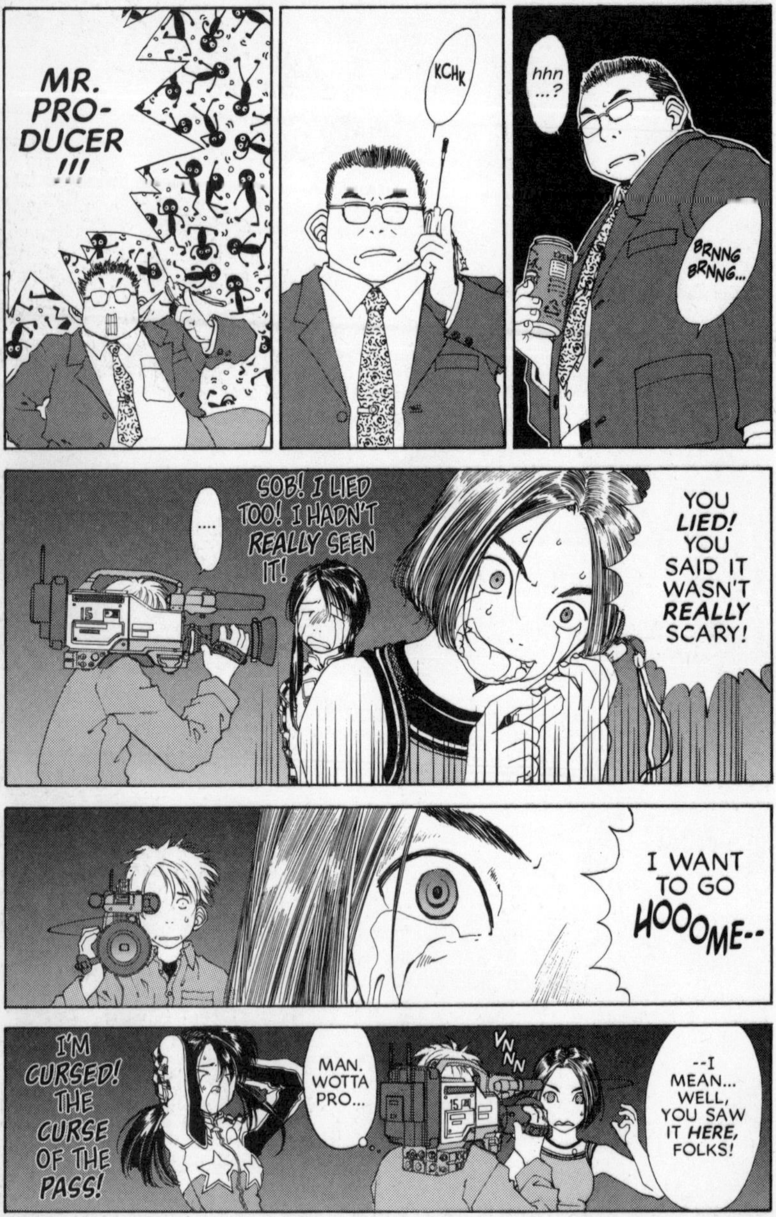
hhn ...?
BRNNG BRNNG...
KCHK
MR. PRO-DUCER!!!
YOU LIED! YOU SAID IT WASN'T REALLY SCARY!
SOB! I LIED TOO! I HADN'T REALLY SEEN IT!
.....
I WANT TO GO HOOOME--
--I MEAN... WELL, YOU SAW IT HERE, FOLKS!
VNNN
MAN. WOTTA PRO...
I'M CURSED! THE CURSE OF THE PASS!

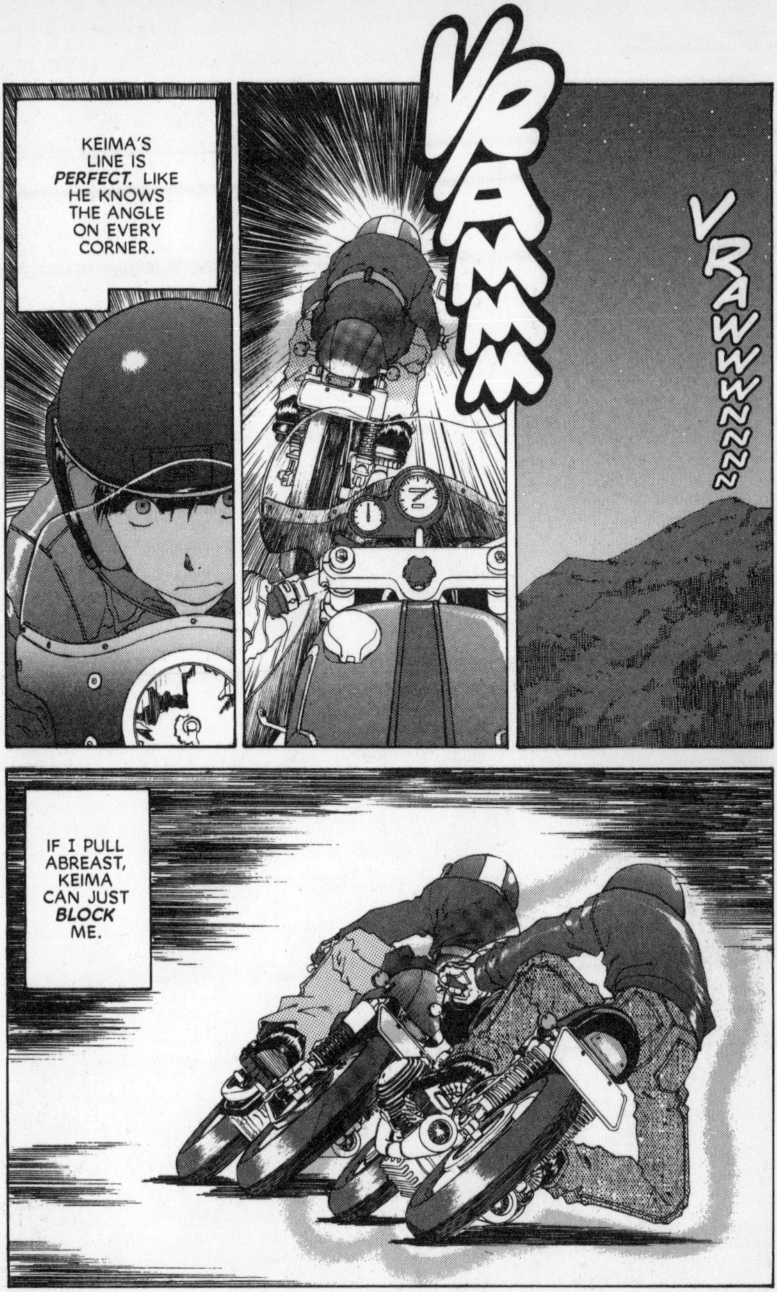
VRAWWWNNNN
VRAMMM
KEIMA'S LINE IS *PERFECT.* LIKE HE KNOWS THE ANGLE ON EVERY CORNER.
IF I PULL ABREAST, KEIMA CAN JUST *BLOCK* ME.

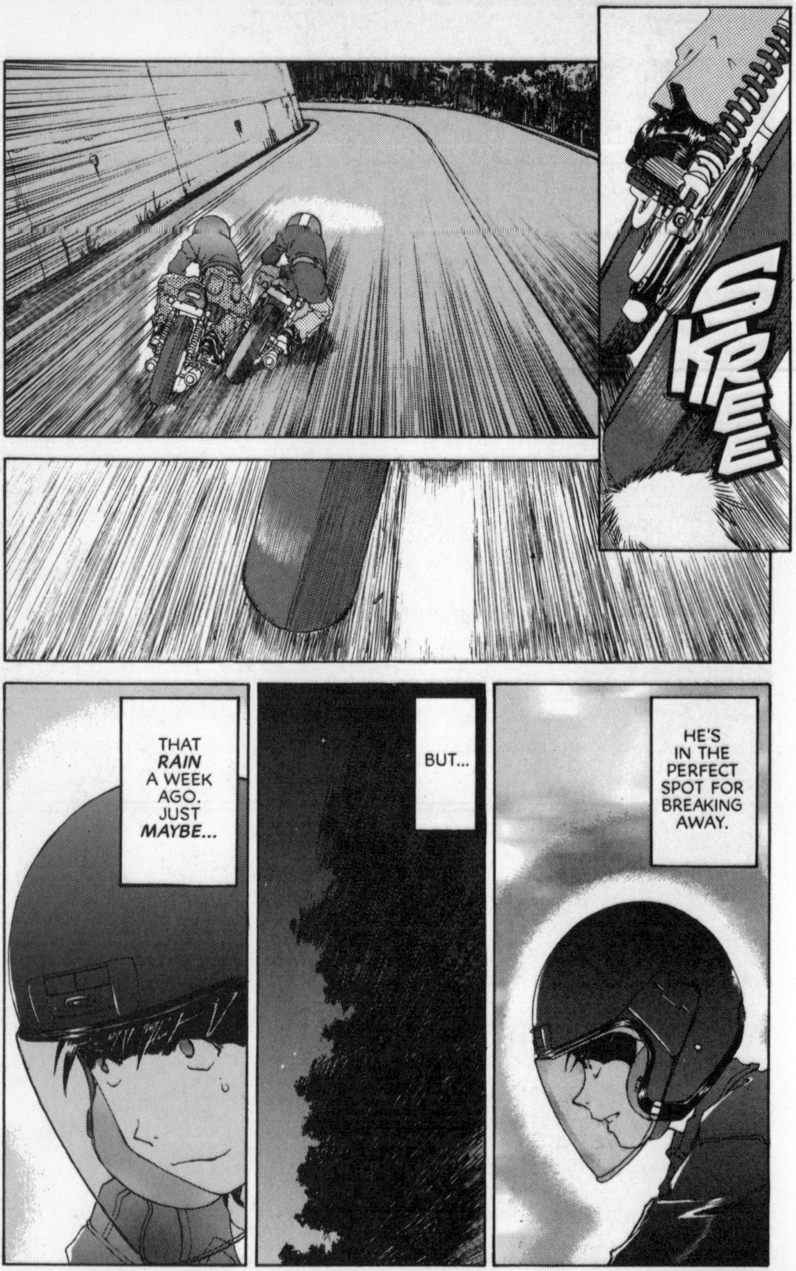
SKREE
HE'S IN THE PERFECT SPOT FOR BREAKING AWAY.
BUT...
THAT *RAIN* A WEEK AGO. JUST *MAYBE...*

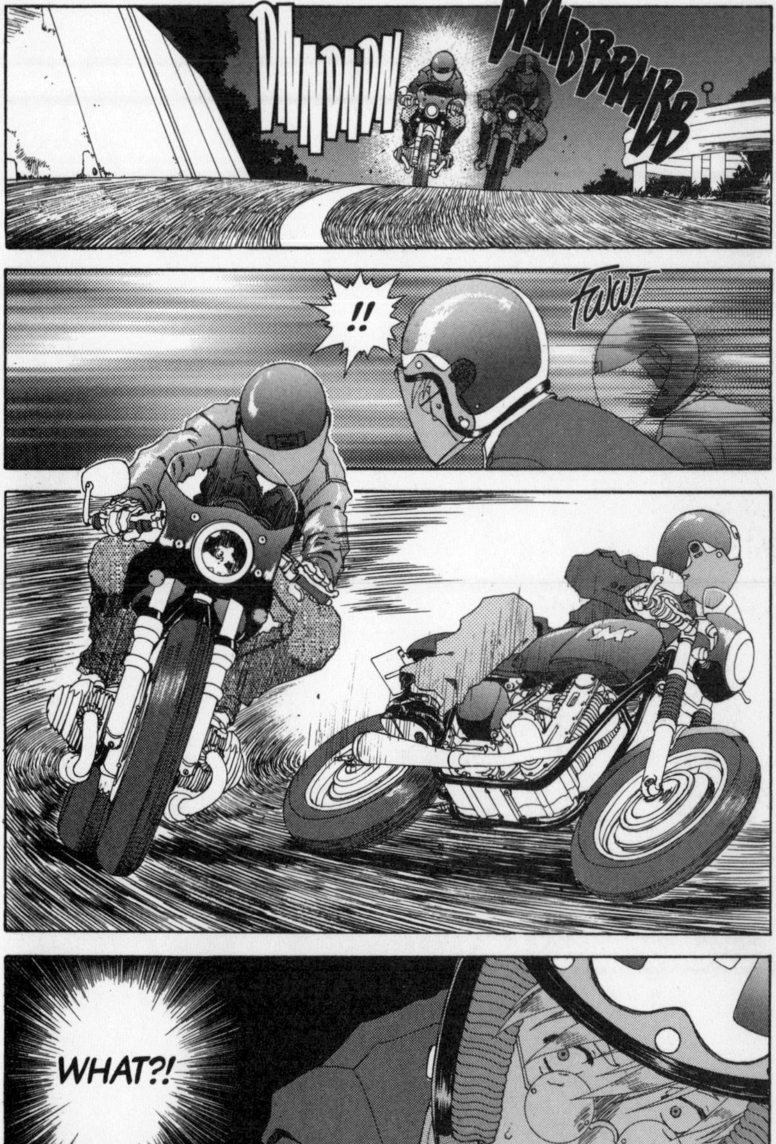

BRMBBRMBB
DNNDNDN
FWUT
!!
WHAT?!

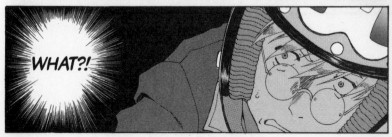

CHAPTER 150

The Path of Belief

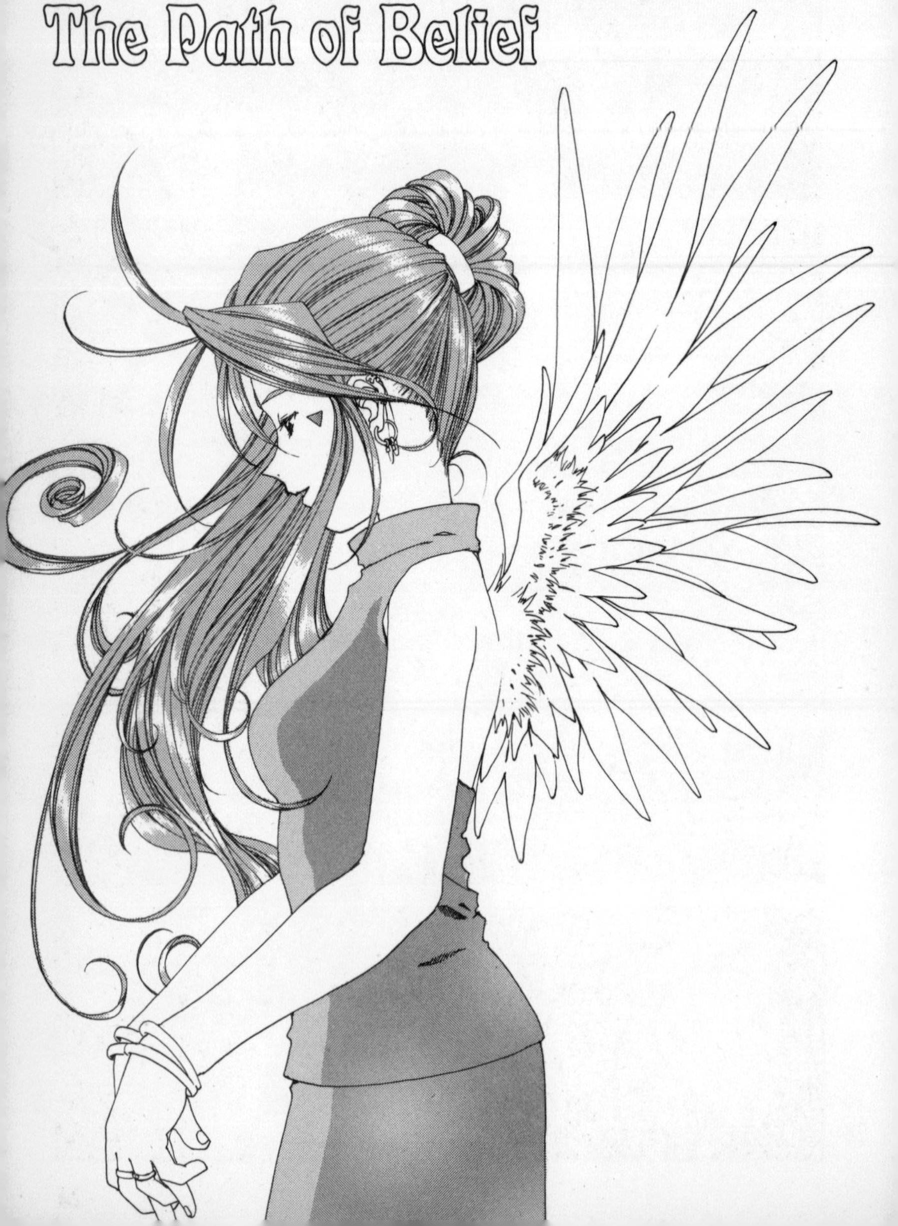

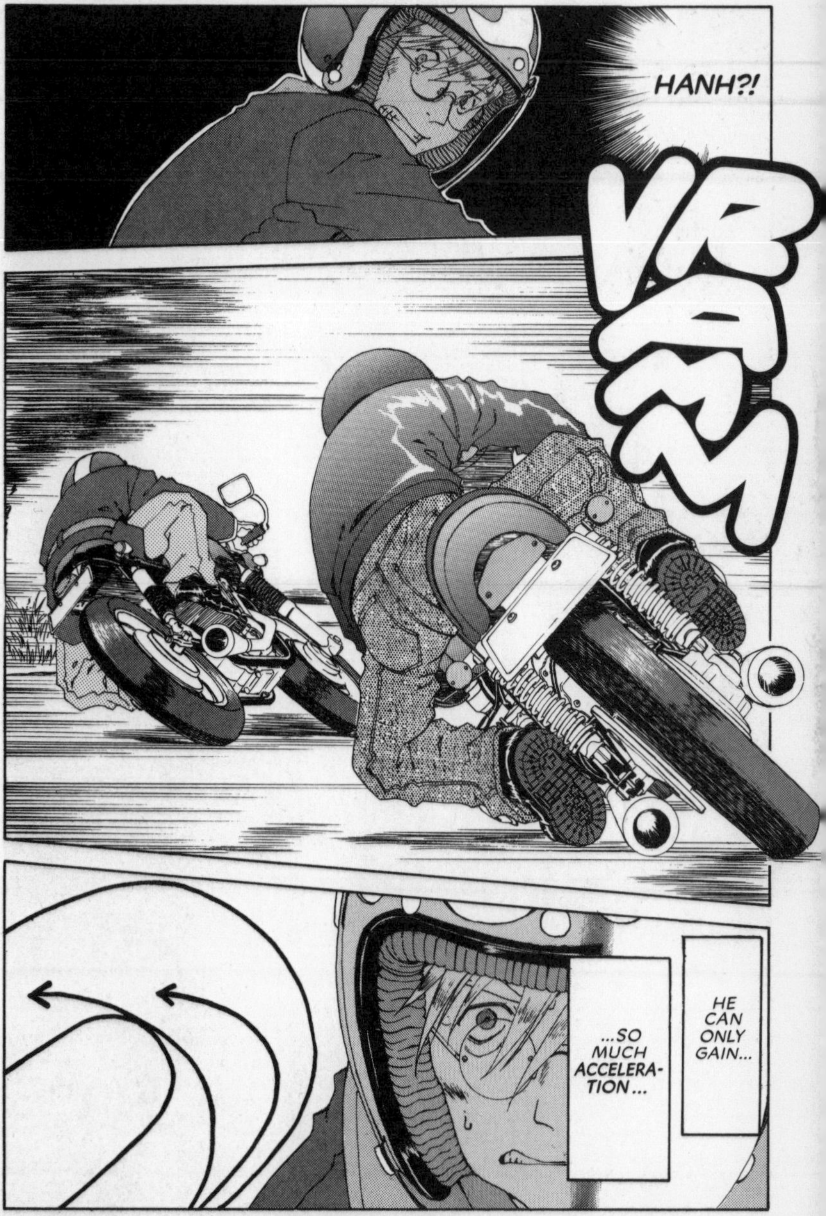
HANH?!
VRAM
HE CAN ONLY GAIN...
...SO MUCH ACCELERATION...

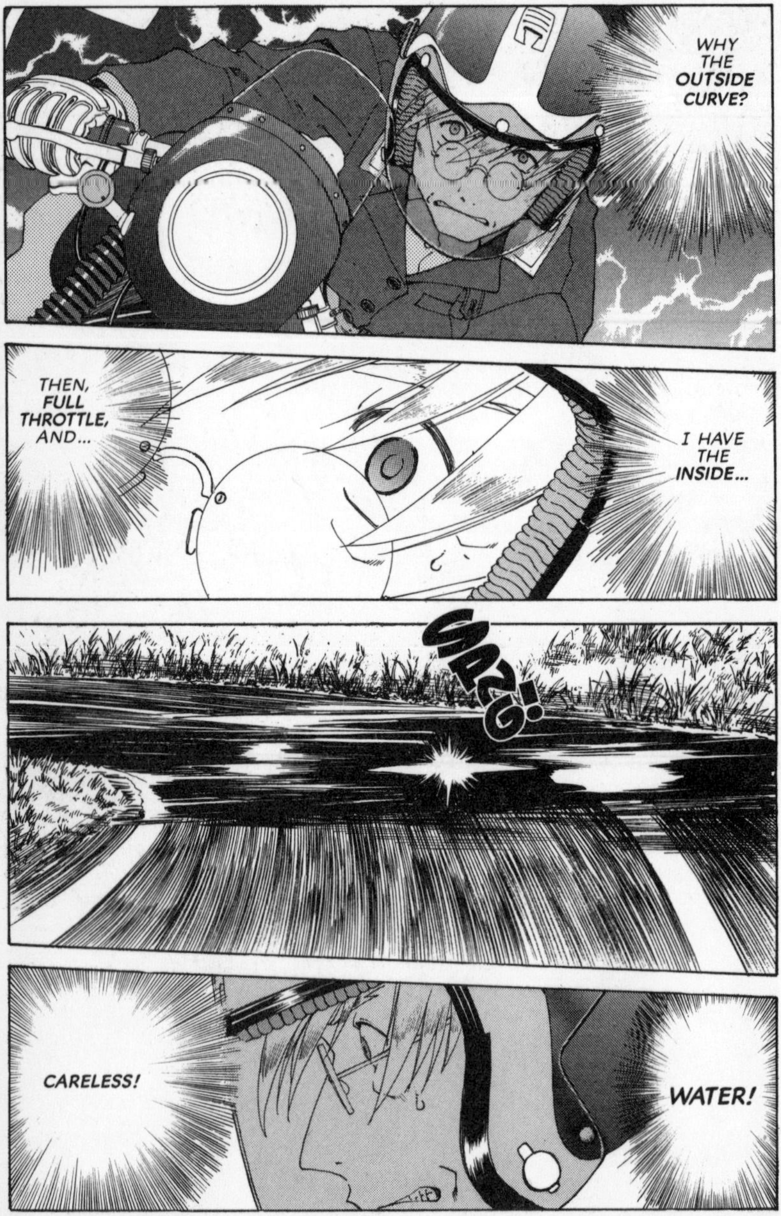
WHY THE OUTSIDE CURVE?
I HAVE THE INSIDE...
THEN, FULL THROTTLE, AND...
SPZG!
WATER!
CARELESS!

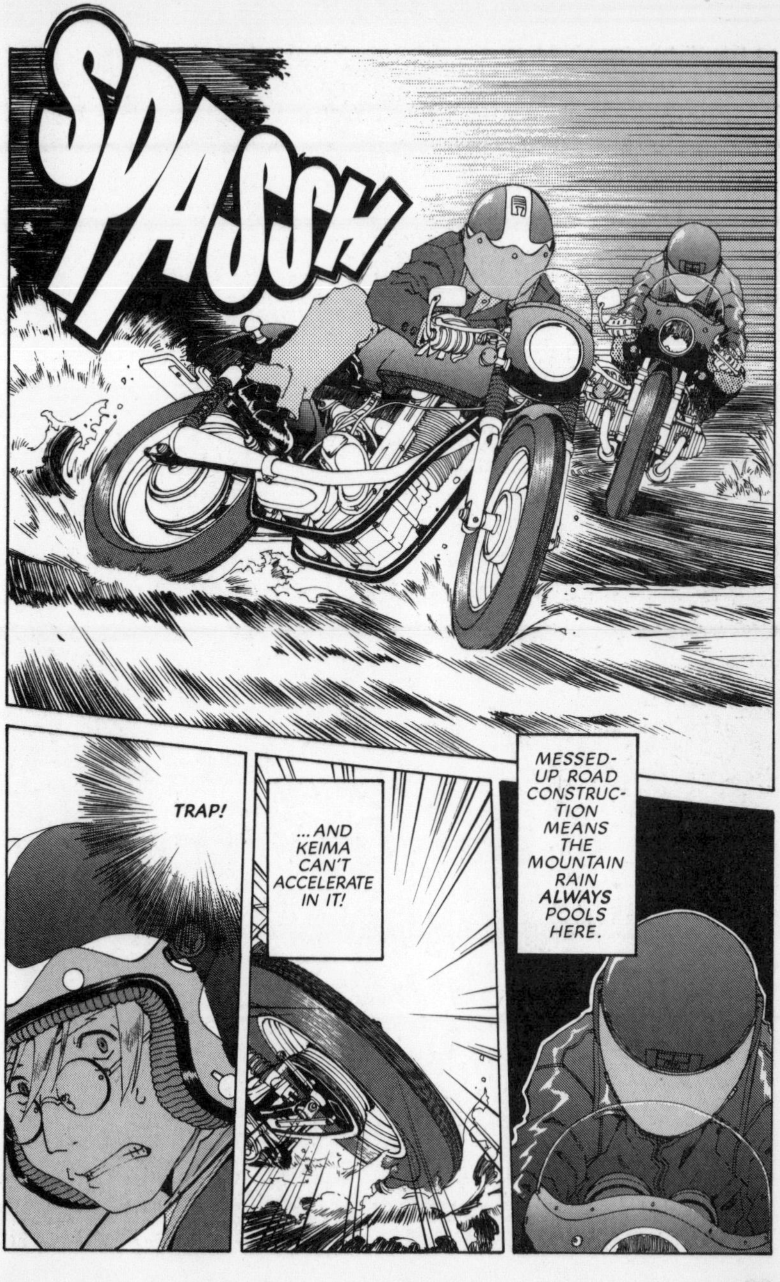
SPASSH
MESSED-UP ROAD CONSTRUCTION MEANS THE MOUNTAIN RAIN **ALWAYS** POOLS HERE.
...AND KEIMA CAN'T ACCELERATE IN IT!
TRAP!

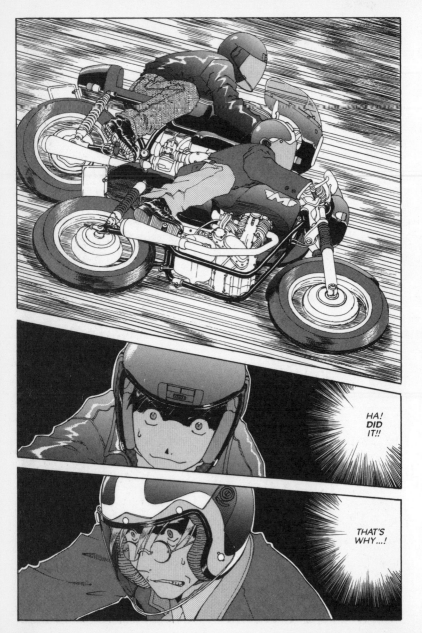

HA!
DID
IT!!

THAT'S
WHY...!

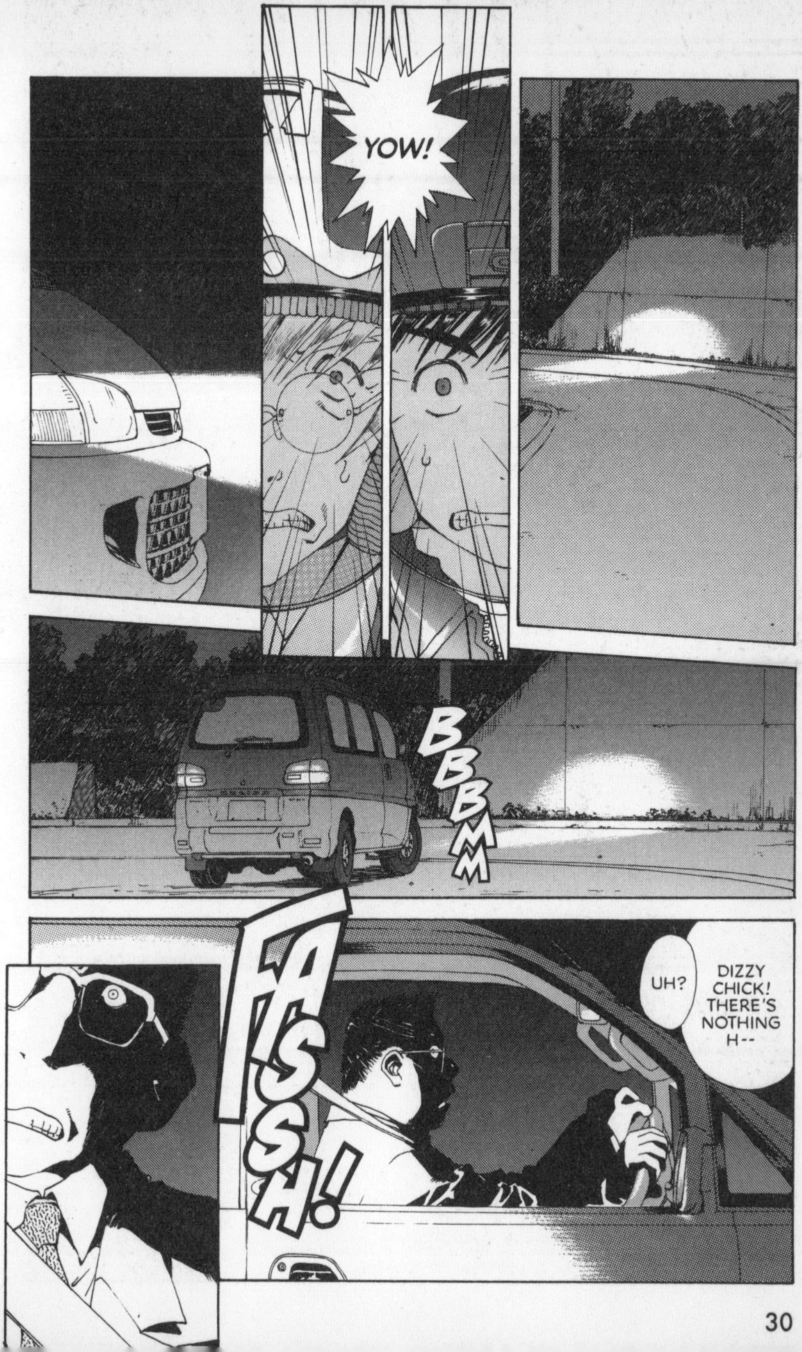
YOW!
BBBMM
DIZZY CHICK! THERE'S NOTHING H--
UH?
FASSH!

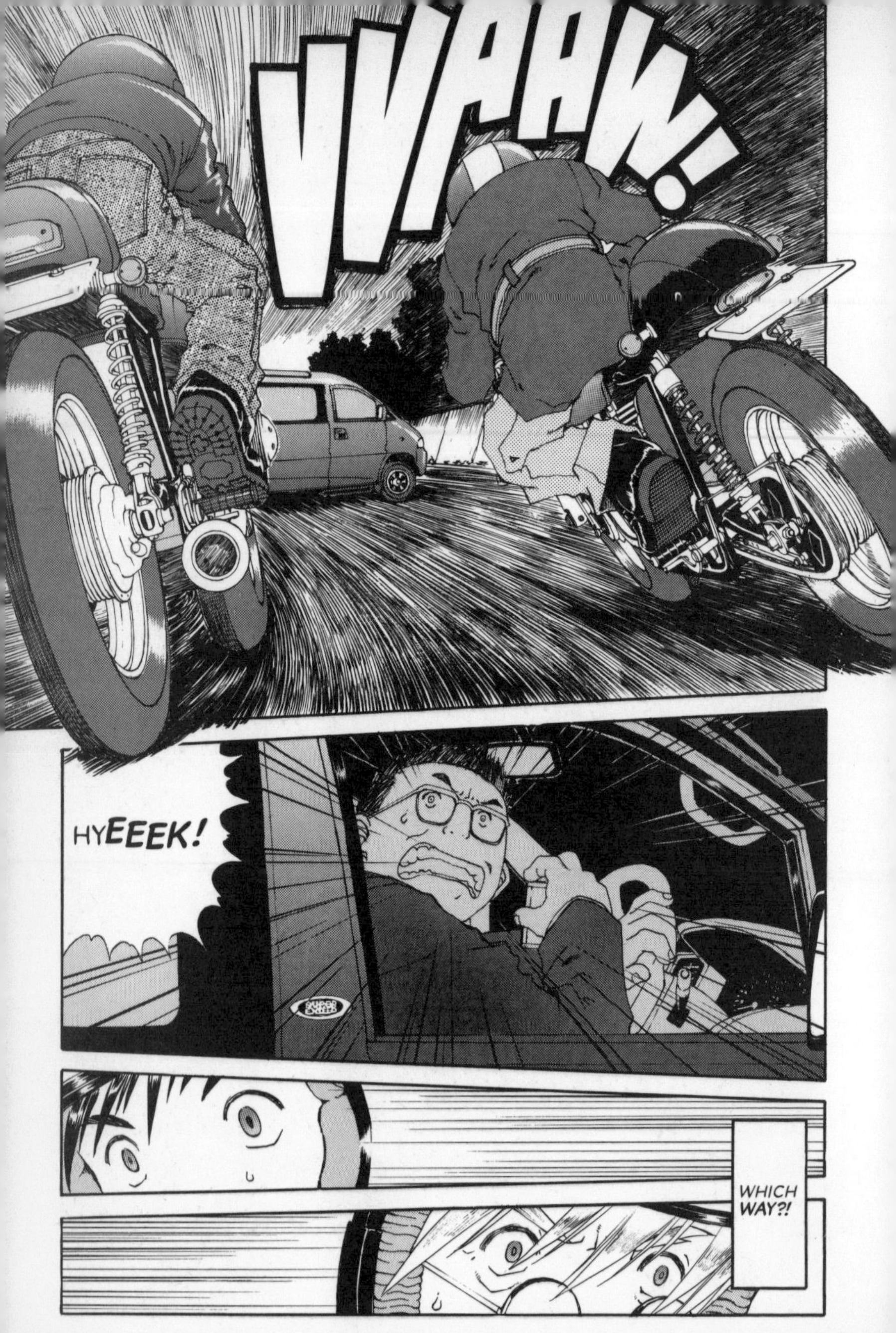
VVAAW!
HYEEEK!
WHICH WAY?!

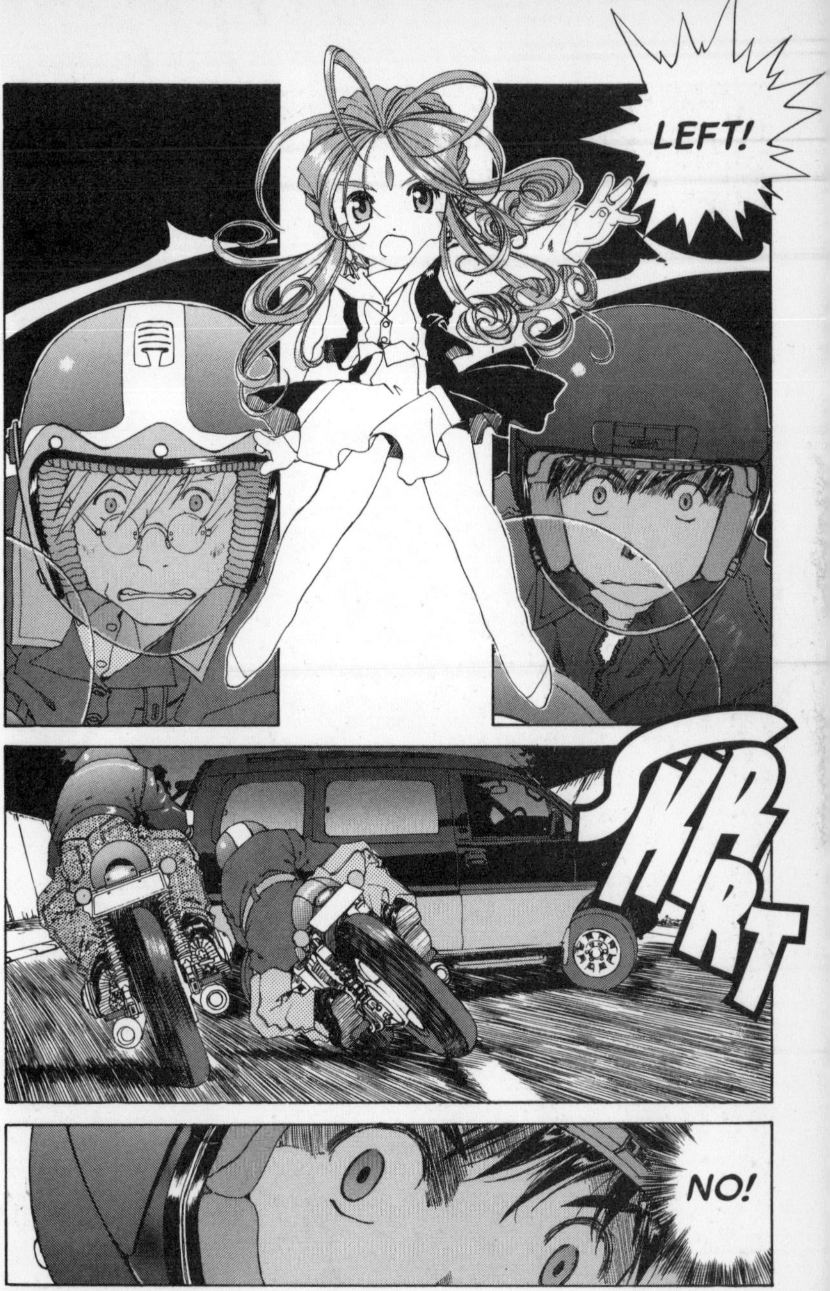
LEFT!
SHRRT
NO!

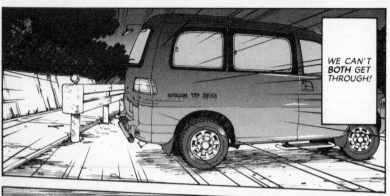

WE CAN'T **BOTH** GET THROUGH!

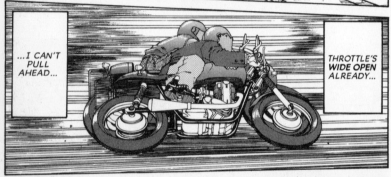

...I CAN'T PULL AHEAD...

THROTTLE'S **WIDE OPEN** ALREADY...

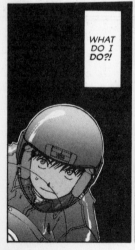

WHAT DO I DO?!

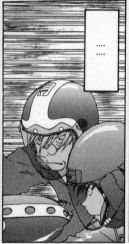

....
....

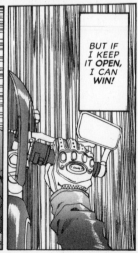

BUT IF I KEEP IT **OPEN**, I CAN **WIN!**

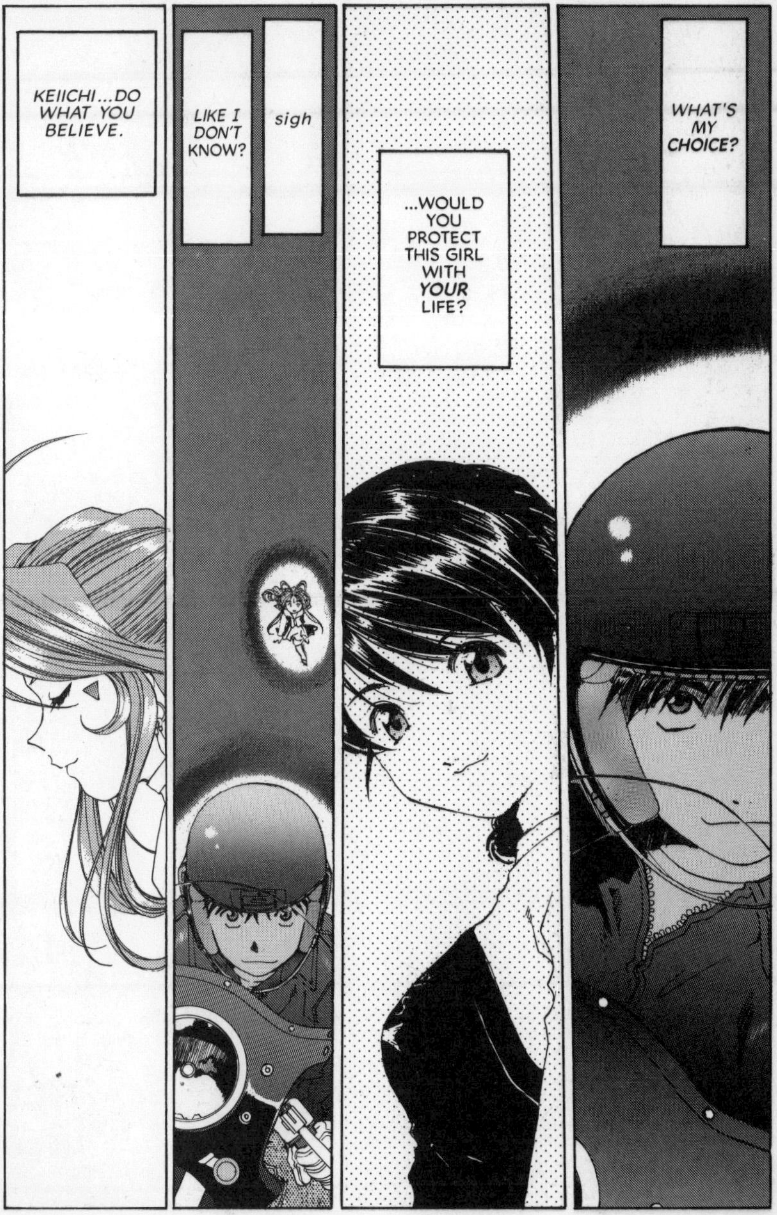
WHAT'S MY CHOICE?
...WOULD YOU PROTECT THIS GIRL WITH *YOUR* LIFE?
sigh
LIKE I DON'T KNOW?
KEIICHI...DO WHAT YOU BELIEVE.

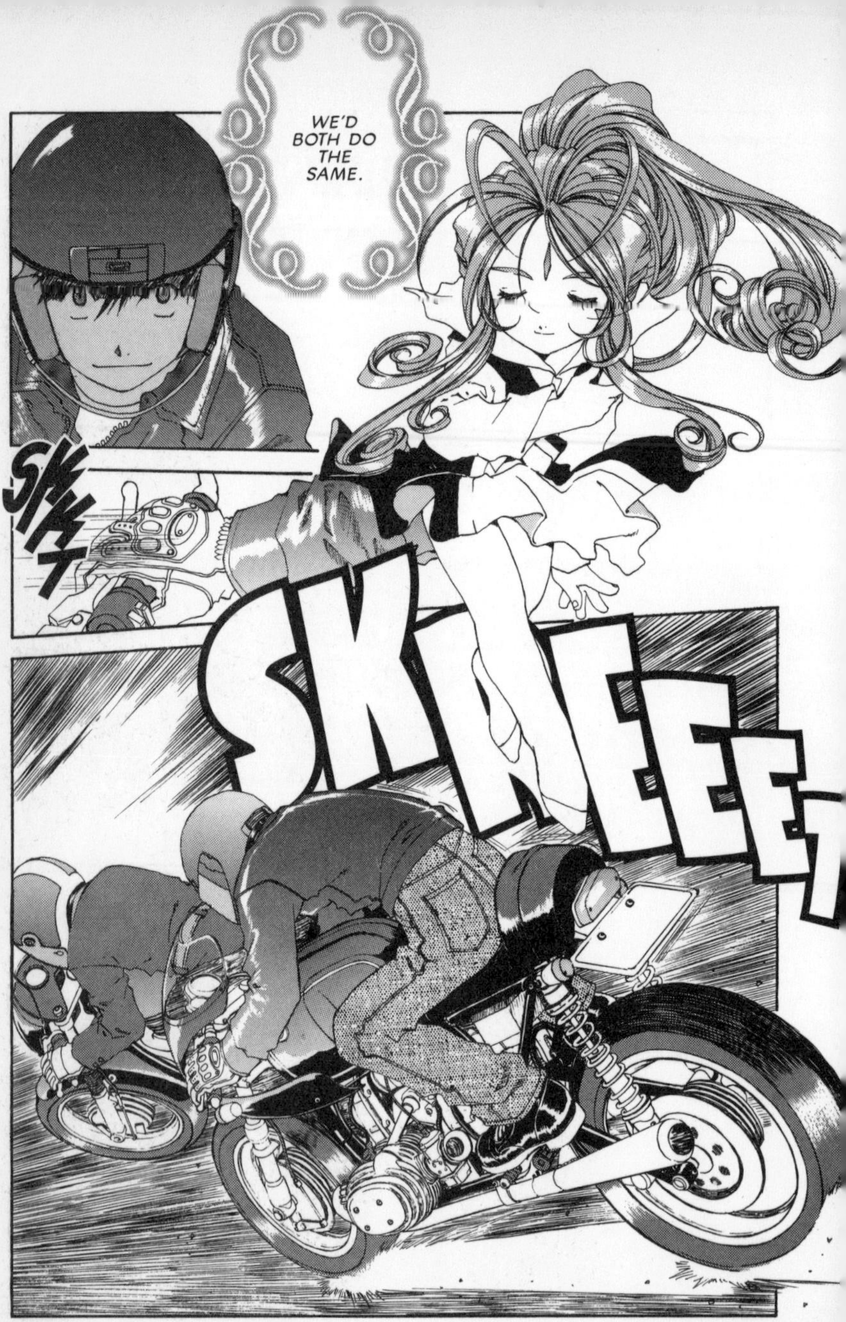
WE'D BOTH DO THE SAME.

OH MY GODDESS!

BELLDANDY

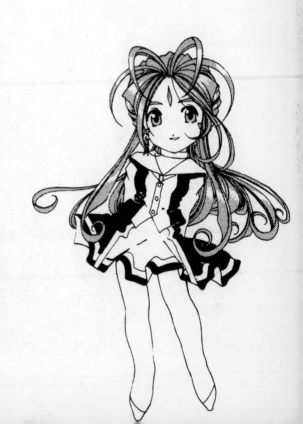

CHAPTER 151

Prepared to Win, Prepared to Lose

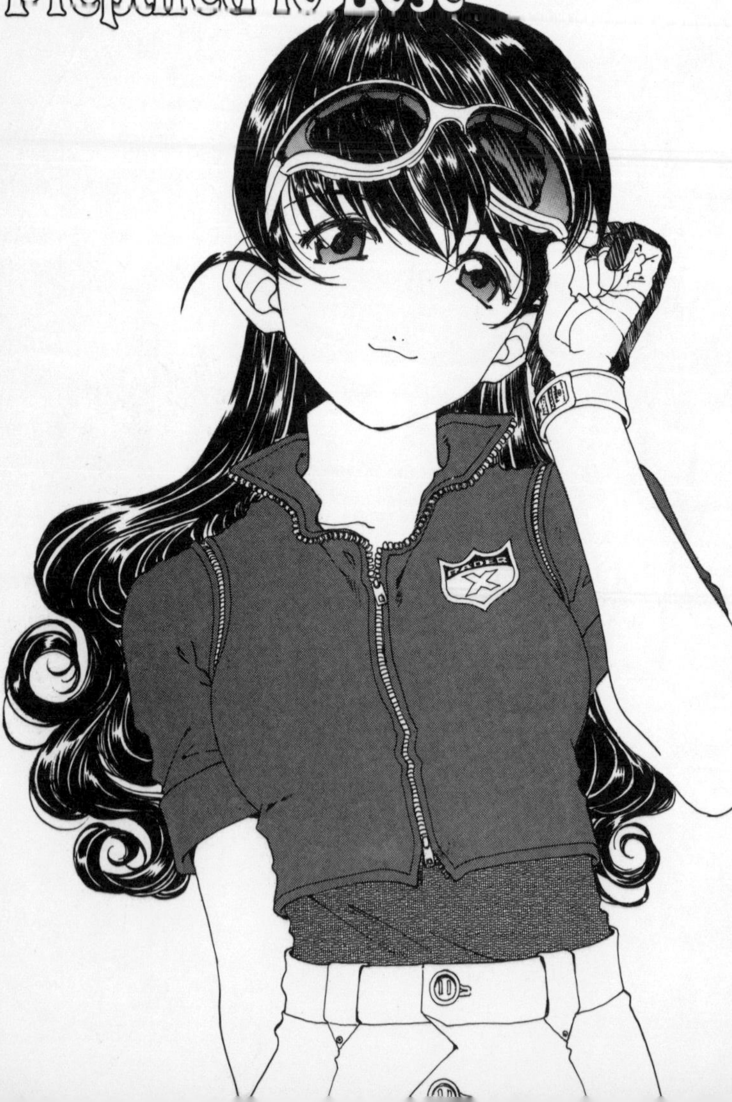

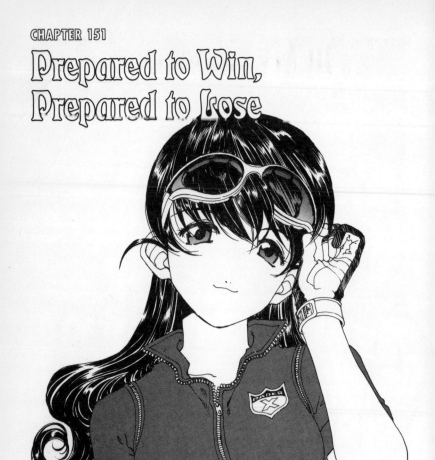

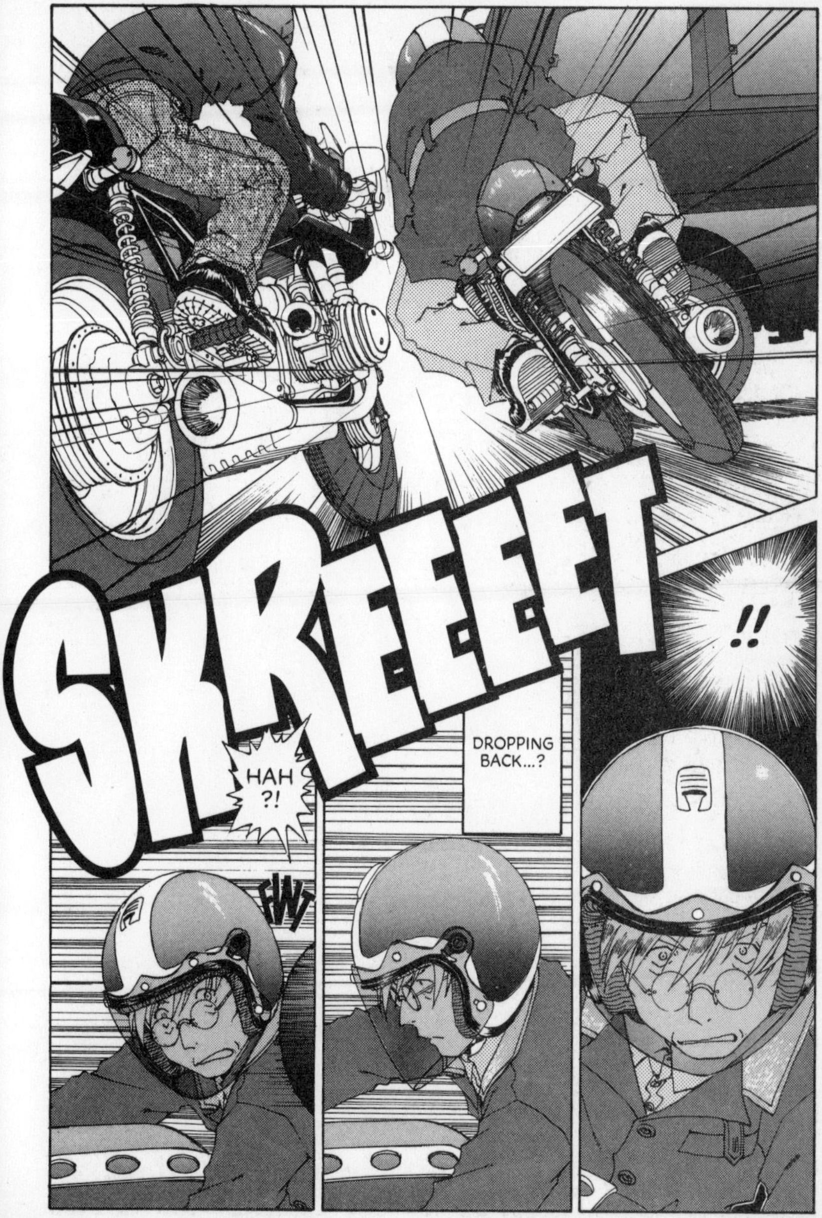
SKREEEET
!!
DROPPING BACK...?
HAH ?!
FWT

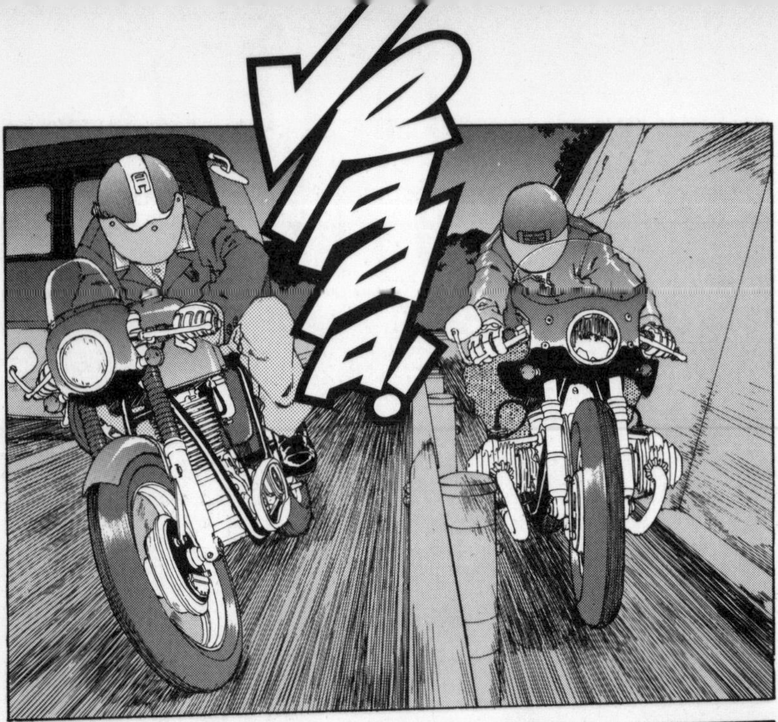
VRAAA!
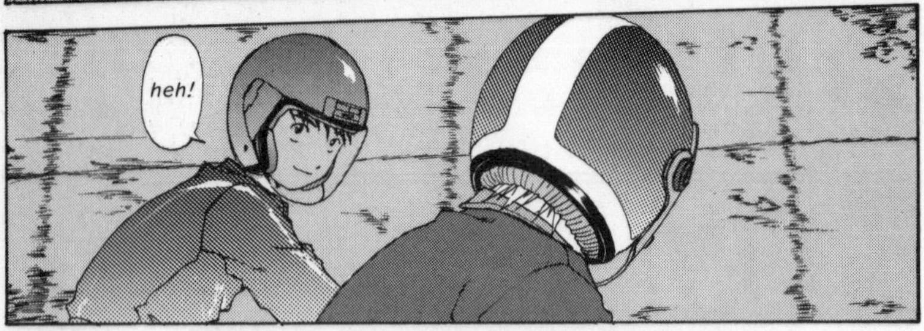
heh!
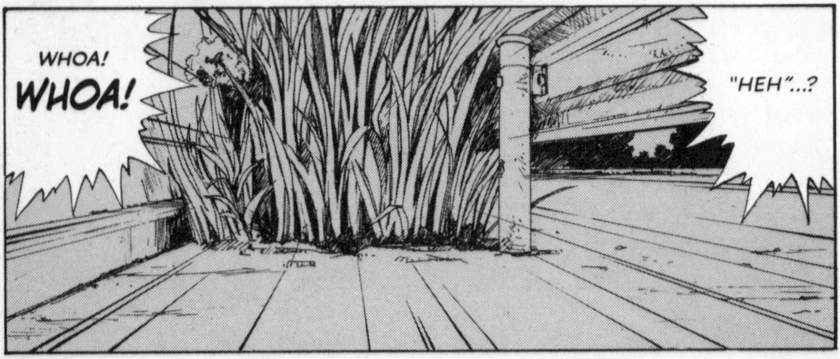
"HEH"...?
WHOA!
WHOA!

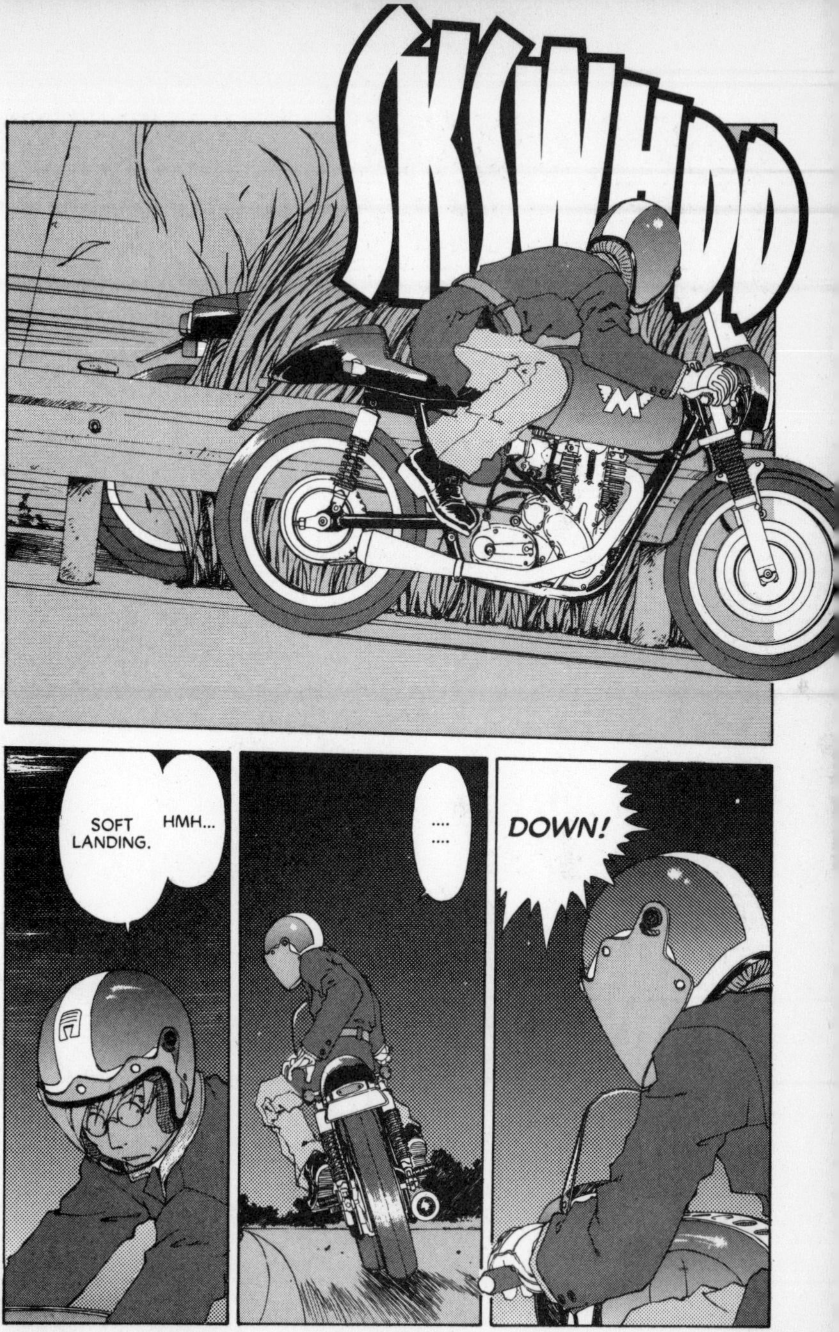

SKSWHDD
DOWN!
....
....
HMH... SOFT LANDING.

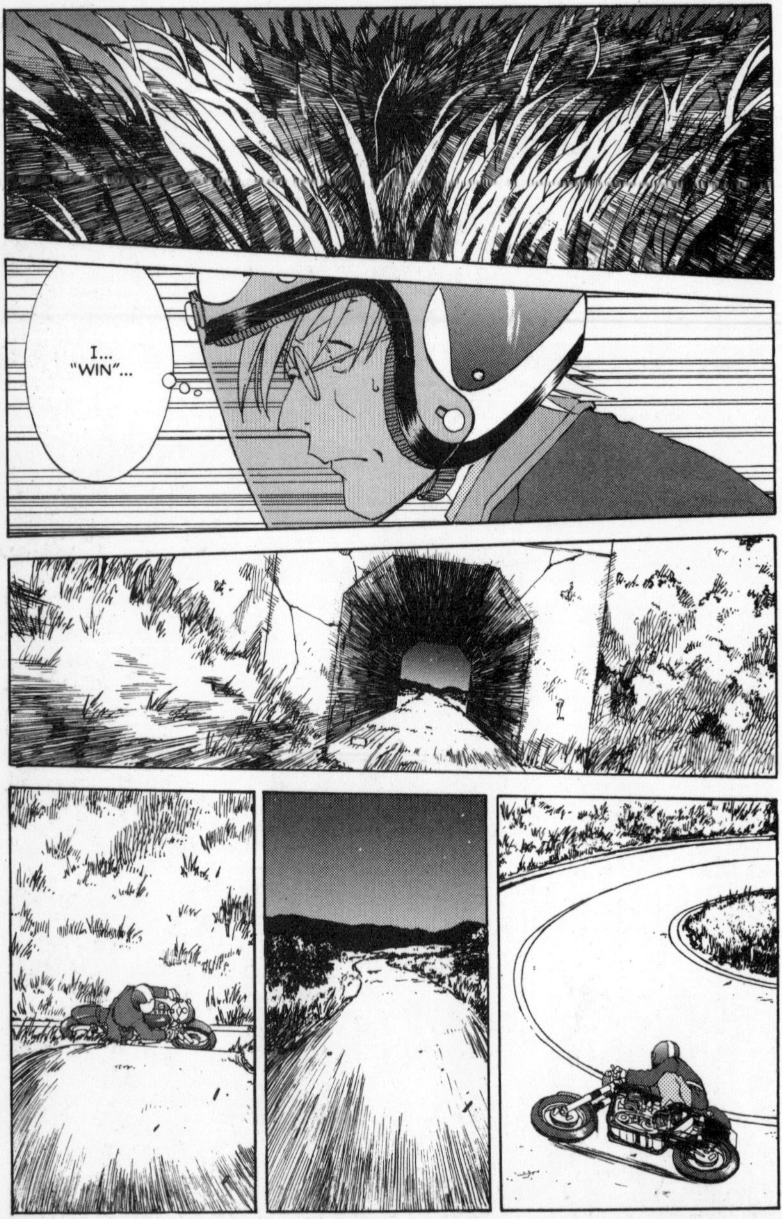
I...
"WIN"...

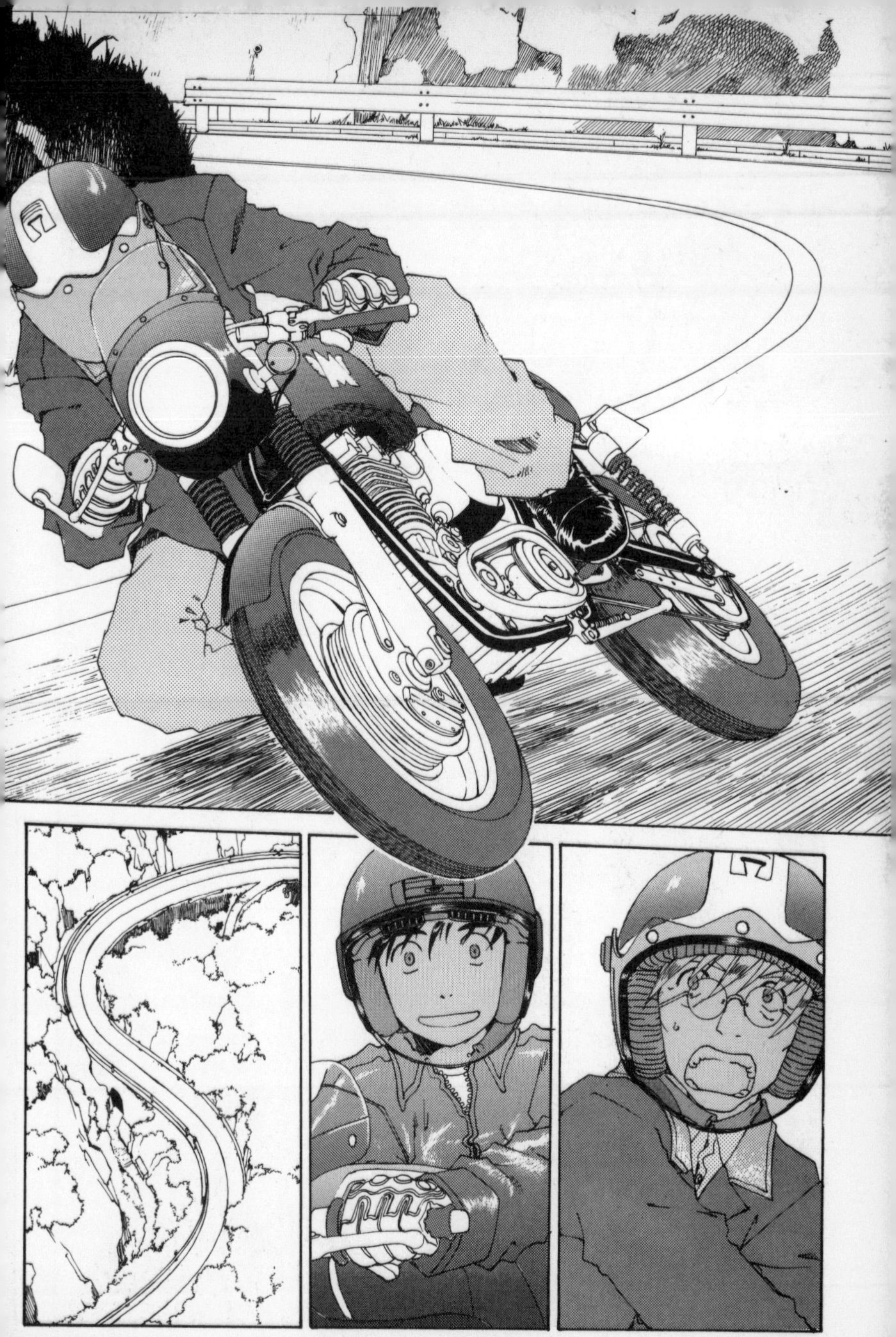

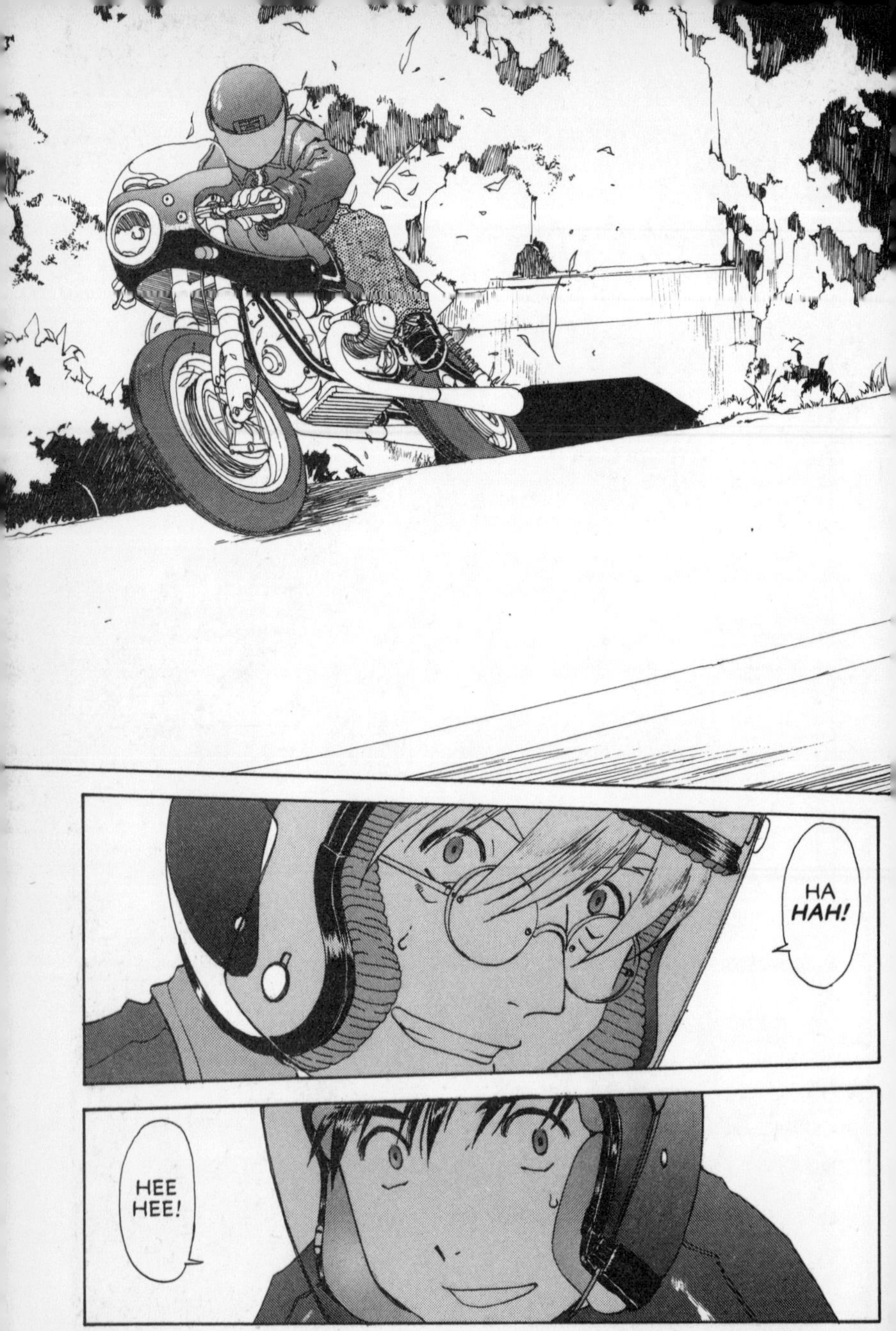
HA HAH!
HEE HEE!

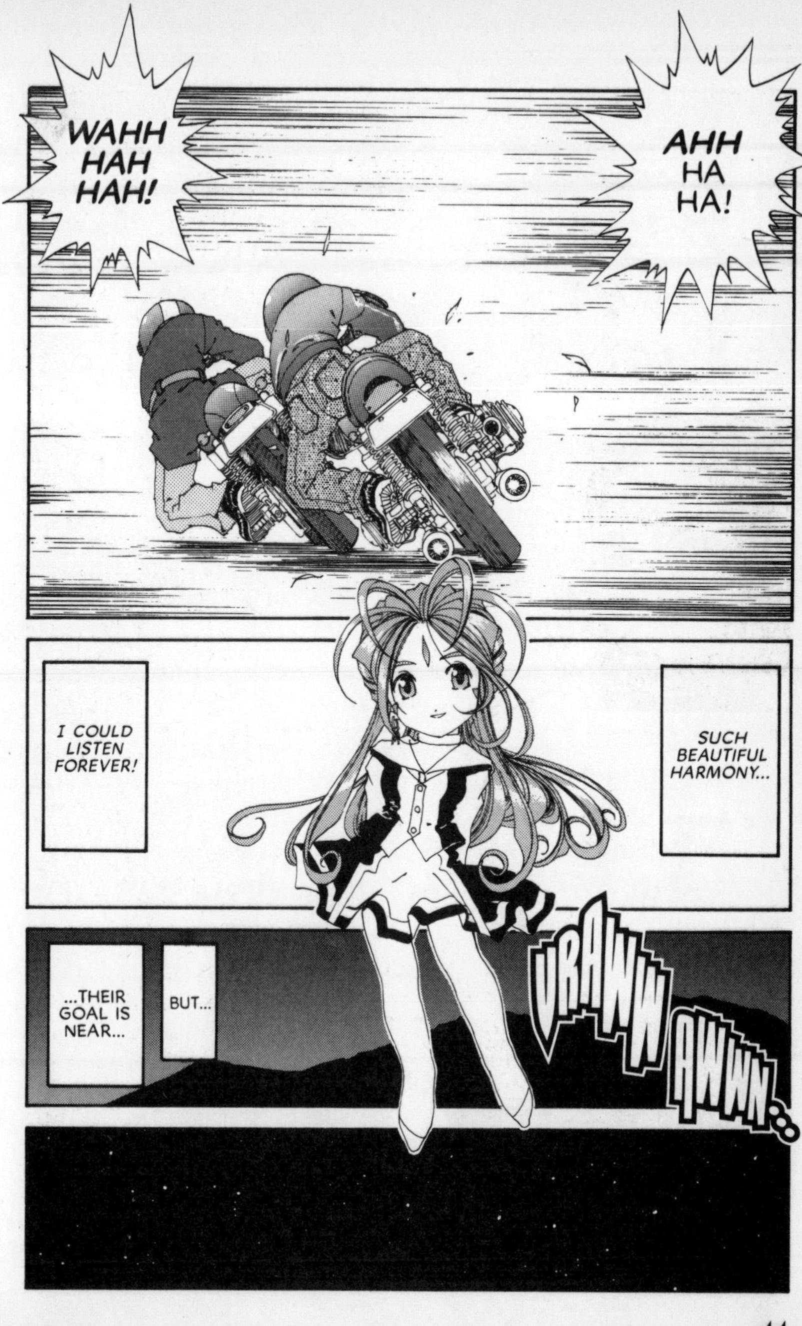
AHH HA HA!
WAHH HAH HAH!
SUCH BEAUTIFUL HARMONY...
I COULD LISTEN FOREVER!
VRAWWN AWWN...
BUT...
...THEIR GOAL IS NEAR...

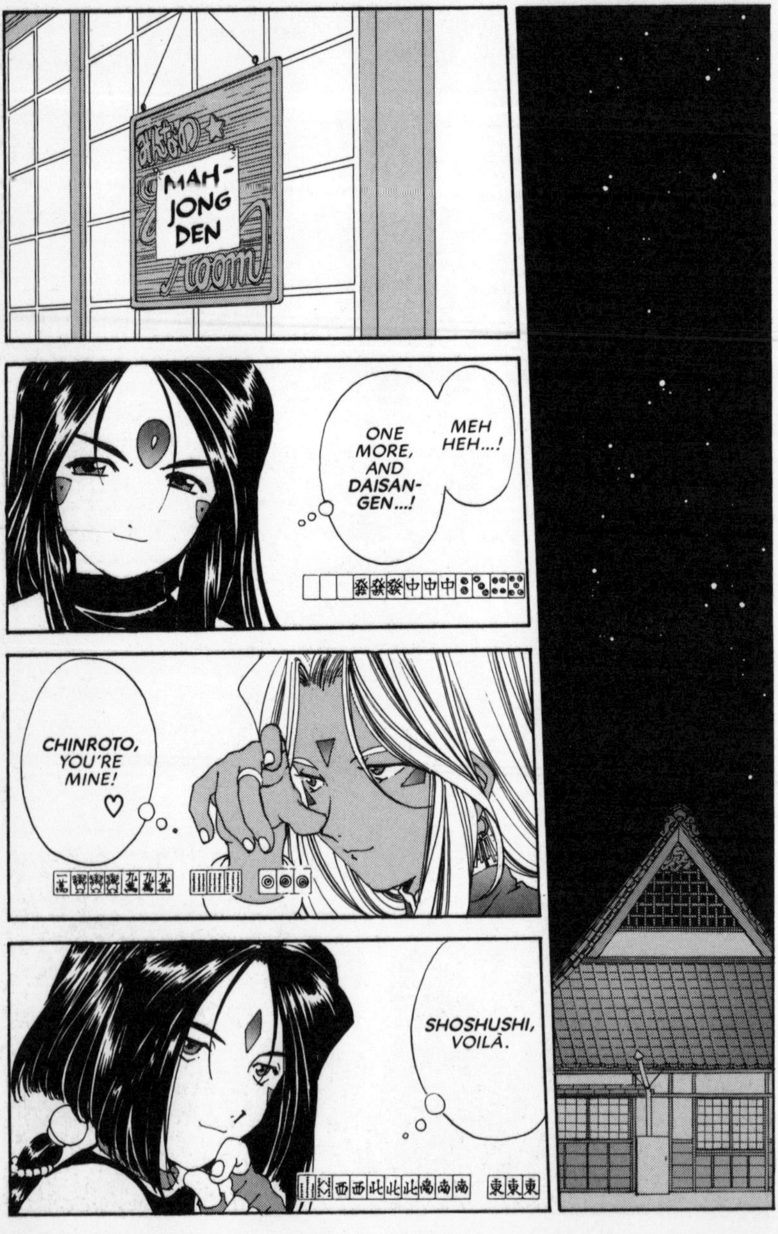
MAH-JONG DEN
MEH HEH...!
ONE MORE, AND DAISAN-GEN...!
CHINROTO, YOU'RE MINE! ♡
SHOSHUSHI, VOILÀ.

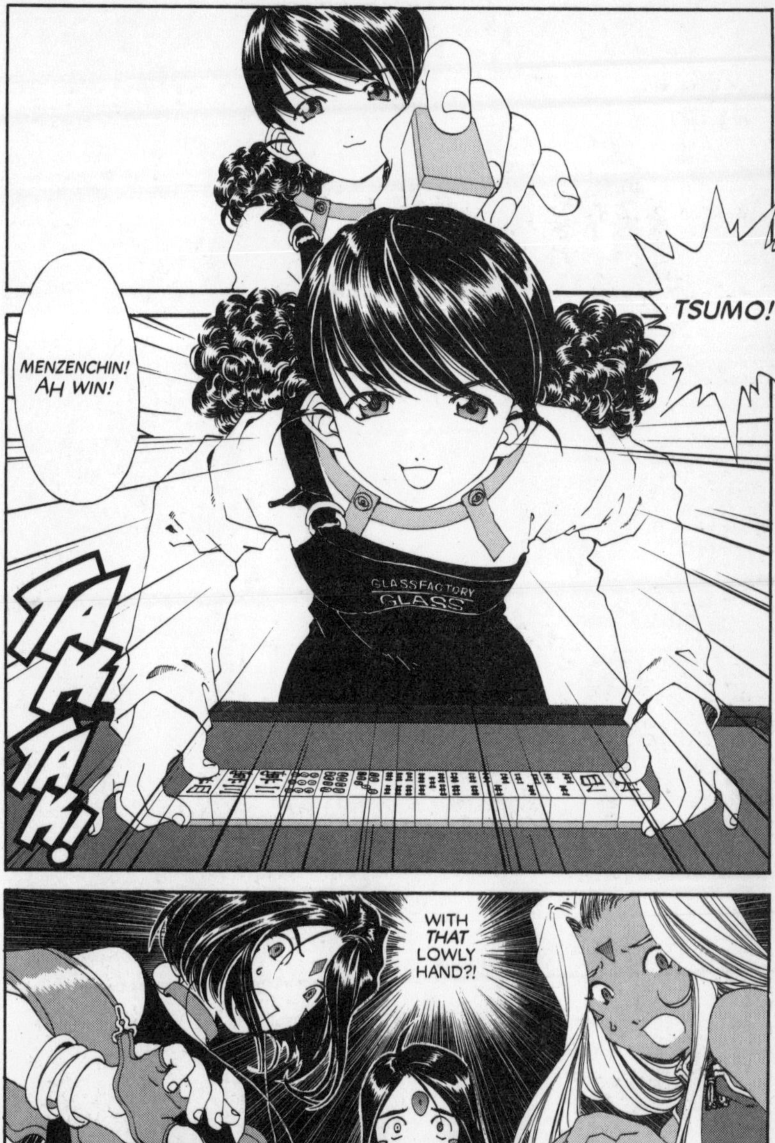
TSUMO!
MENZENCHIN! AH WIN!
GLASSFACTORY GLASS
TAK TAK!
WITH THAT LOWLY HAND?!

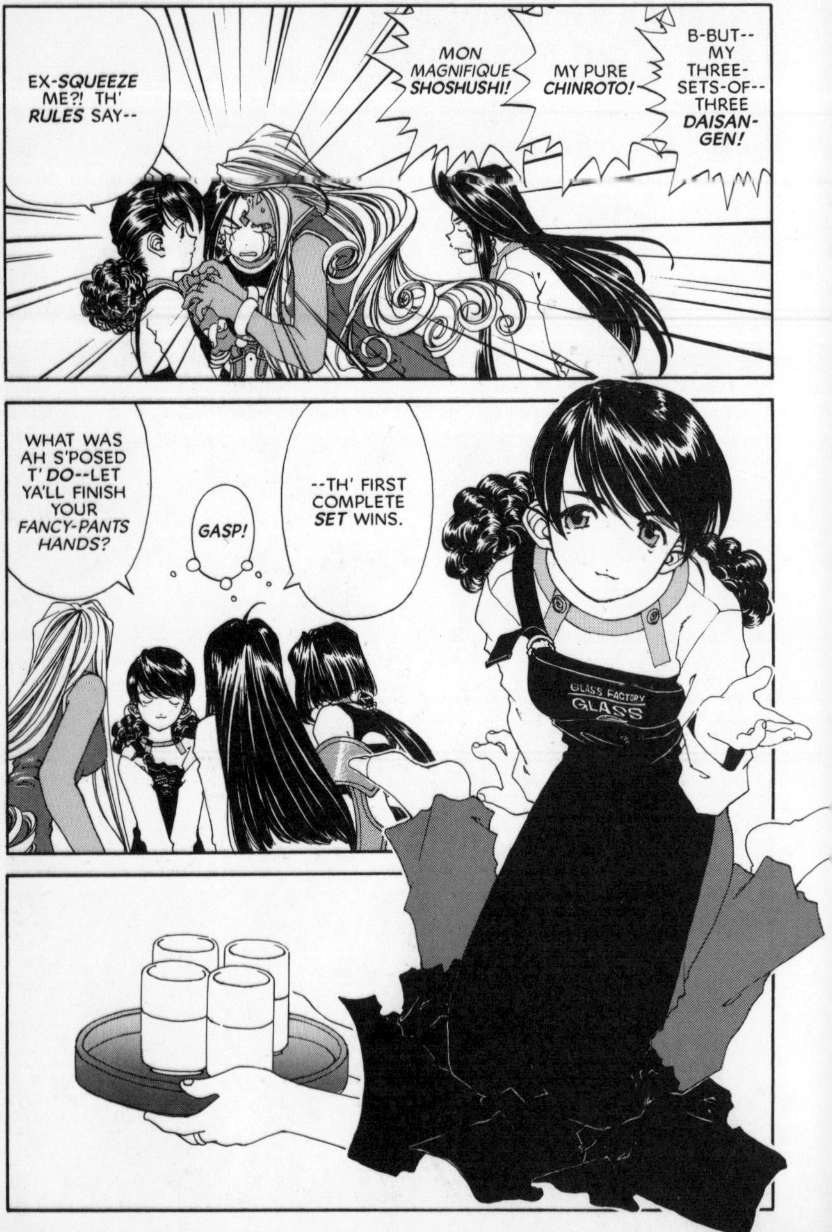
B-BUT-- MY THREE-SETS-OF-- THREE DAISAN-GEN!
MY PURE CHINROTO!
MON MAGNIFIQUE SHOSHUSHI!
EX-SQUEEZE ME?! TH' RULES SAY--
--TH' FIRST COMPLETE SET WINS.
GASP!
WHAT WAS AH S'POSED T' DO--LET YA'LL FINISH YOUR FANCY-PANTS HANDS?
GLASS FACTORY
GLASS

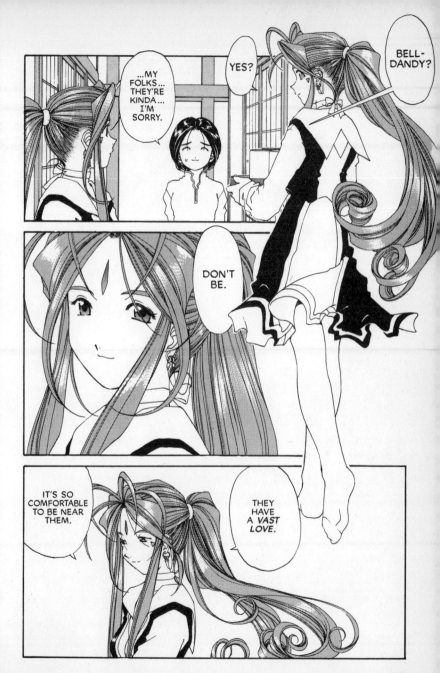

...MY FOLKS... THEY'RE KINDA... I'M SORRY.

YES?

BELL-DANDY?

DON'T BE.

IT'S SO COMFORTABLE TO BE NEAR THEM.

THEY HAVE A *VAST* LOVE.

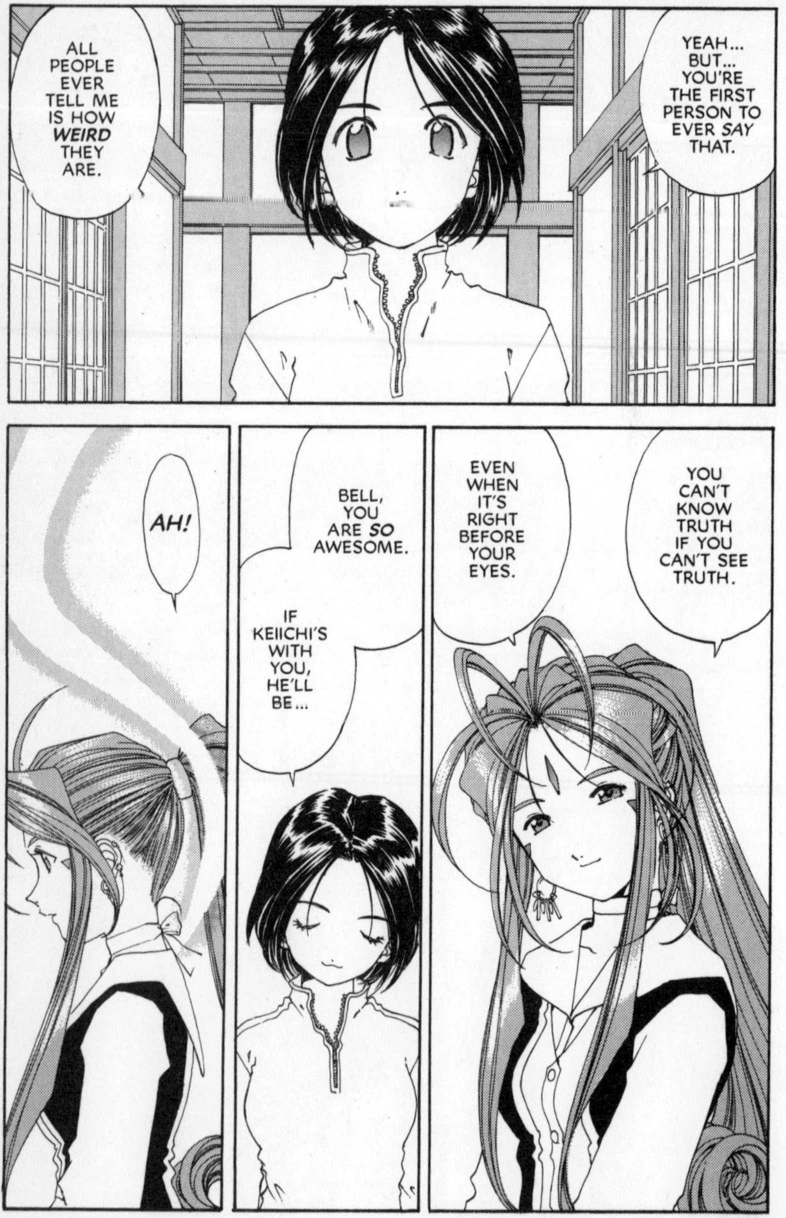
YEAH... BUT... YOU'RE THE FIRST PERSON TO EVER *SAY* THAT.
ALL PEOPLE EVER TELL ME IS HOW ***WEIRD*** THEY ARE.
YOU CAN'T KNOW TRUTH IF YOU CAN'T SEE TRUTH.
EVEN WHEN IT'S RIGHT BEFORE YOUR EYES.
BELL, YOU ARE *SO* AWESOME.
IF KEIICHI'S WITH YOU, HE'LL BE...
AH!

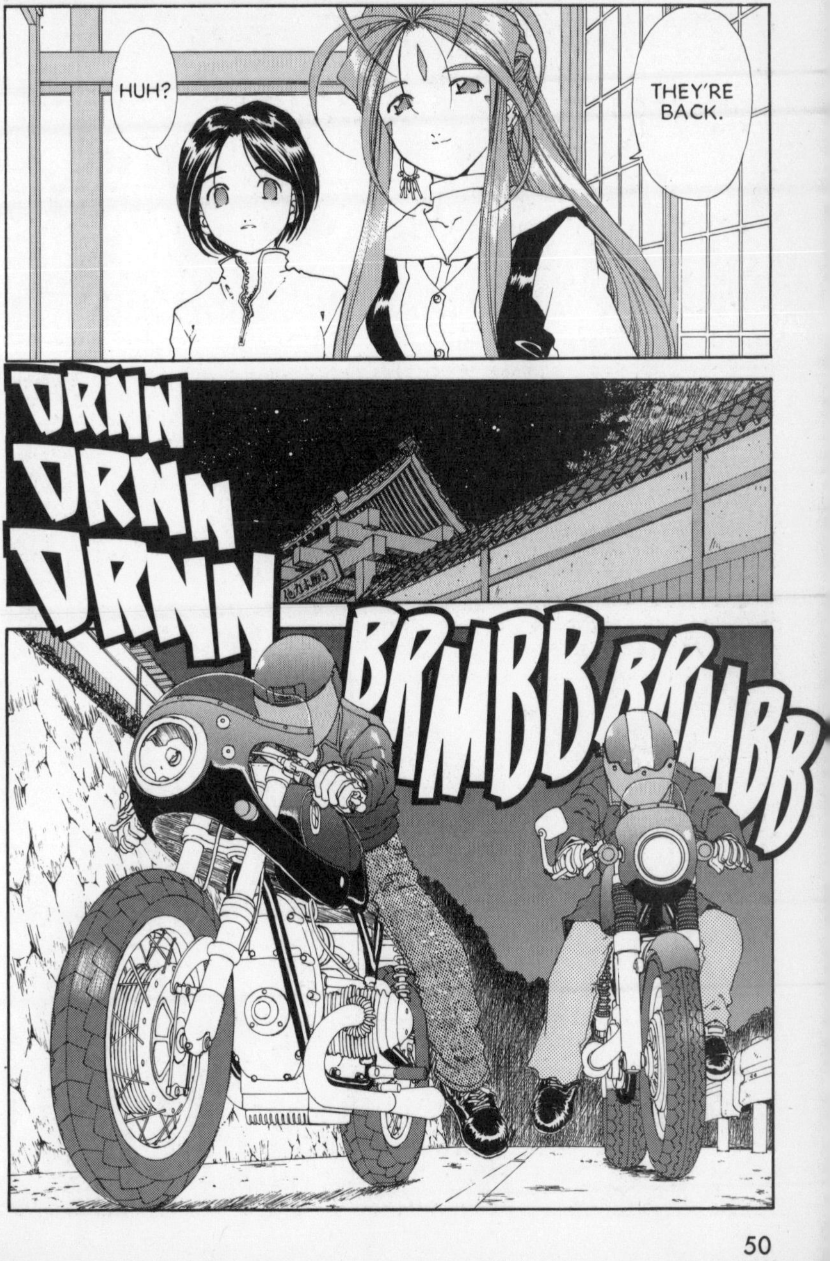
THEY'RE BACK.
HUH?
DRNN
DRNN
DRNN
BRMBB
BRMBB

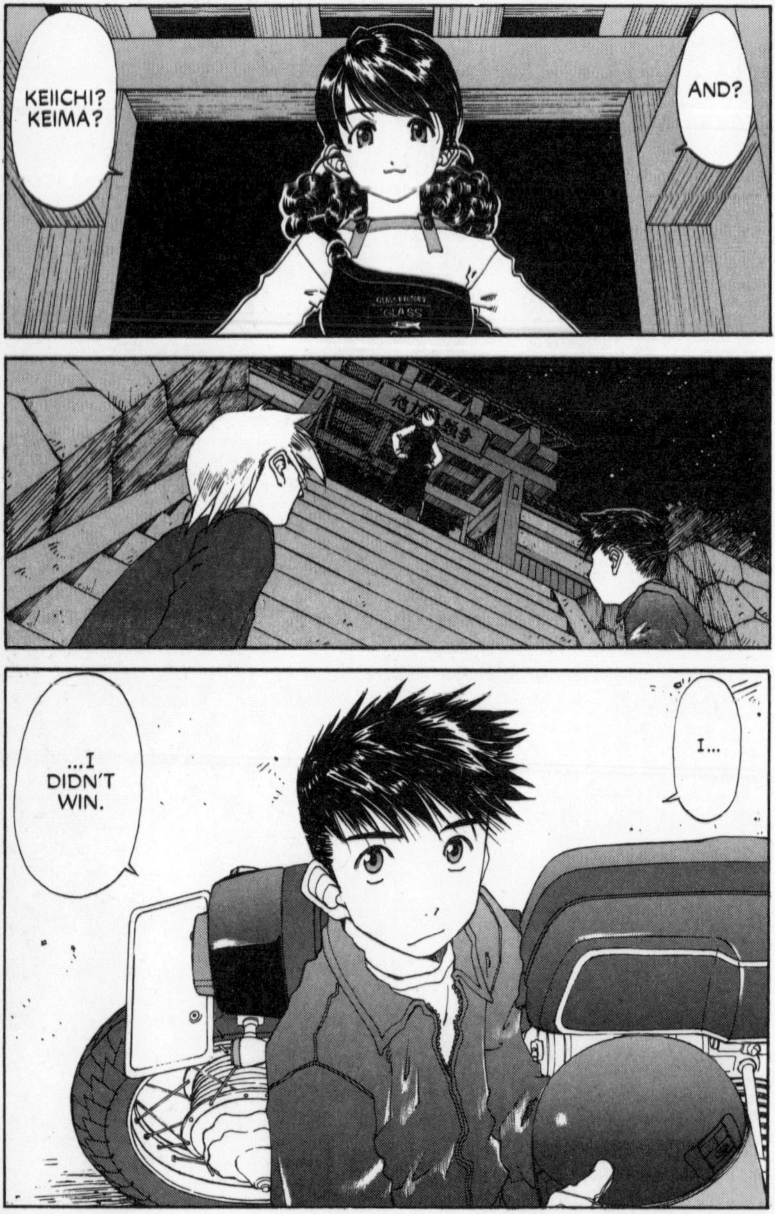
AND?
KEIICHI? KEIMA?
I...
...I DIDN'T WIN.

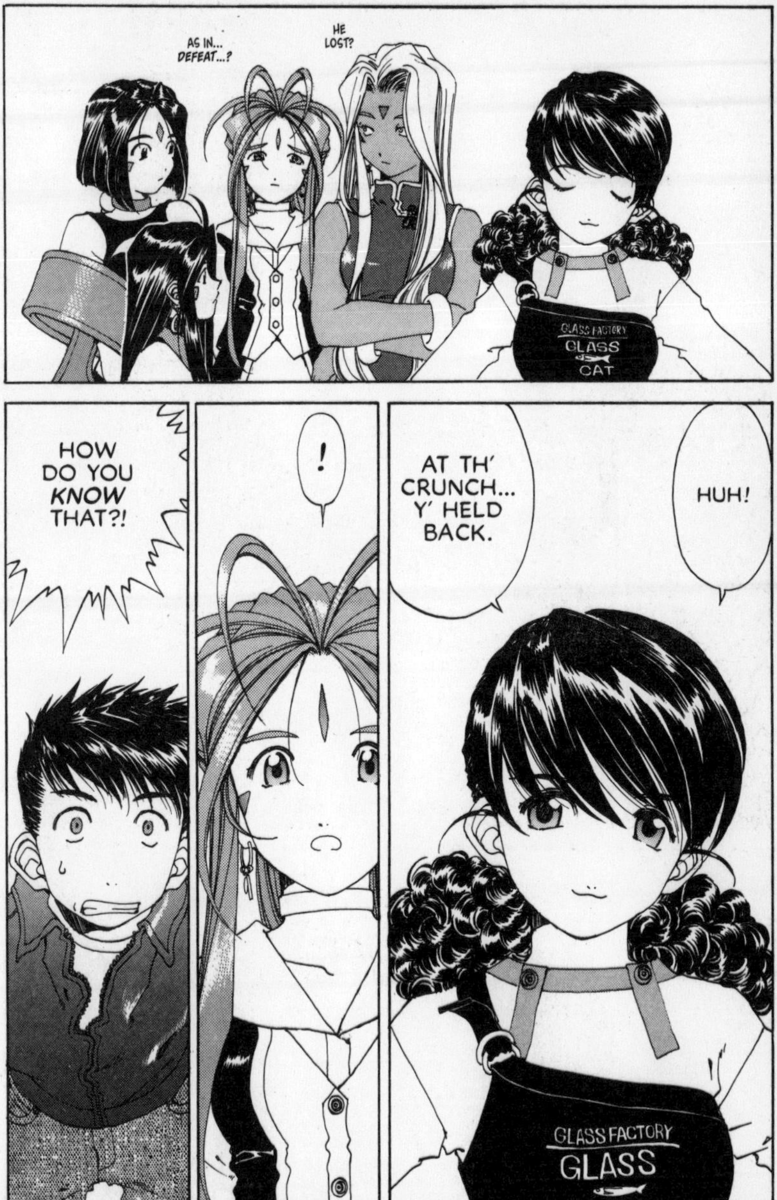
HE LOST?
AS IN... DEFEAT...?
GLASS FACTORY GLASS CAT
HUH!
AT TH' CRUNCH... Y' HELD BACK.
GLASS FACTORY GLASS
!
HOW DO YOU *KNOW* THAT?!

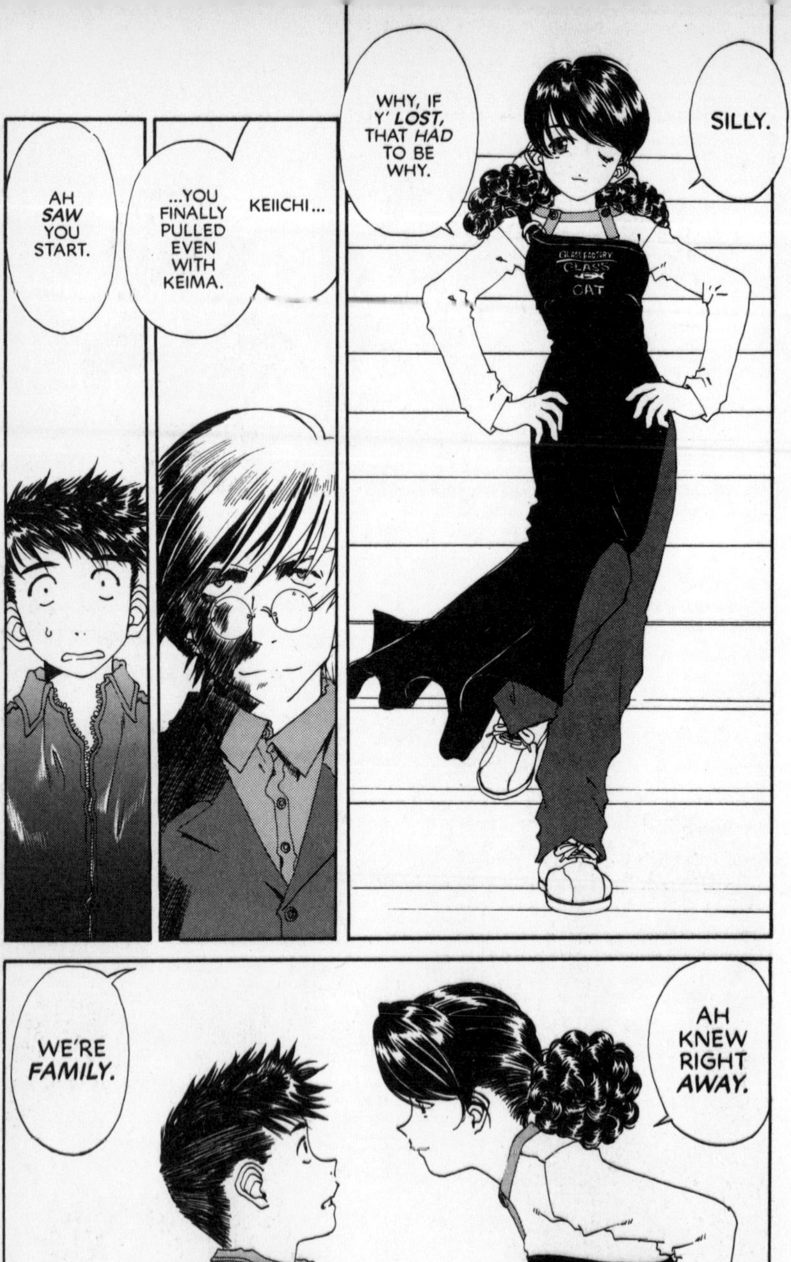
SILLY.
WHY, IF Y' *LOST,* THAT *HAD* TO BE WHY.
GLASS FACTORY GLASS CAT
KEIICHI...
...YOU FINALLY PULLED EVEN WITH KEIMA.
AH *SAW* YOU START.
AH KNEW RIGHT *AWAY.*
WE'RE *FAMILY.*

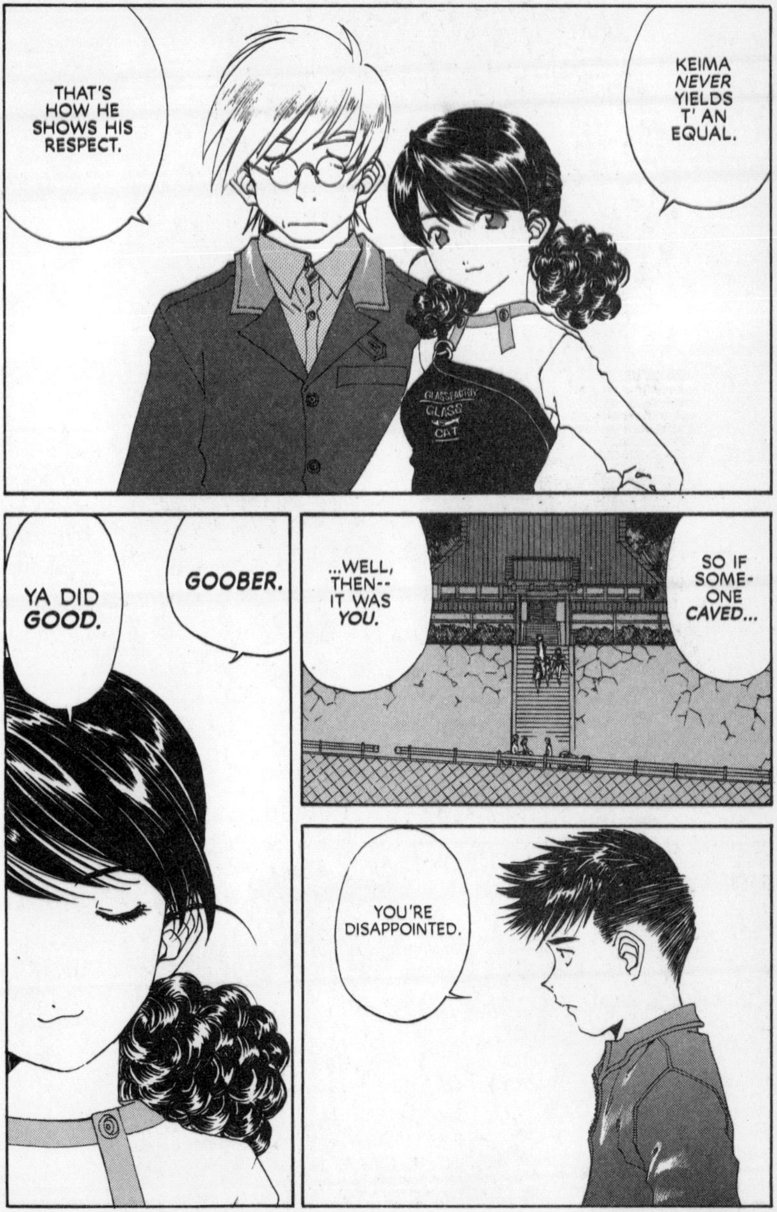
KEIMA NEVER YIELDS T' AN EQUAL.
THAT'S HOW HE SHOWS HIS RESPECT.
SO IF SOME-ONE CAVED...
...WELL, THEN-- IT WAS YOU.
YOU'RE DISAPPOINTED.
GOOBER.
YA DID GOOD.

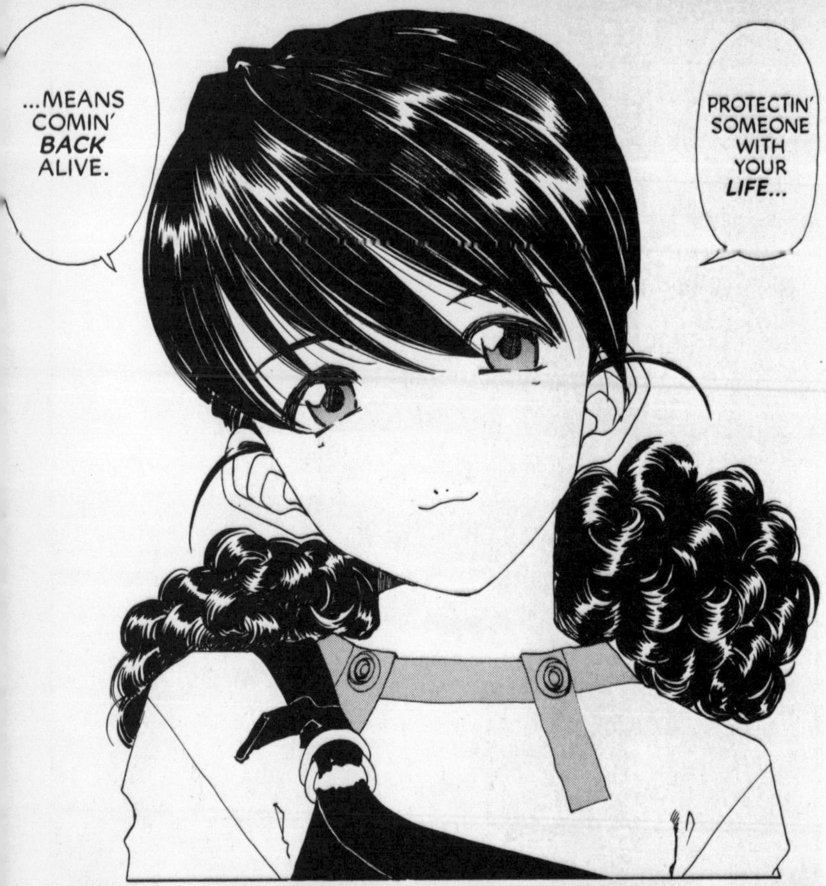
PROTECTIN' SOMEONE WITH YOUR *LIFE*...
...MEANS COMIN' *BACK* ALIVE.

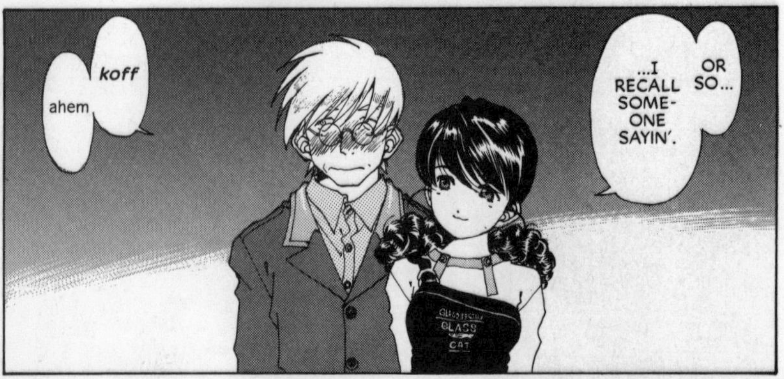
...I RECALL SOME-ONE SAYIN'.
OR SO...
koff
ahem

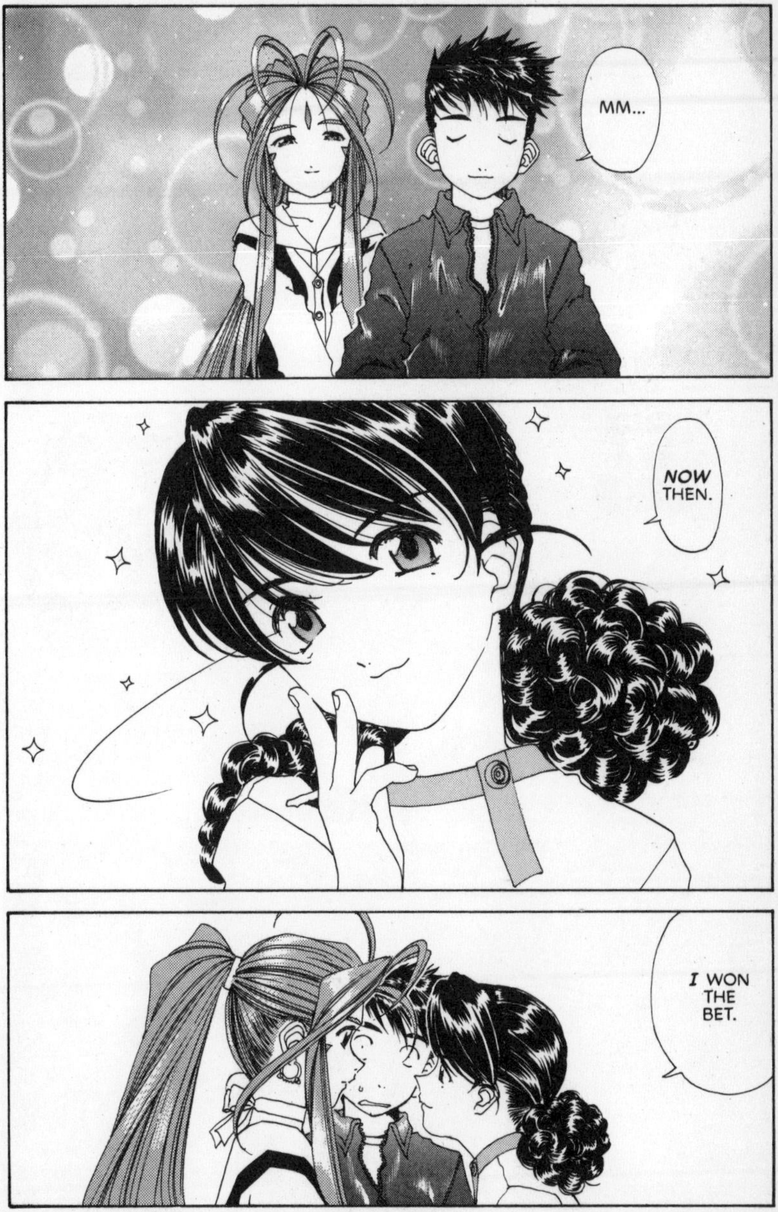
MM...
NOW THEN.
I WON THE BET.

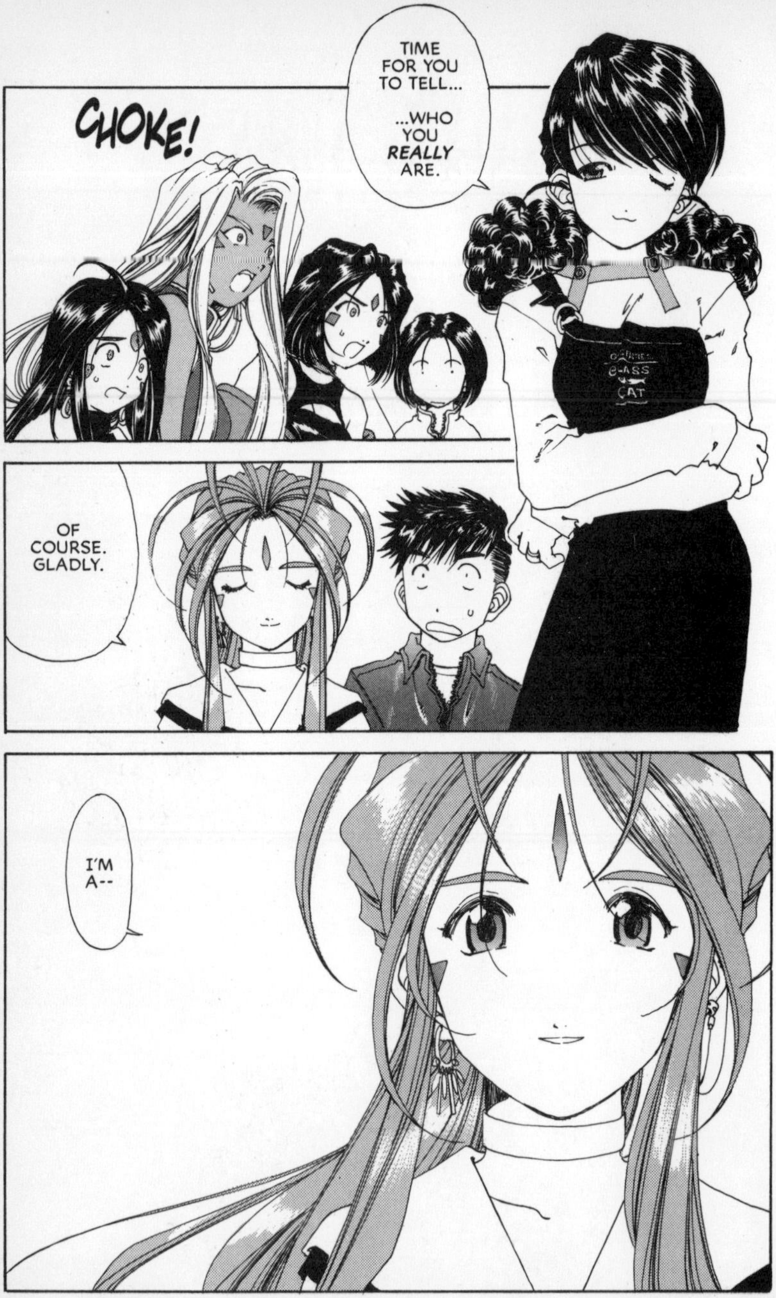
TIME FOR YOU TO TELL... ...WHO YOU *REALLY* ARE.
CHOKE!
OF COURSE. GLADLY.
I'M A--

OH MY GODDESS!
CHIHIRO

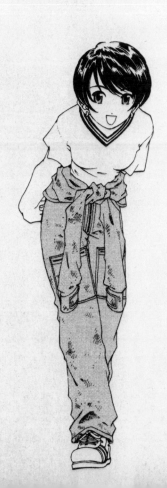

CHAPTER 152

The Real You

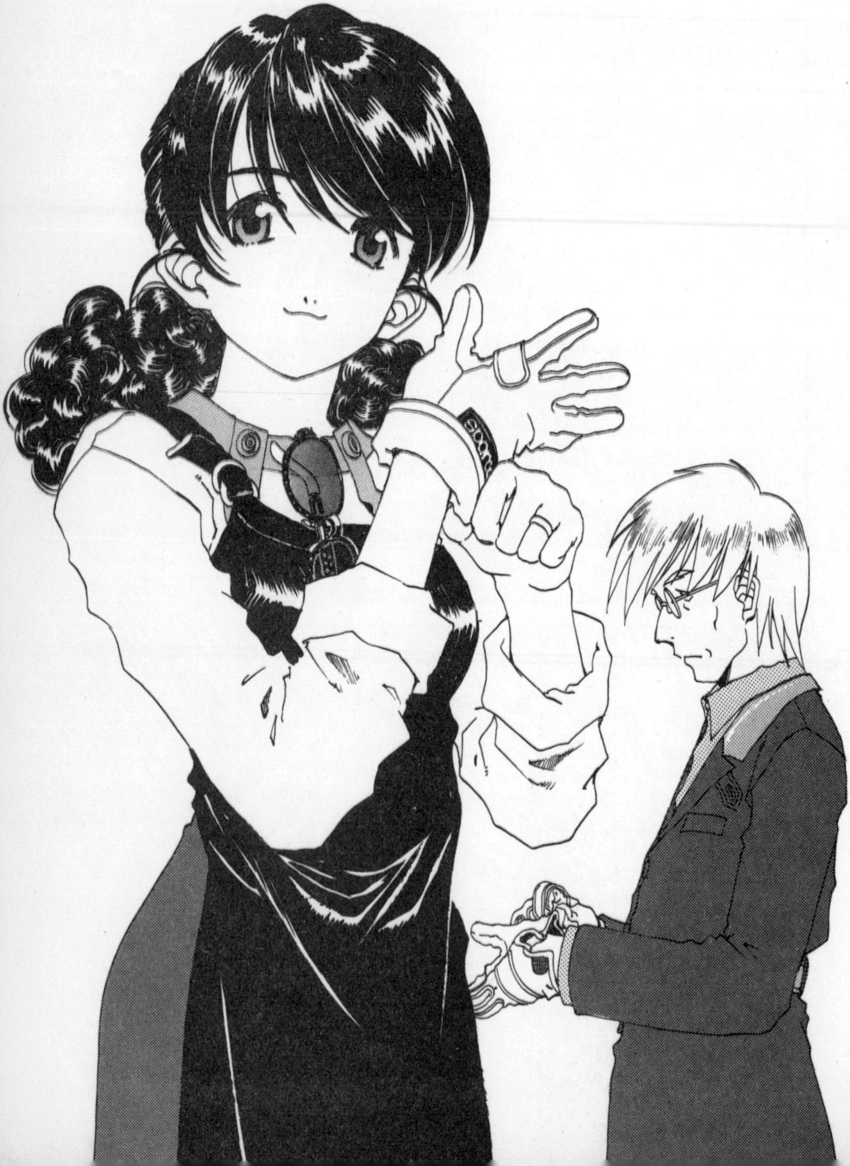

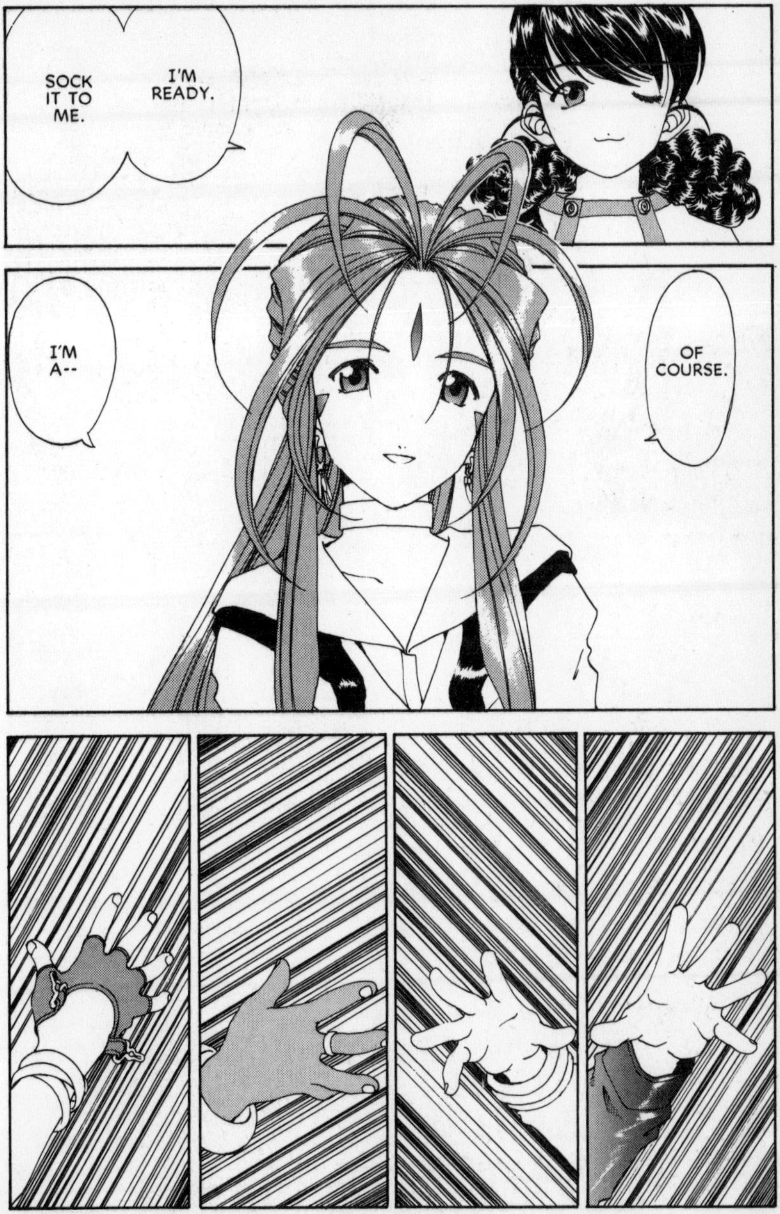
I'M READY.
SOCK IT TO ME.
OF COURSE.
I'M A--

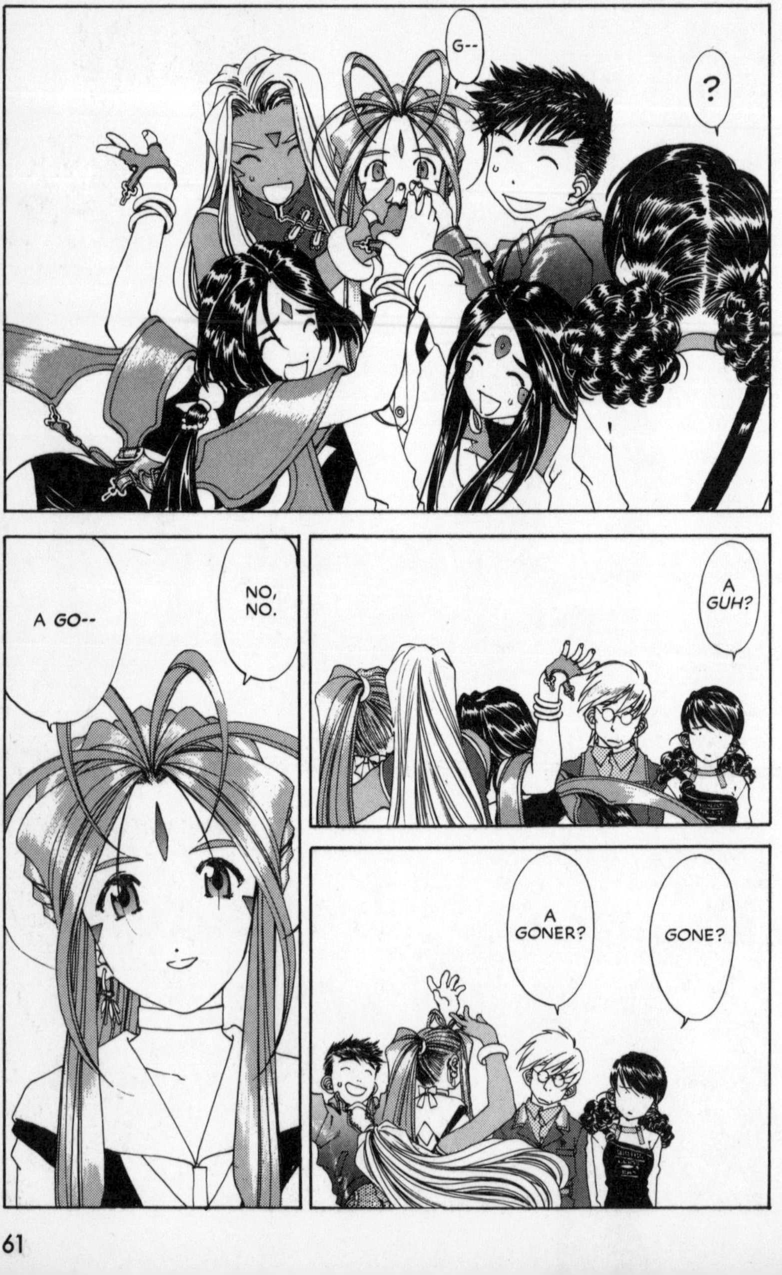
G--
?
A GUH?
GONE?
A GONER?
NO, NO.
A GO--

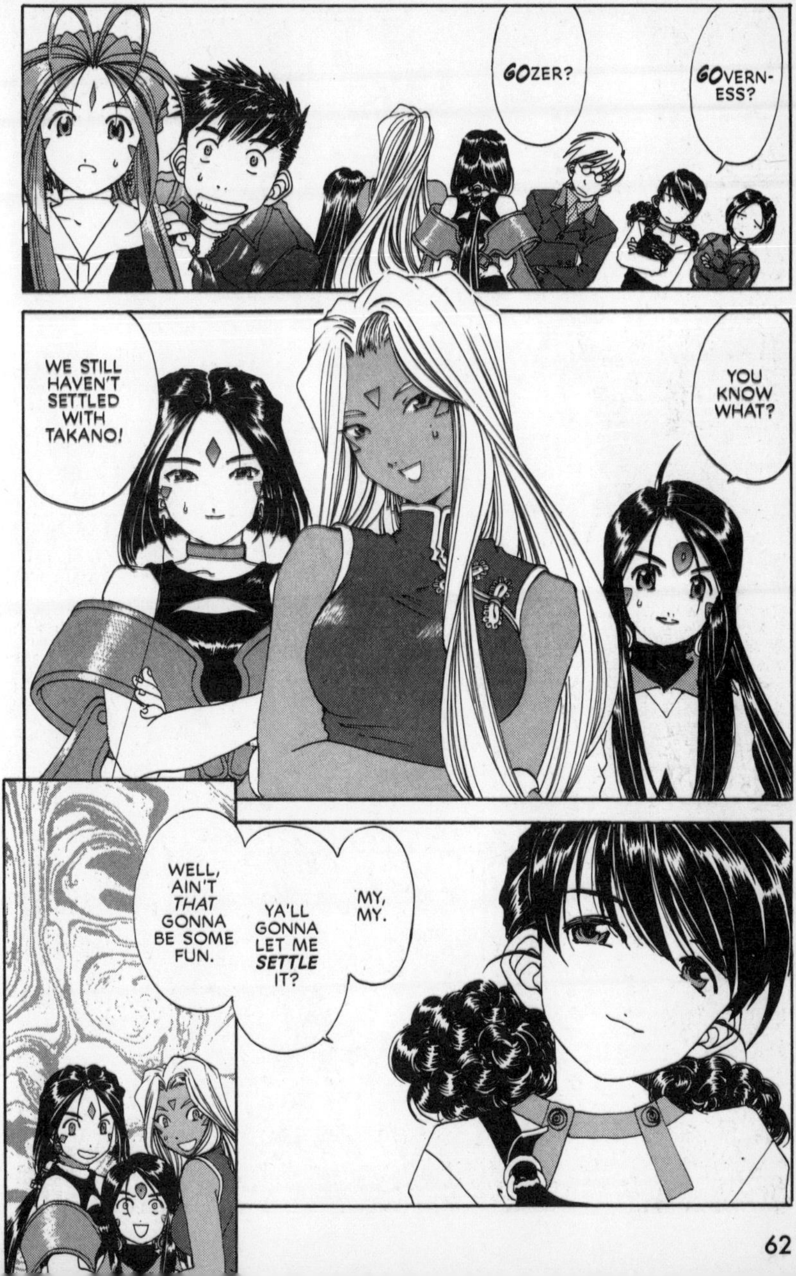
GOVERN-ESS?
GOZER?
YOU KNOW WHAT?
WE STILL HAVEN'T SETTLED WITH TAKANO!
MY, MY.
YA'LL GONNA LET ME *SETTLE* IT?
WELL, AIN'T *THAT* GONNA BE SOME FUN.

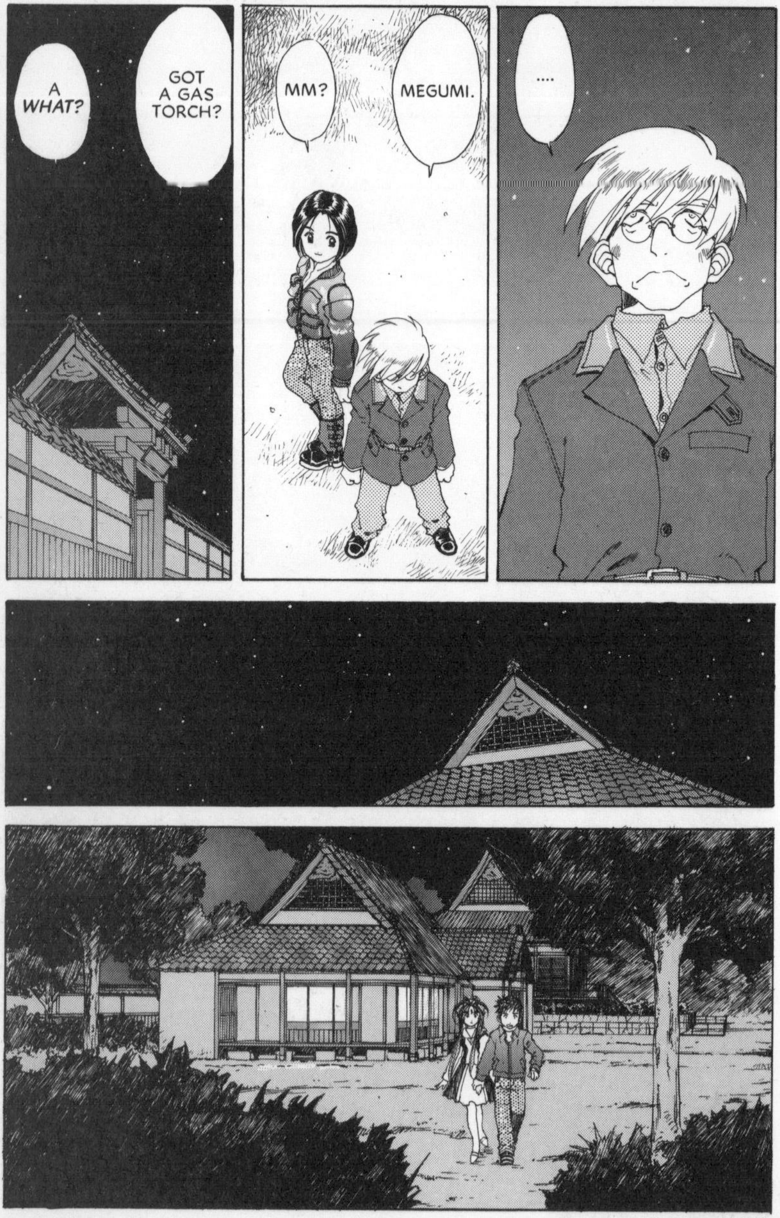
....
MEGUMI.
MM?
GOT A GAS TORCH?
A WHAT?

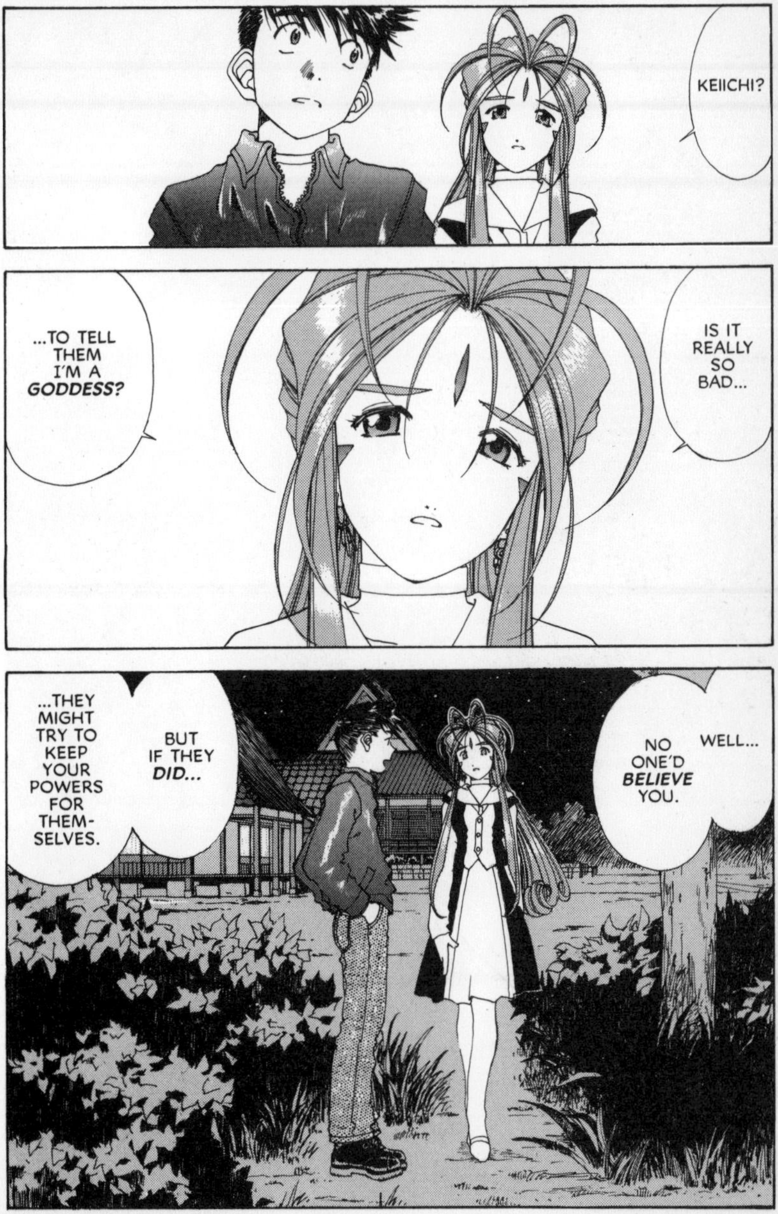
KEIICHI?
IS IT REALLY SO BAD...
...TO TELL THEM I'M A *GODDESS?*
WELL...
NO ONE'D *BELIEVE* YOU.
BUT IF THEY *DID...*
...THEY MIGHT TRY TO KEEP YOUR POWERS FOR THEM-SELVES.

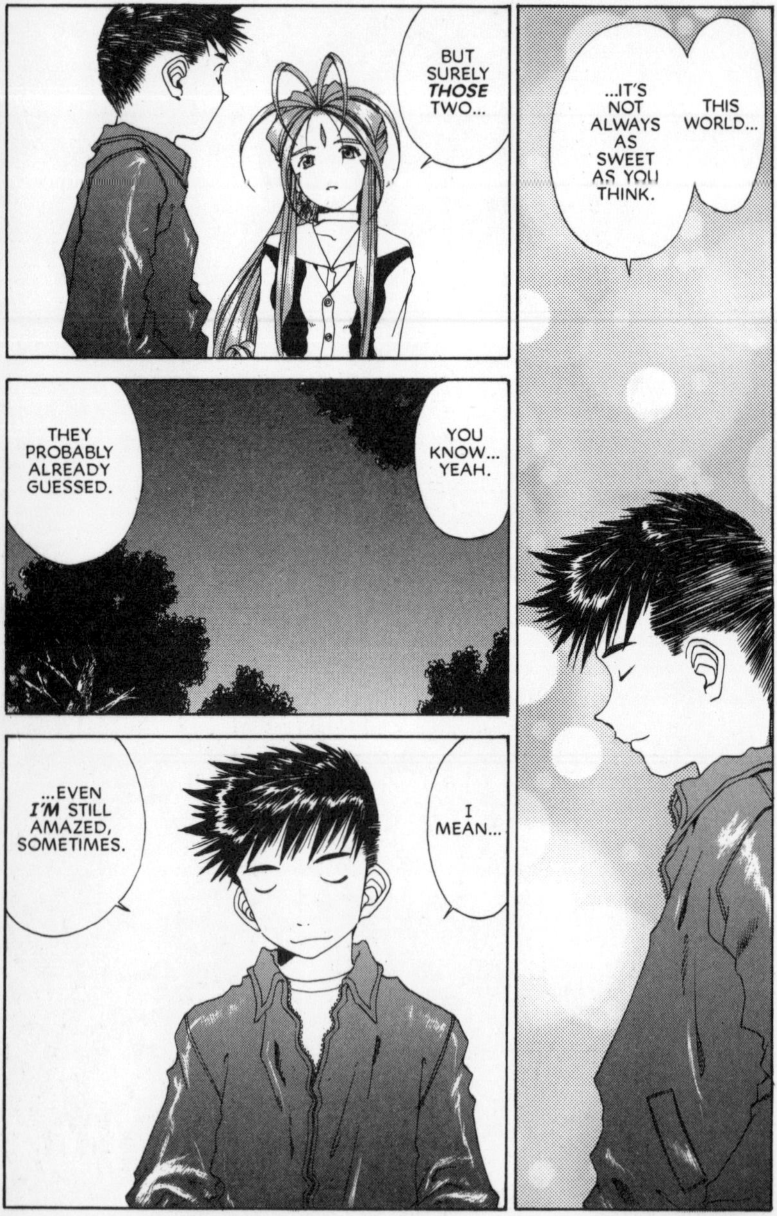
THIS WORLD...
...IT'S NOT ALWAYS AS SWEET AS YOU THINK.
BUT SURELY *THOSE* TWO...
YOU KNOW... YEAH.
THEY PROBABLY ALREADY GUESSED.
I MEAN...
...EVEN *I'M* STILL AMAZED, SOMETIMES.

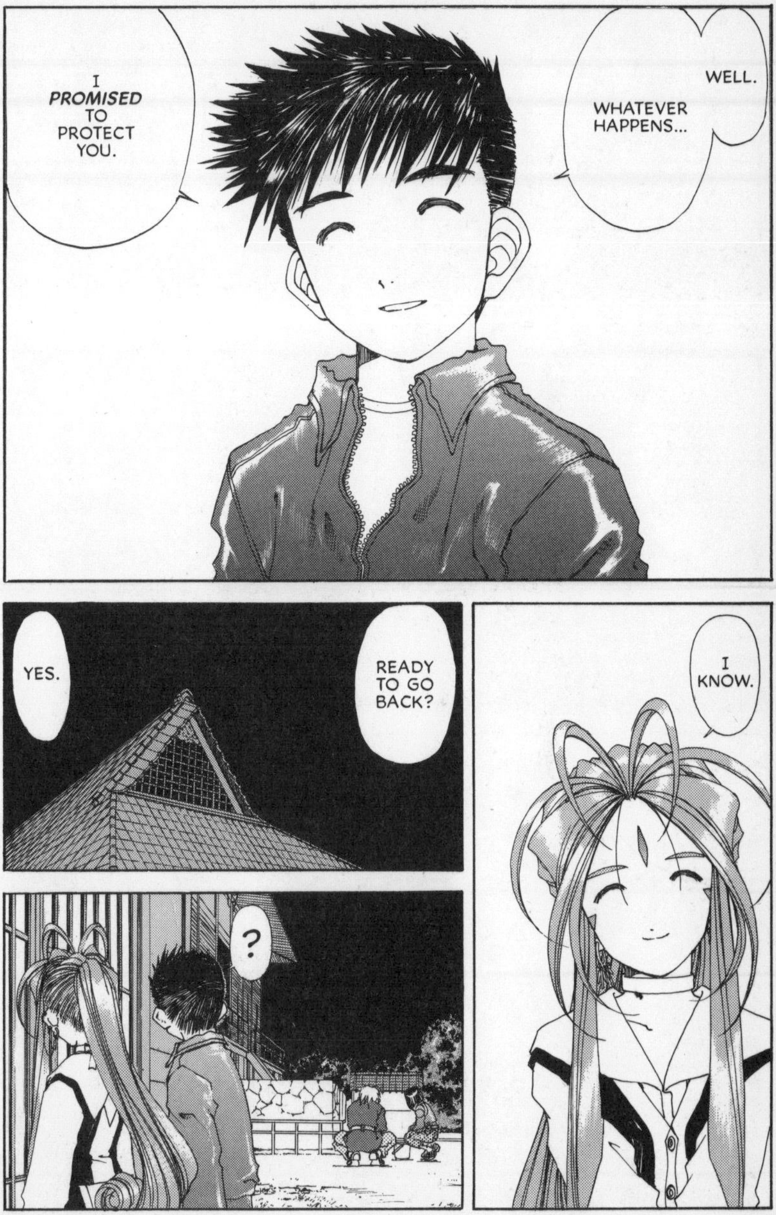
WELL.
WHATEVER HAPPENS...
I *PROMISED* TO PROTECT YOU.
I KNOW.
READY TO GO BACK?
YES.
?

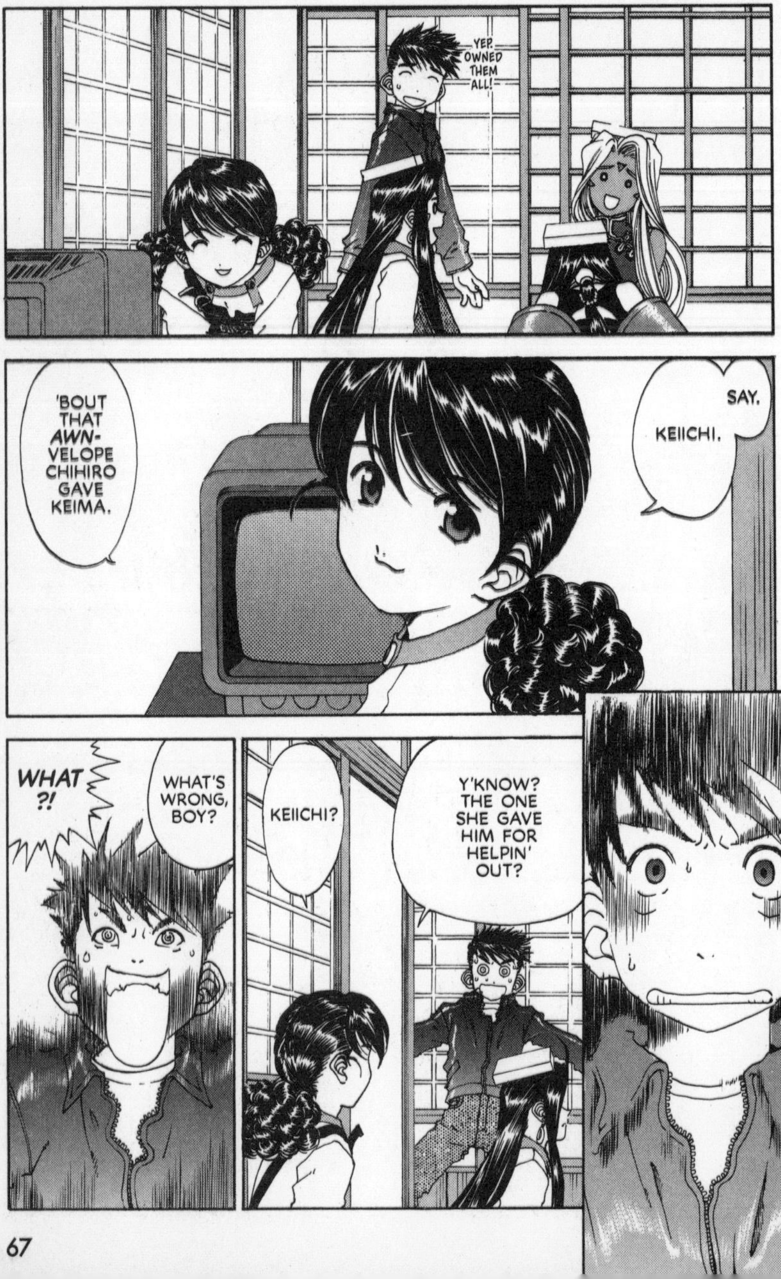
YEP. OWNED THEM ALL!
SAY. KEIICHI.
'BOUT THAT AWN-VELOPE CHIHIRO GAVE KEIMA.
Y'KNOW? THE ONE SHE GAVE HIM FOR HELPIN' OUT?
KEIICHI?
WHAT'S WRONG, BOY?
WHAT ?!

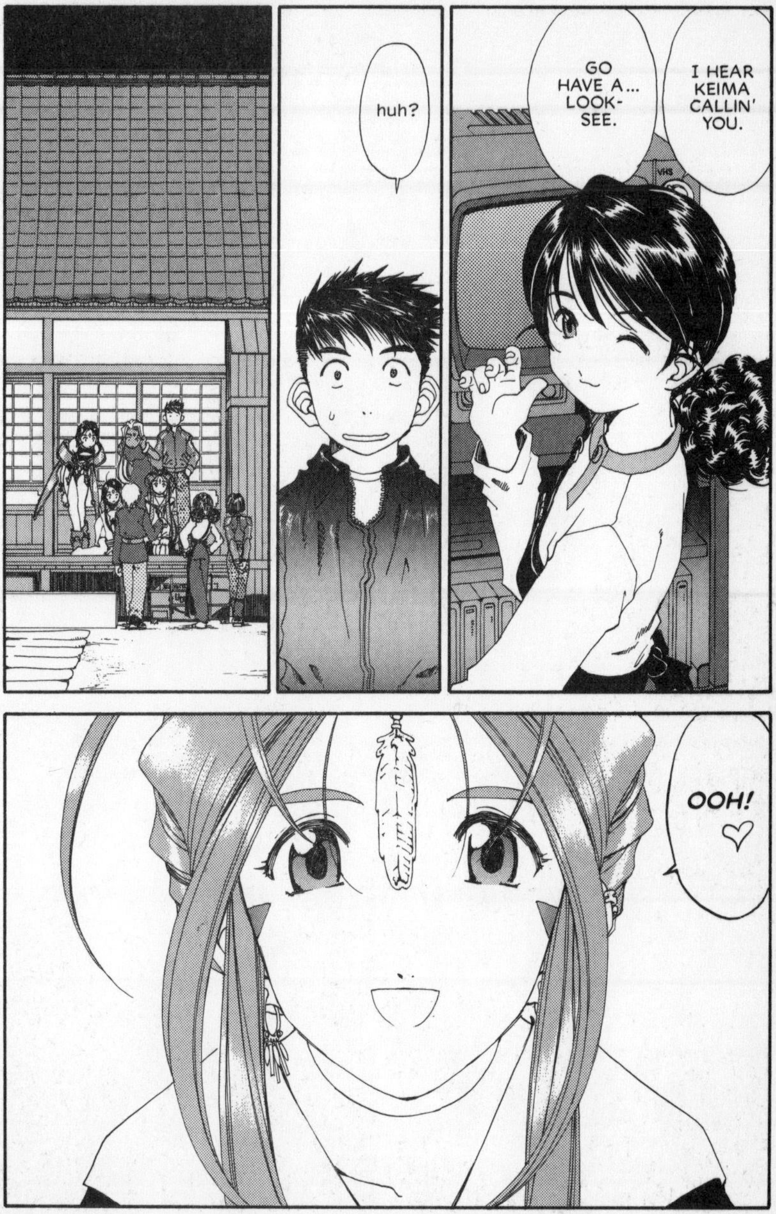
I HEAR KEIMA CALLIN' YOU.
GO HAVE A... LOOK-SEE.
huh?
OOH! ♥

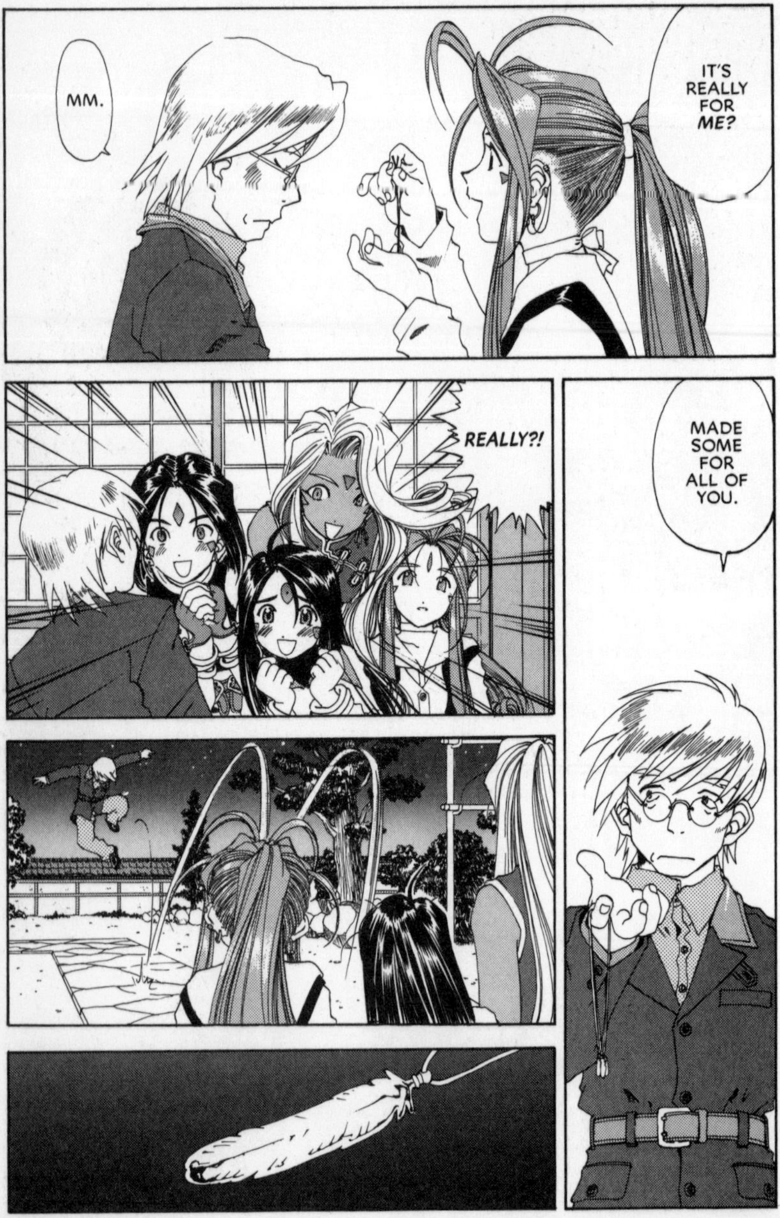
IT'S REALLY FOR ME?
MM.
MADE SOME FOR ALL OF YOU.
REALLY?!

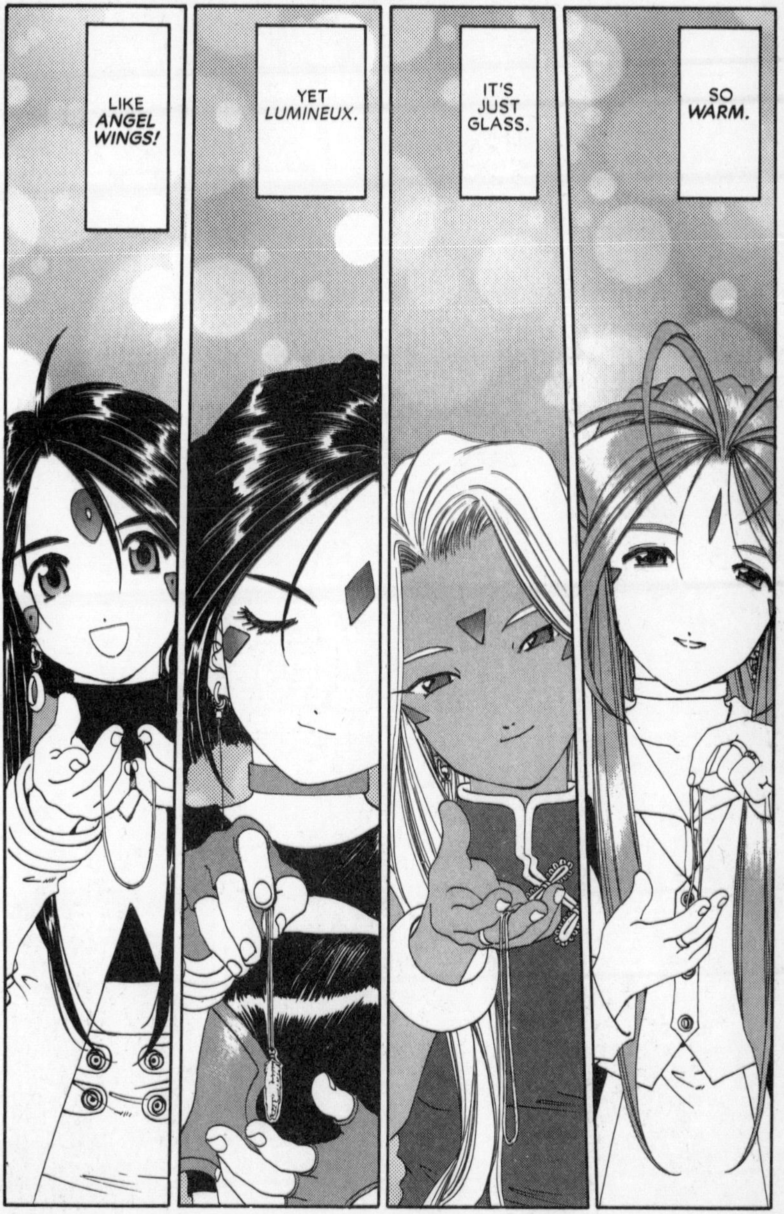
SO *WARM.*
IT'S JUST GLASS.
YET *LUMINEUX.*
LIKE *ANGEL WINGS!*

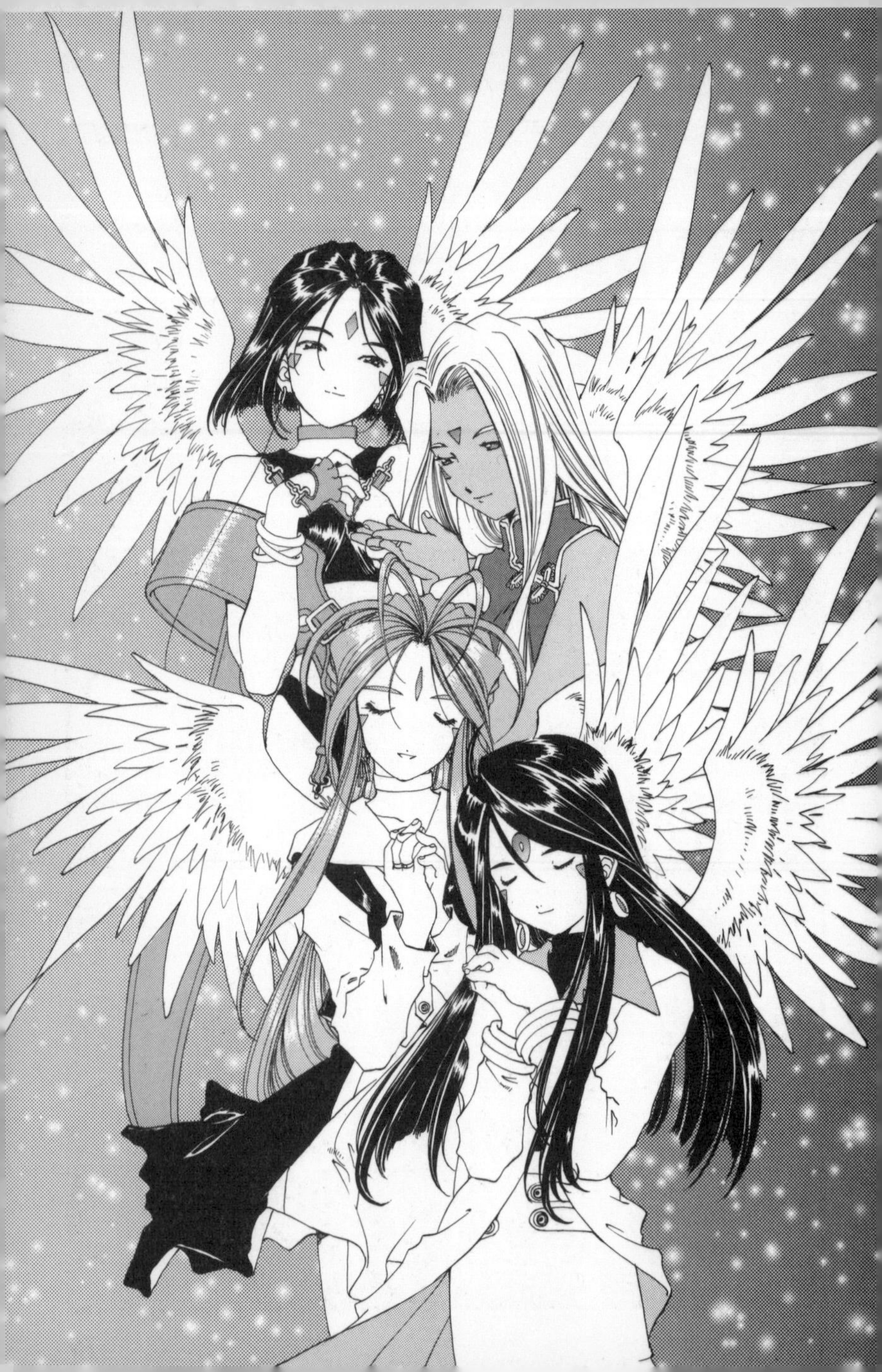

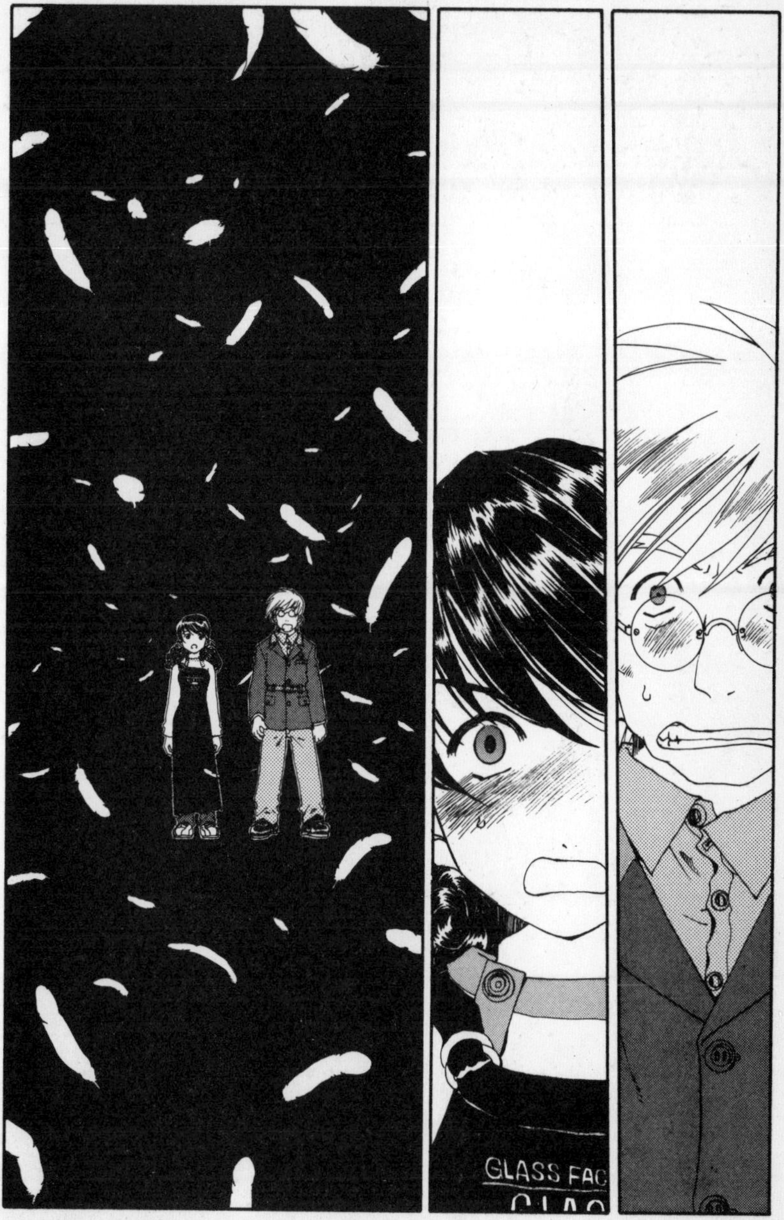
GLASS FAC

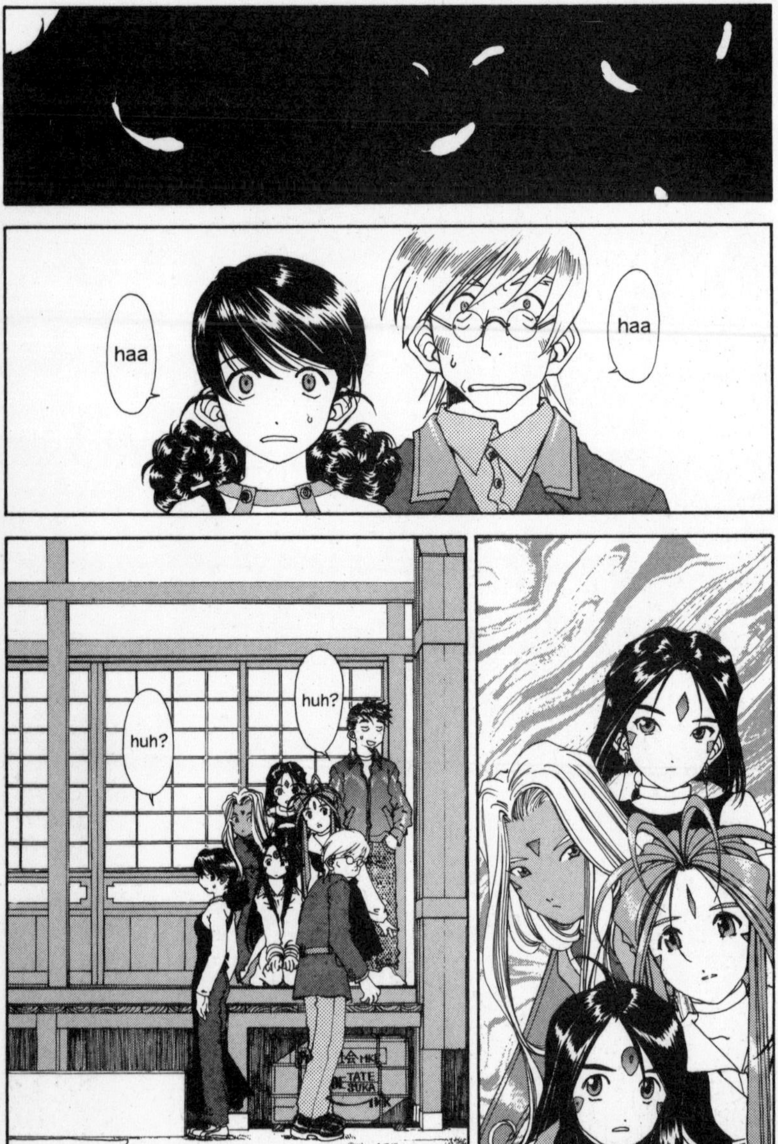
haa
haa
huh?
huh?

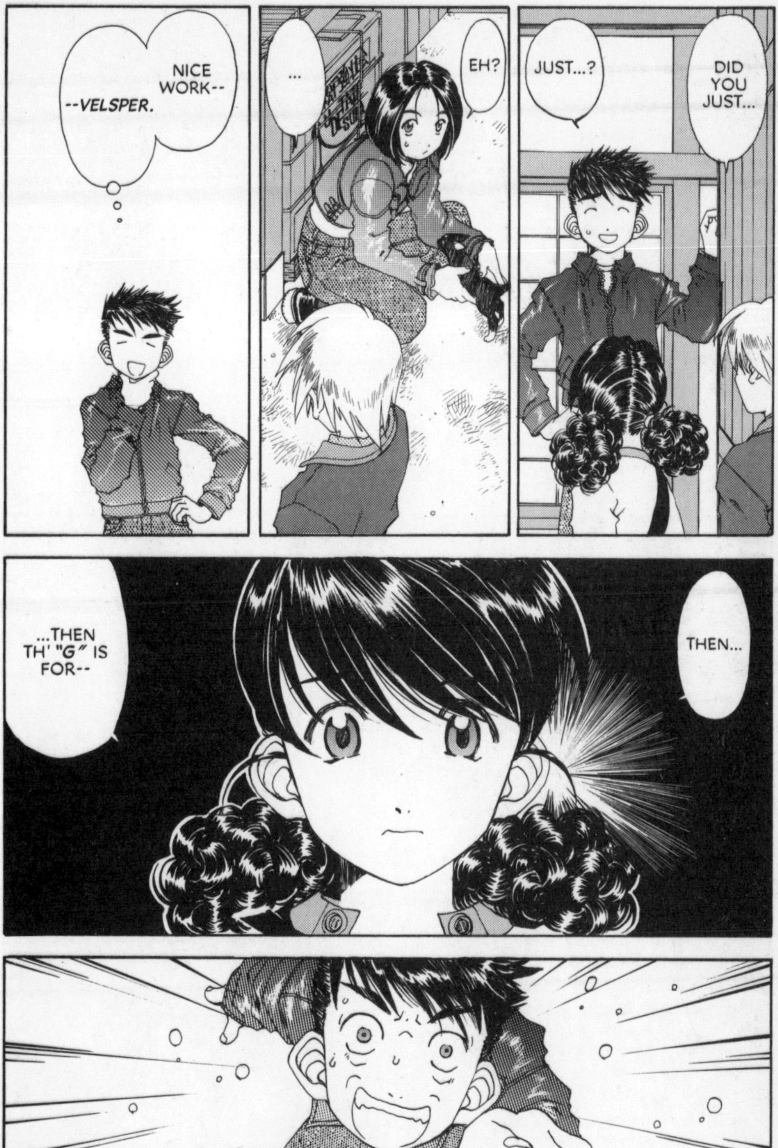
DID YOU JUST...
JUST...?
EH?
...
NICE WORK-- --VELSPER.
THEN...
...THEN TH' "G" IS FOR--

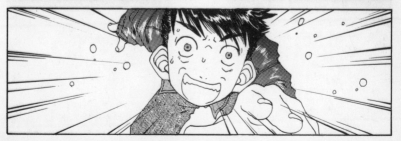

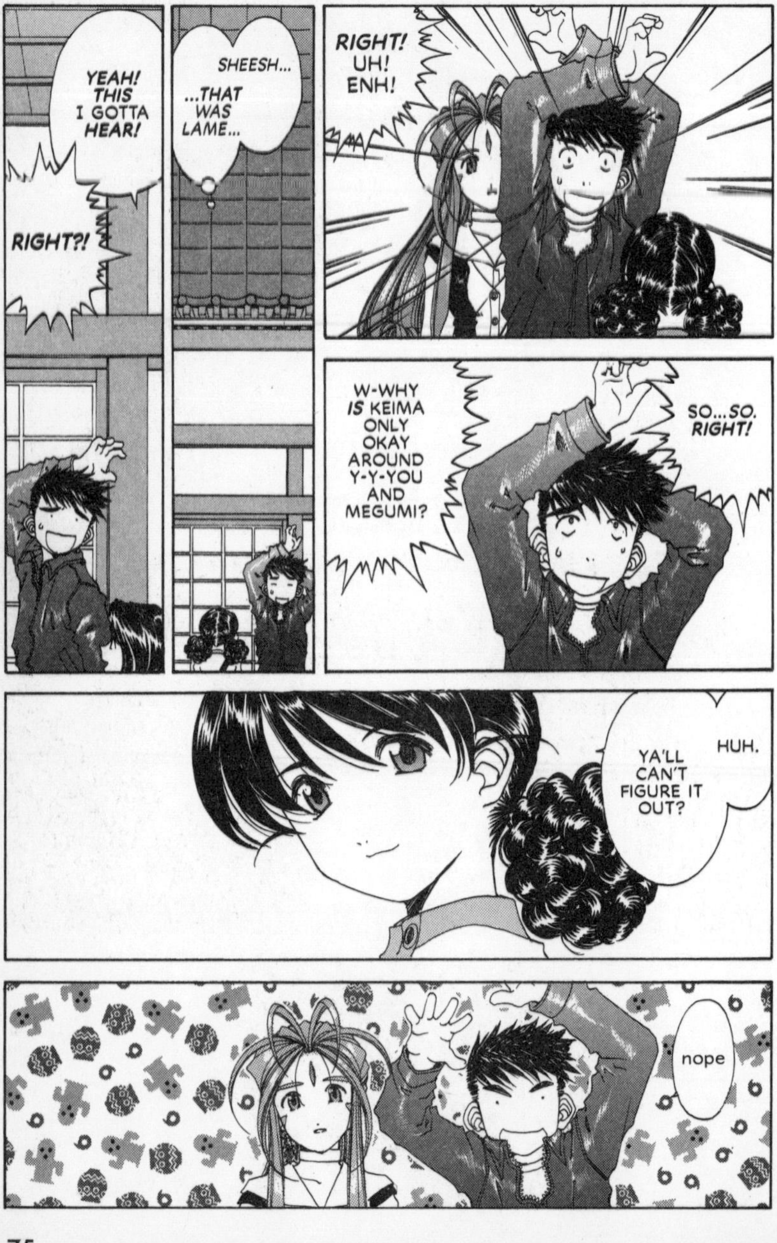
RIGHT! UH! ENH!
SO...SO. RIGHT!
W-WHY IS KEIMA ONLY OKAY AROUND Y-Y-YOU AND MEGUMI?
SHEESH...
...THAT WAS LAME...
YEAH! THIS I GOTTA HEAR!
RIGHT?!
HUH.
YA'LL CAN'T FIGURE IT OUT?
nope

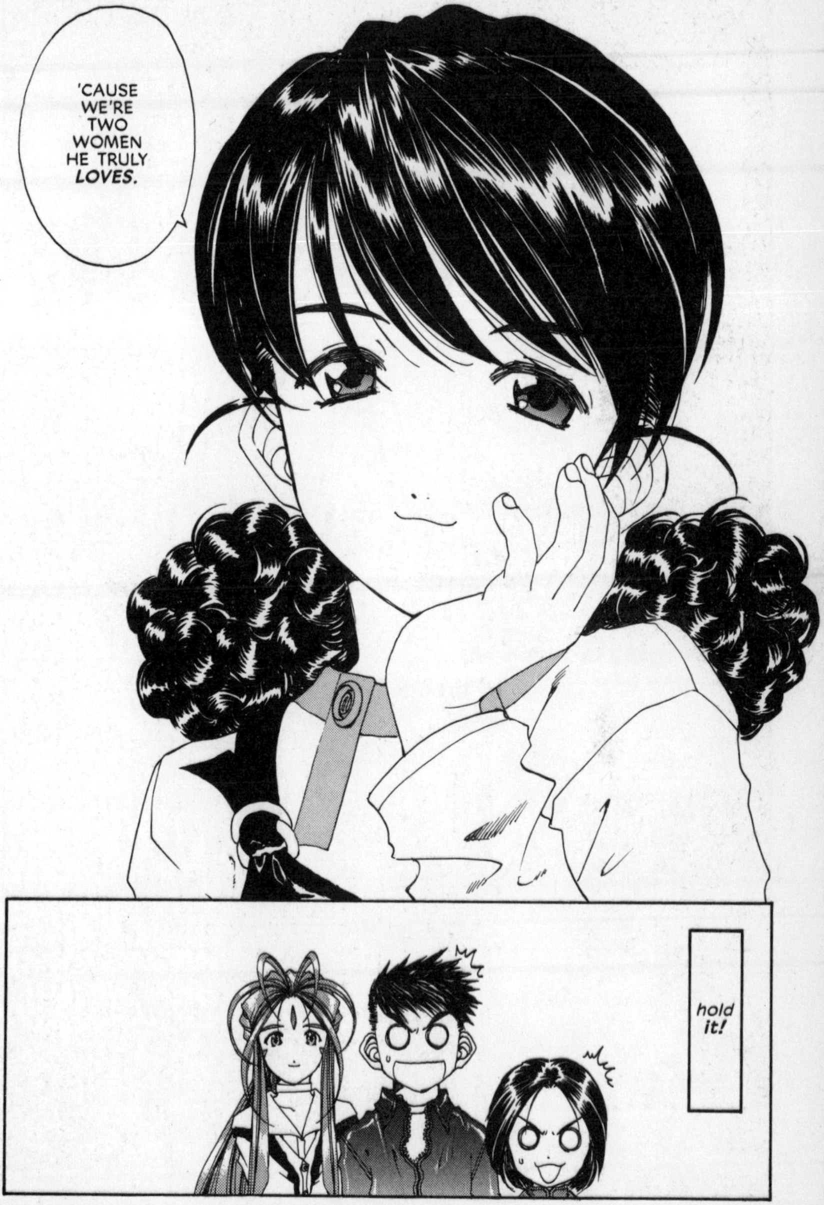
'CAUSE WE'RE TWO WOMEN HE TRULY *LOVES*.
hold it!

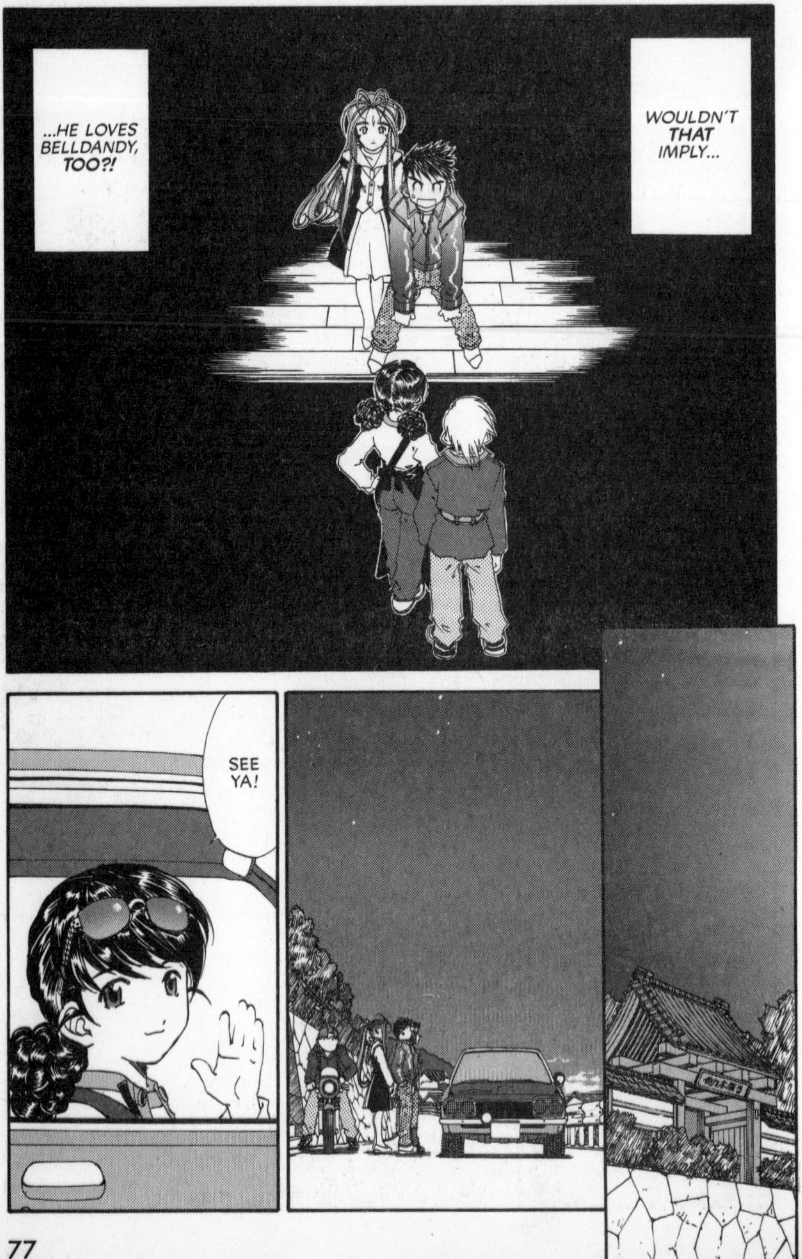
WOULDN'T THAT IMPLY...
...HE LOVES BELLDANDY, TOO?!
SEE YA!

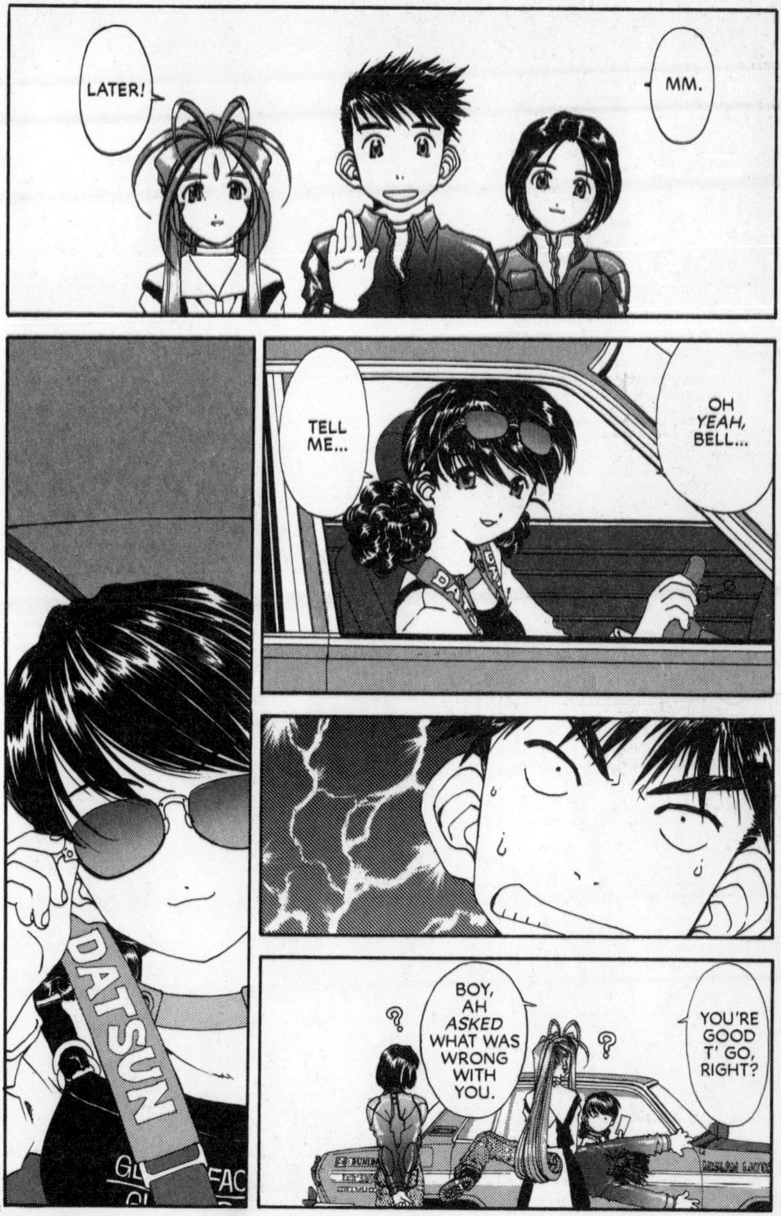
MM.
LATER!
OH *YEAH*, BELL...
TELL ME...
YOU'RE GOOD T' GO, RIGHT?
BOY, AH *ASKED* WHAT WAS WRONG WITH YOU.
DATSUN

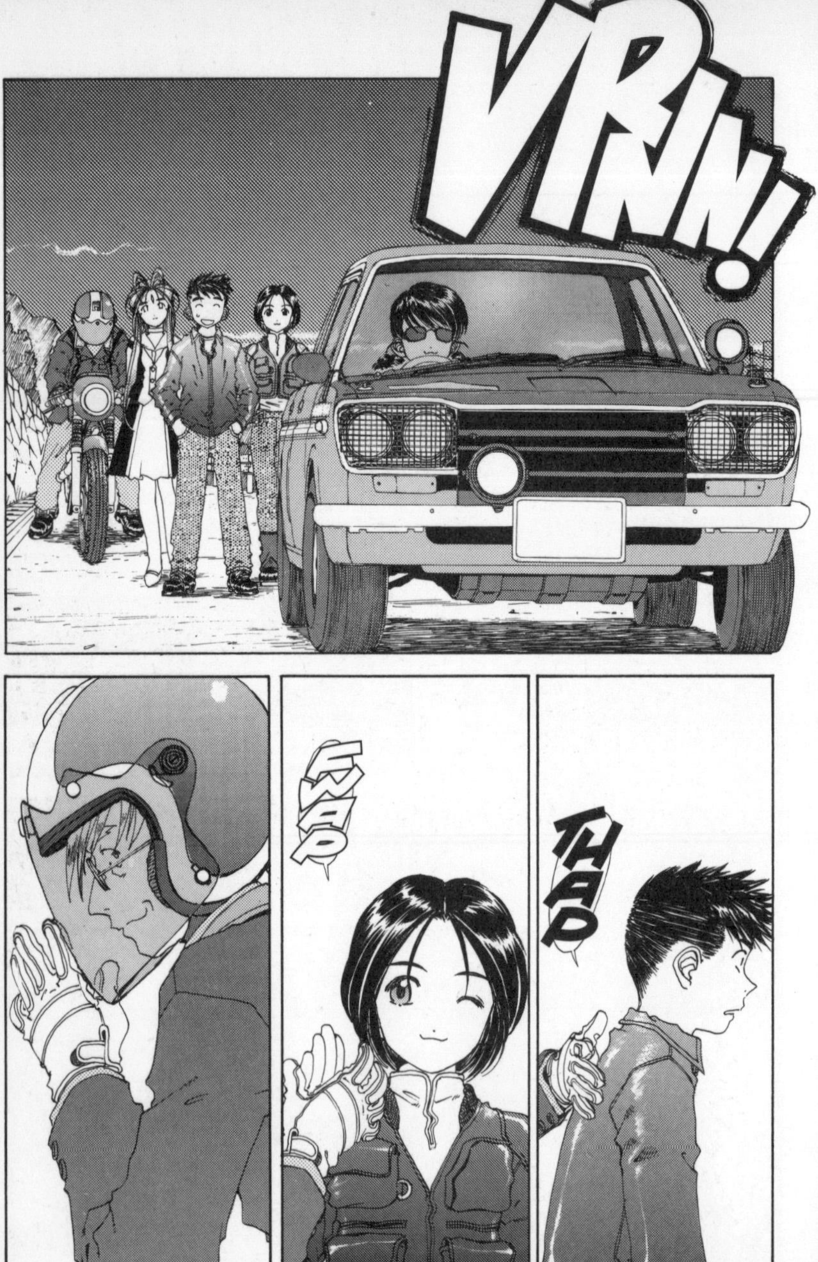
VRNN!
THAP
FWAP

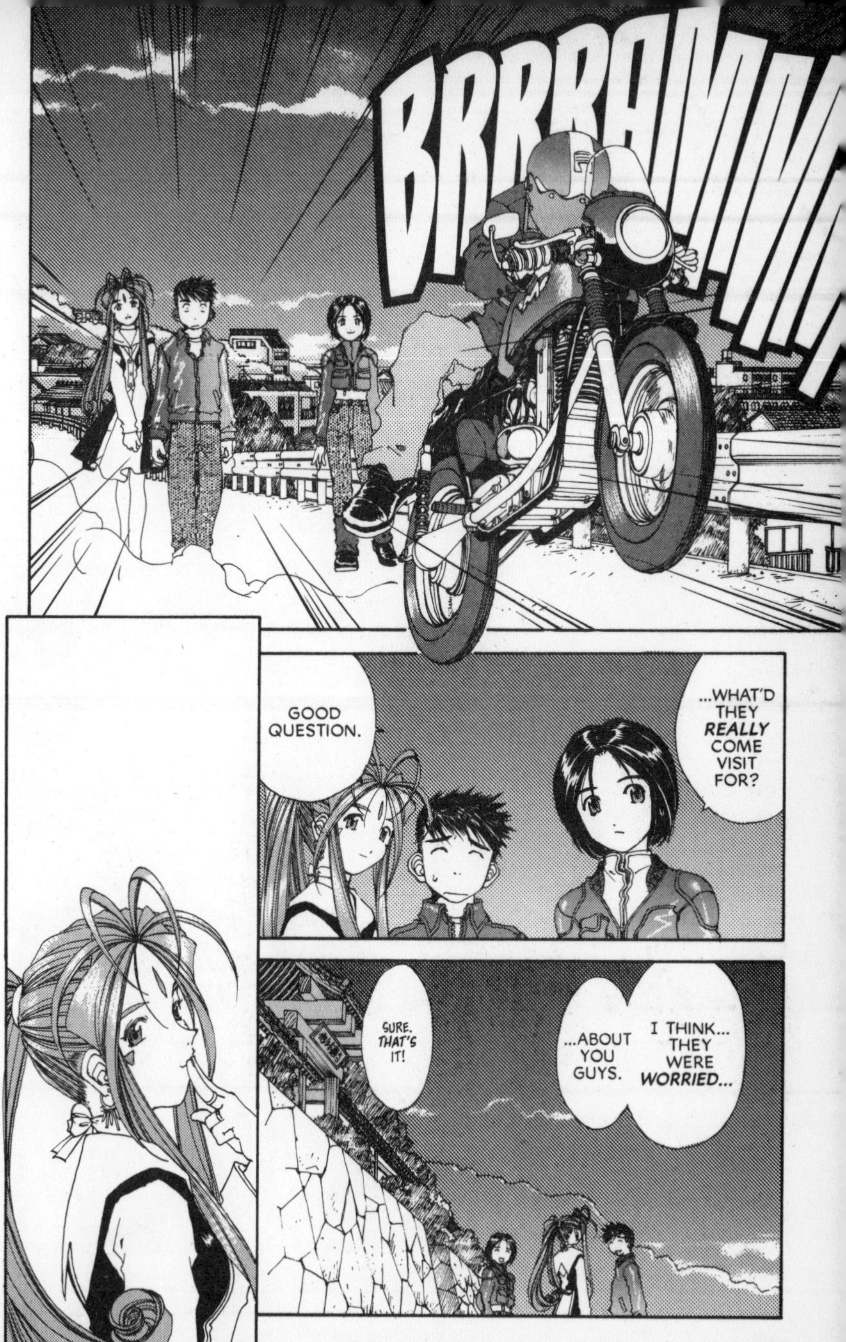
BRRRAMM
...WHAT'D THEY *REALLY* COME VISIT FOR?
GOOD QUESTION.
I THINK... THEY WERE *WORRIED...*
...ABOUT YOU GUYS.
SURE. *THAT'S* IT!

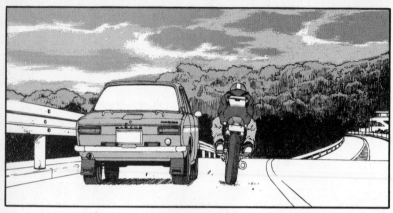

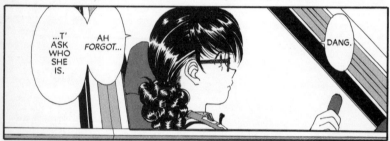

DANG.

...T' ASK WHO SHE IS.

AH FORGOT...

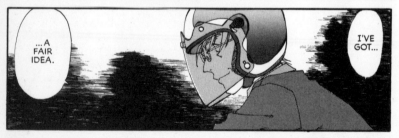

I'VE GOT...

...A FAIR IDEA.

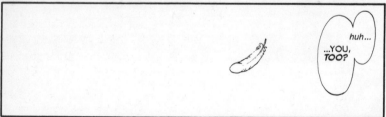

huh...

...YOU, TOO?

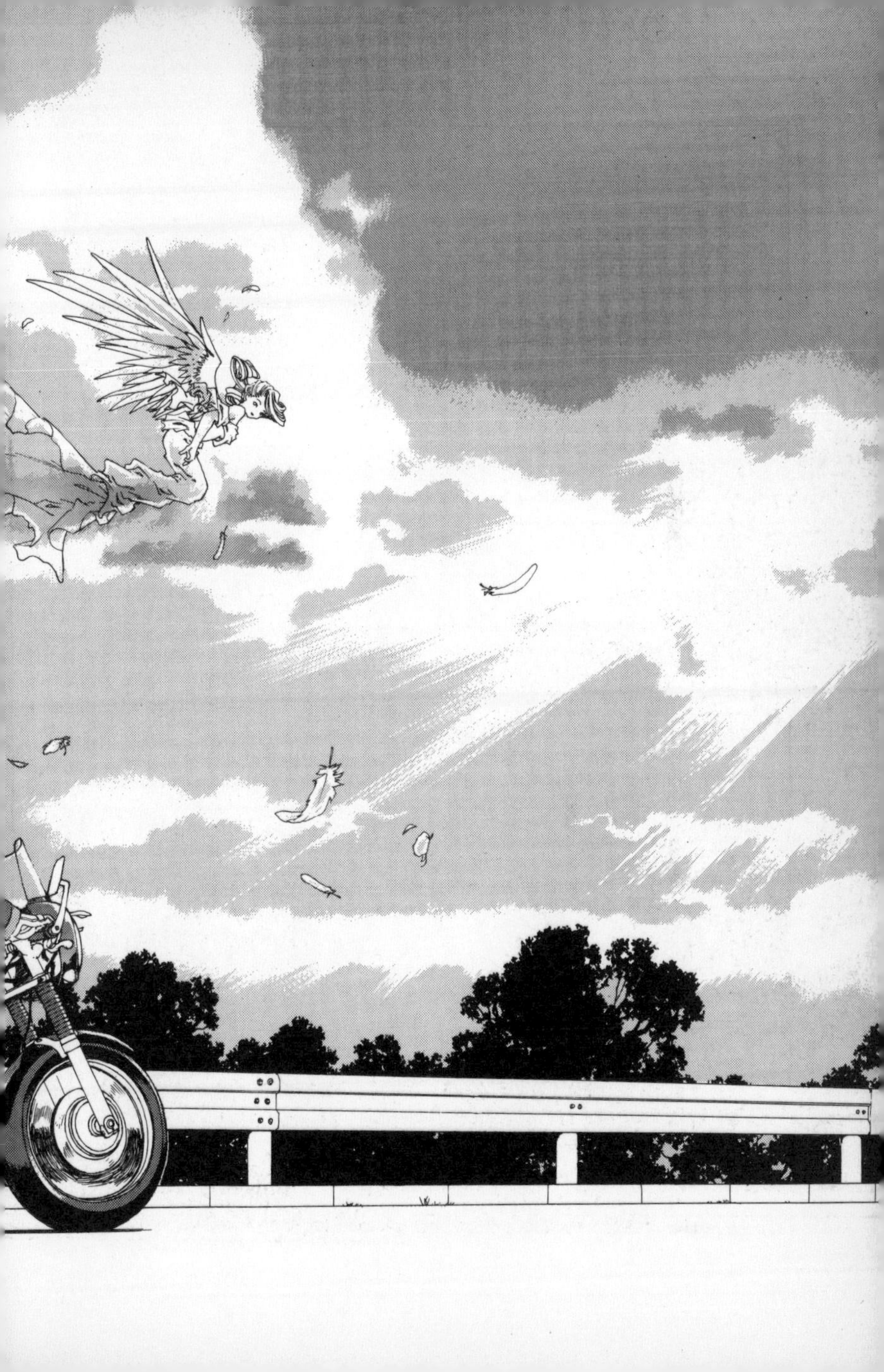

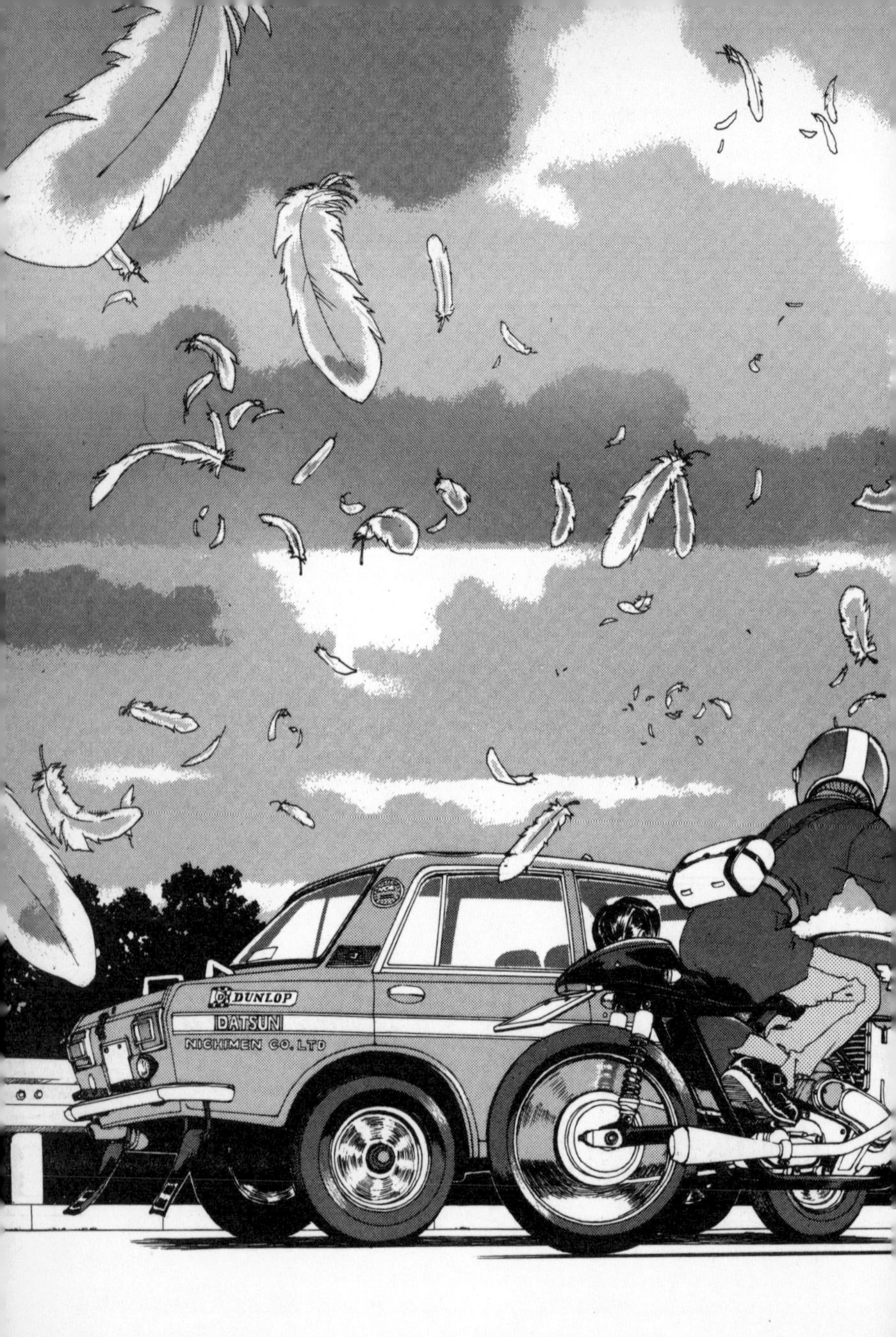
DUNLOP
DATSUN
NICHIMEN CO. LTD

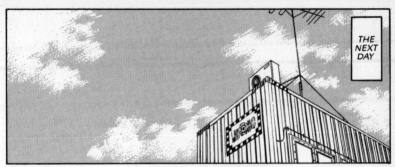

THE NEXT DAY
YOU PAID MY DAD WITH THIS?!
WELL, HE DIDN'T WANT TO ACCEPT IT...
CHIHIRO... HOW SHALL I PUT THIS... YOU'RE SO... SO...
...BUT I HAD TO MAKE HIM. HE DESERVED IT!
WIN A STAY AT
YUUFUIN
HOT SPRINGS RESORT
ONE COUPLE
WILL WIN
FOUR DAYS, THREE NIGHTS
0913864178
NOW IF THE TICKET WINS, WOULDN'T THAT BE COOL?
...SO CHEAP.

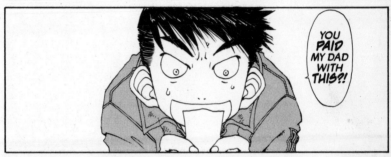

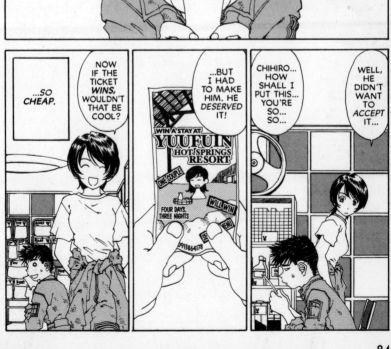

CHAPTER 153

The Hot Springs Episode

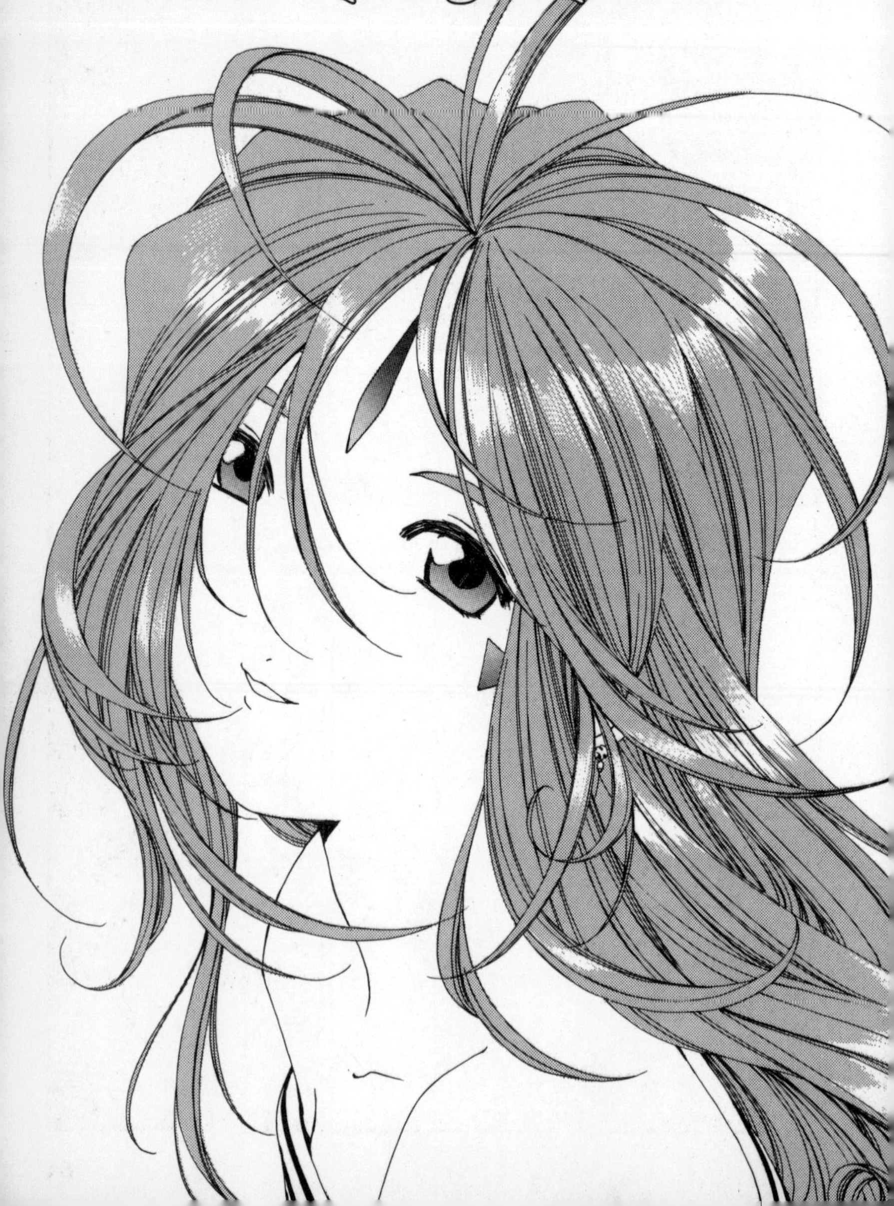

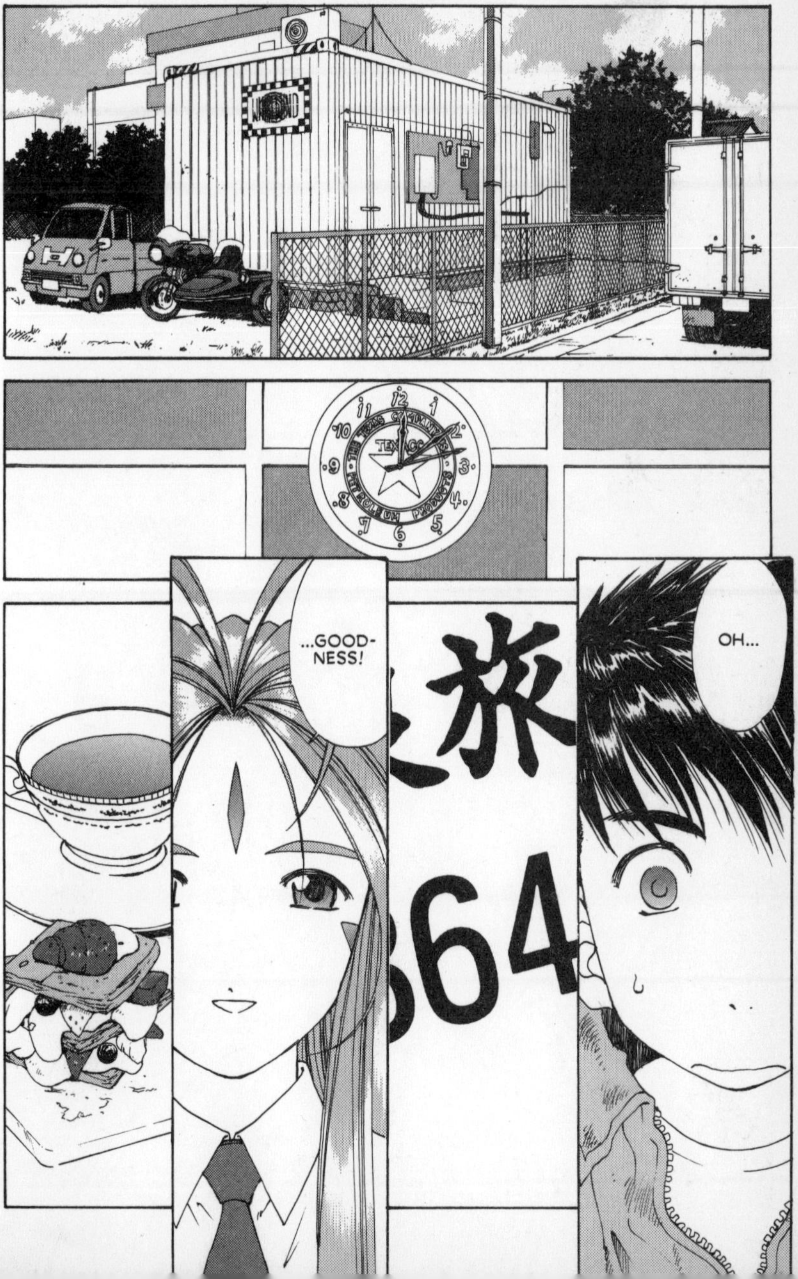
OH...
...GOOD-
NESS!

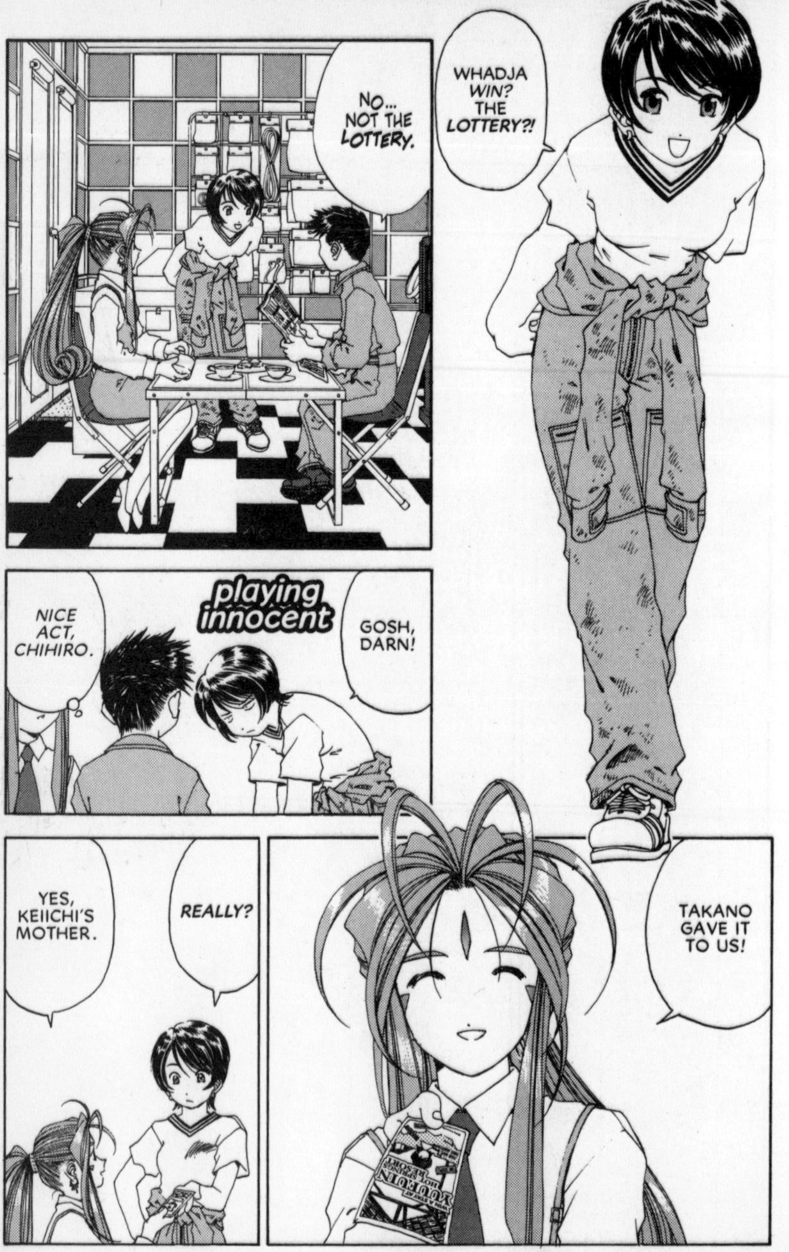
WHADJA WIN? THE LOTTERY?!
NO... NOT THE LOTTERY.
GOSH, DARN!
playing innocent
NICE ACT, CHIHIRO.
TAKANO GAVE IT TO US!
REALLY?
YES, KEIICHI'S MOTHER.

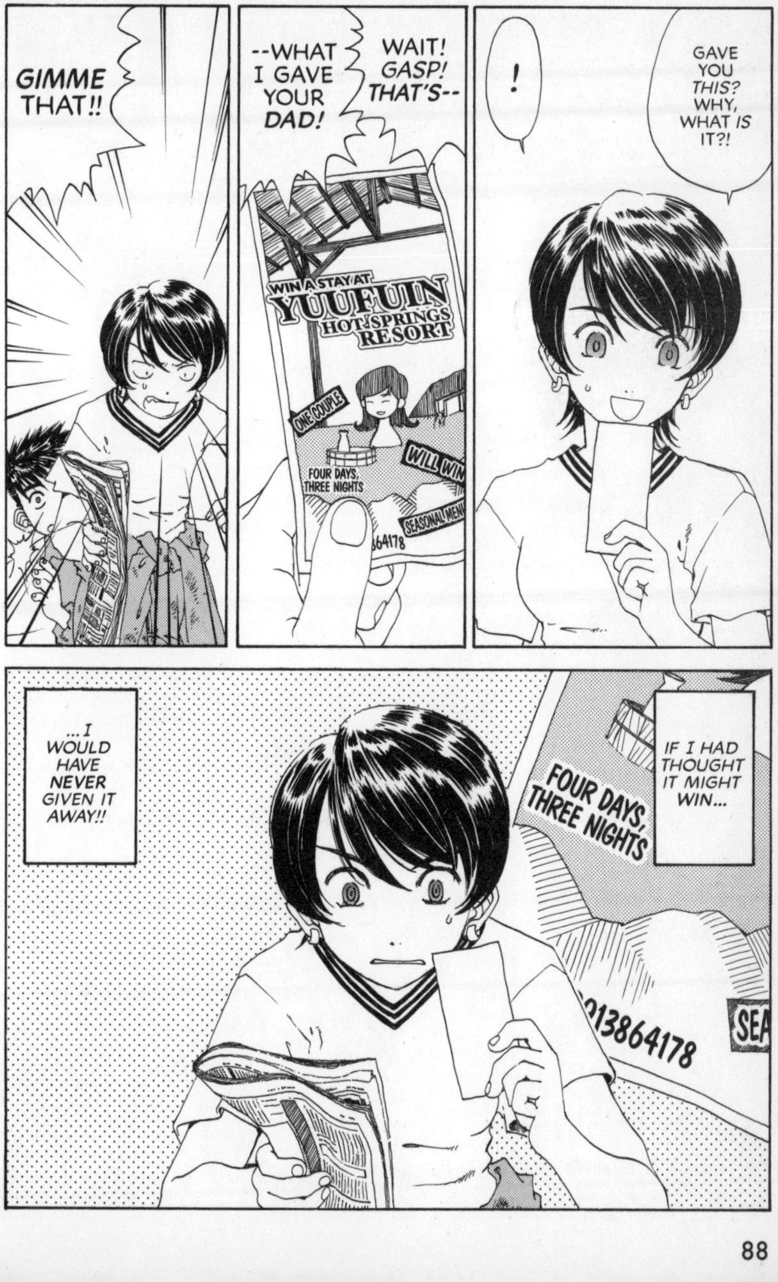
GAVE YOU THIS? WHY, WHAT IS IT?!
!
WAIT! GASP! THAT'S--
--WHAT I GAVE YOUR DAD!
WIN A STAY AT
YUUFUIN HOT SPRINGS RESORT
ONE COUPLE
WILL WIN
FOUR DAYS, THREE NIGHTS
GIMME THAT!!
IF I HAD THOUGHT IT MIGHT WIN...
FOUR DAYS, THREE NIGHTS
...I WOULD HAVE NEVER GIVEN IT AWAY!!

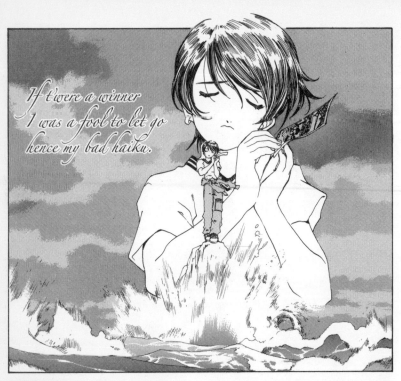

*If t'were a winner
I was a fool to let go
hence my bad haiku.*

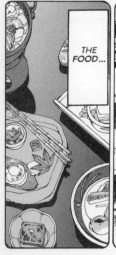

THE FOOD...

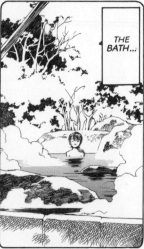

THE BATH...

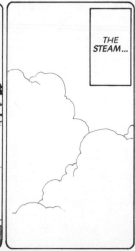

THE STEAM...

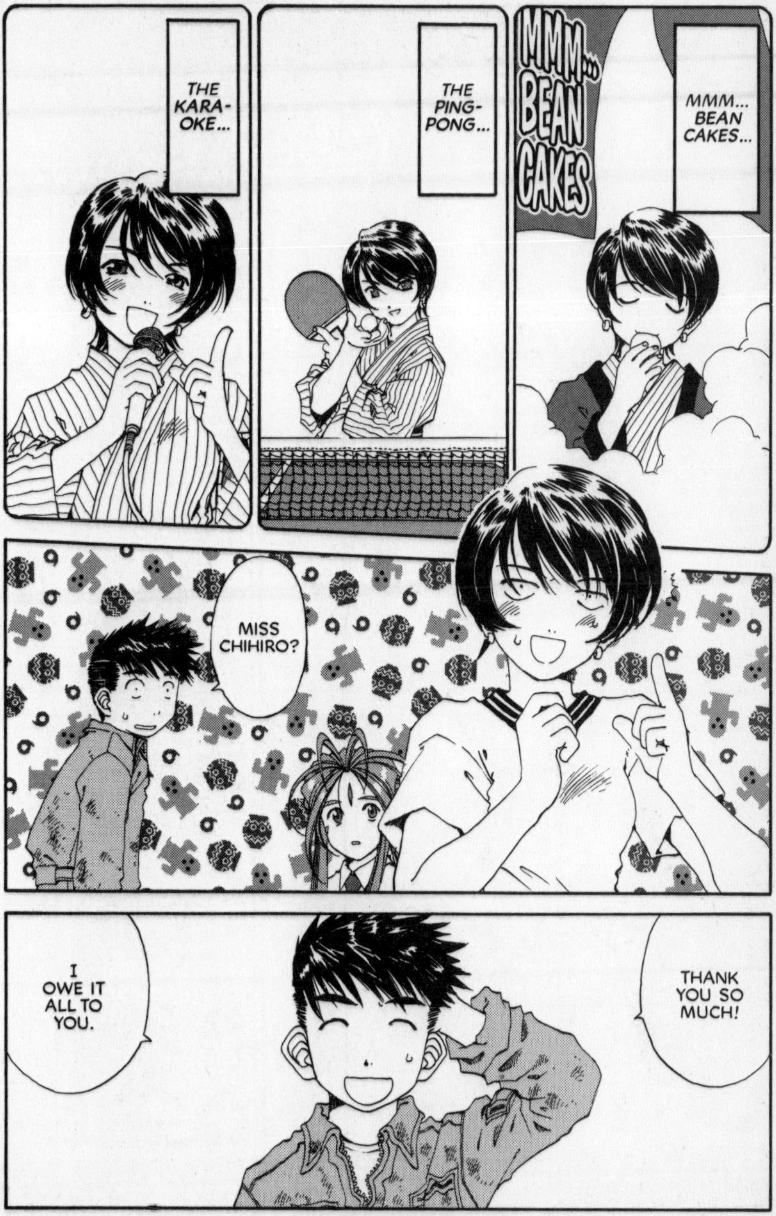
MMM... BEAN CAKES...
MMM... BEAN CAKES
THE PING-PONG...
THE KARA-OKE...
MISS CHIHIRO?
THANK YOU SO MUCH!
I OWE IT ALL TO YOU.

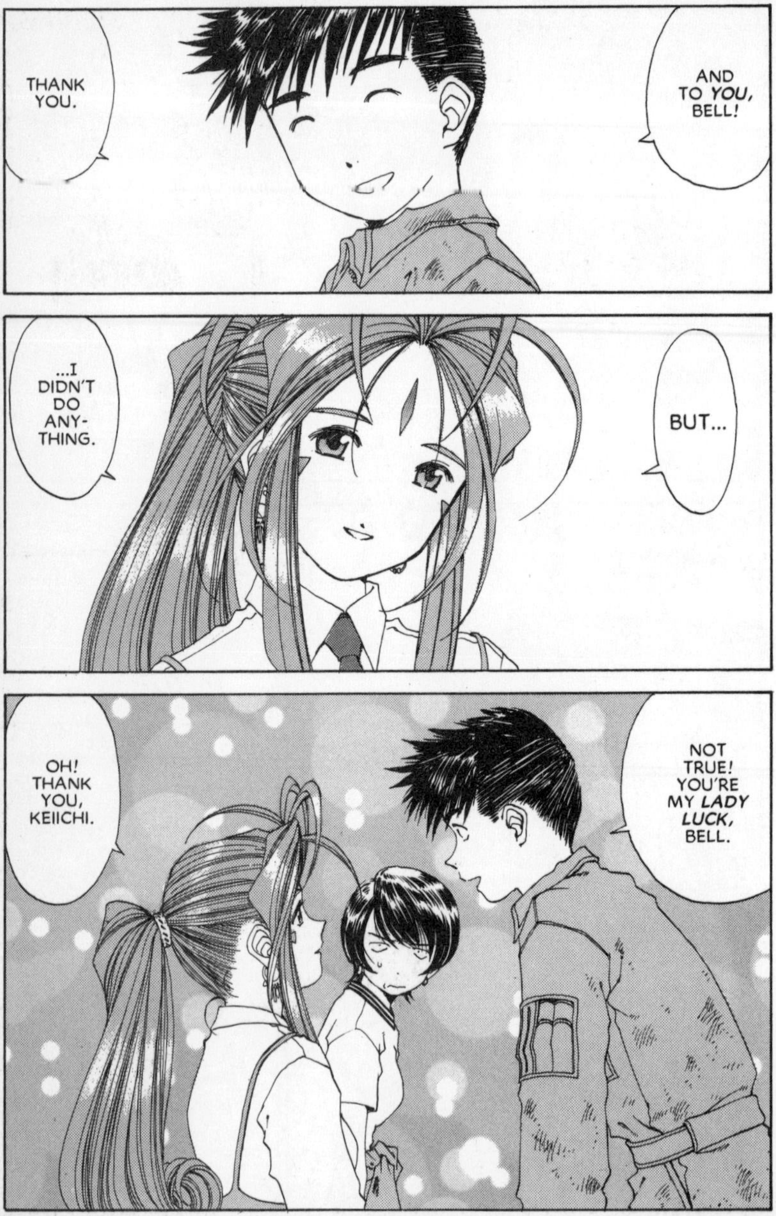
AND TO *YOU*, BELL!
THANK YOU.
BUT...
...I DIDN'T DO ANY-THING.
NOT TRUE! YOU'RE MY *LADY LUCK*, BELL.
OH! THANK YOU, KEIICHI.

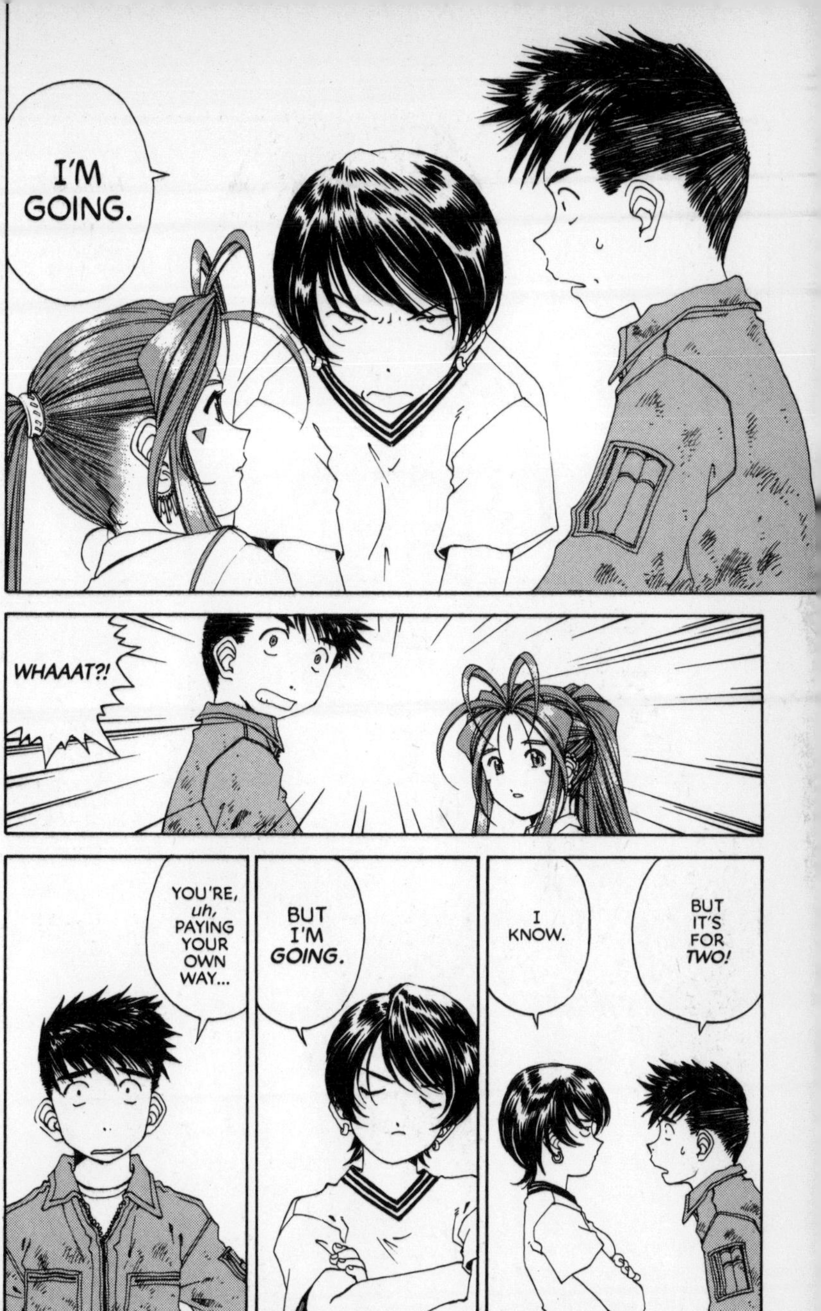
I'M GOING.
WHAAAT?!
BUT IT'S FOR *TWO!*
I KNOW.
BUT I'M *GOING*.
YOU'RE, *uh*, PAYING YOUR OWN WAY...

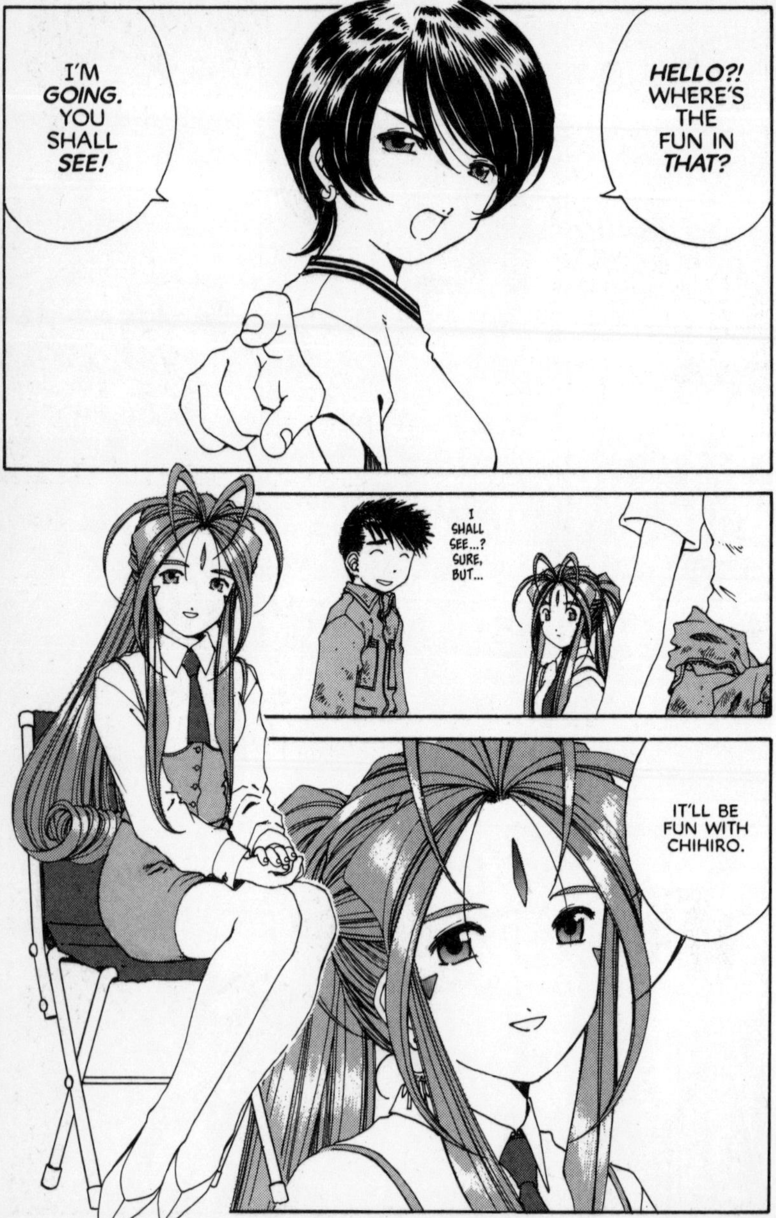
HELLO?! WHERE'S THE FUN IN THAT?
I'M GOING. YOU SHALL SEE!
I SHALL SEE...? SURE, BUT...
IT'LL BE FUN WITH CHIHIRO.

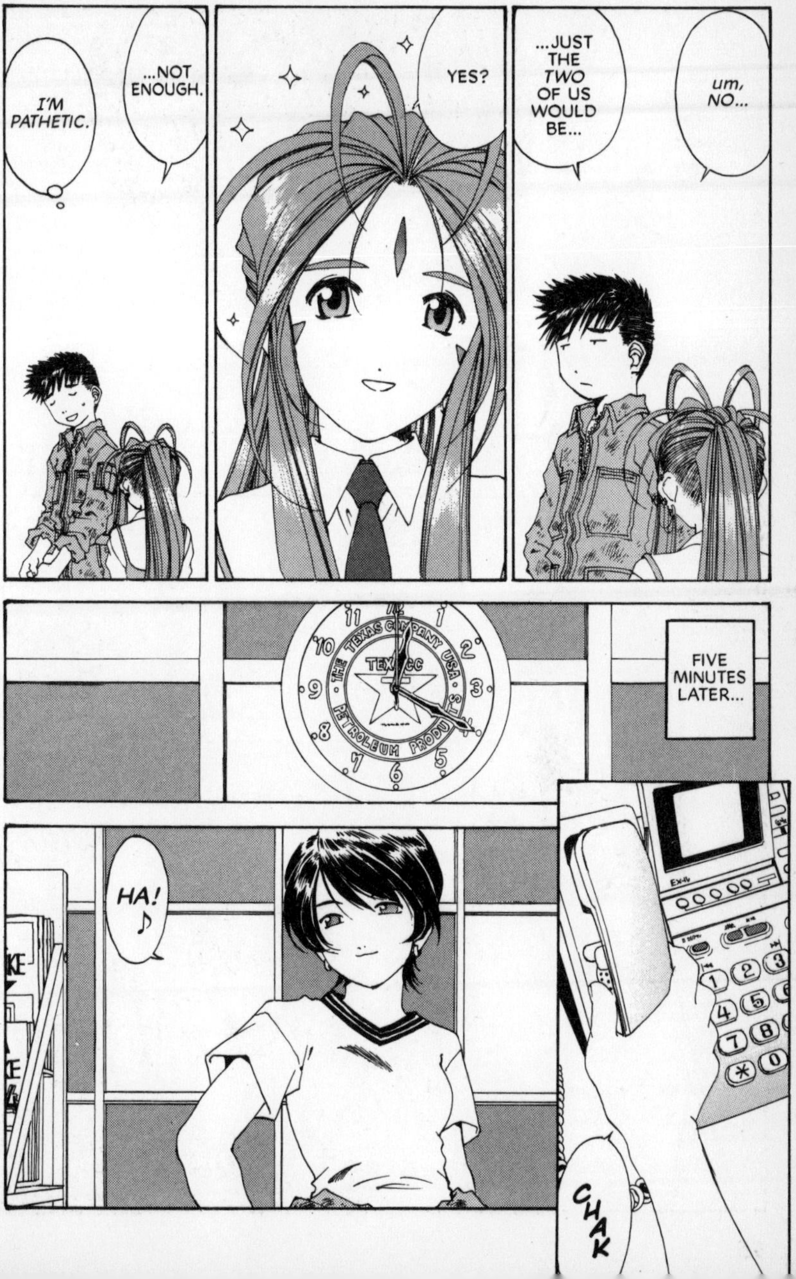
um, NO...
...JUST THE *TWO* OF US WOULD BE...
YES?
...NOT ENOUGH.
I'M PATHETIC.
FIVE MINUTES LATER...
CHAK
HA! ♪

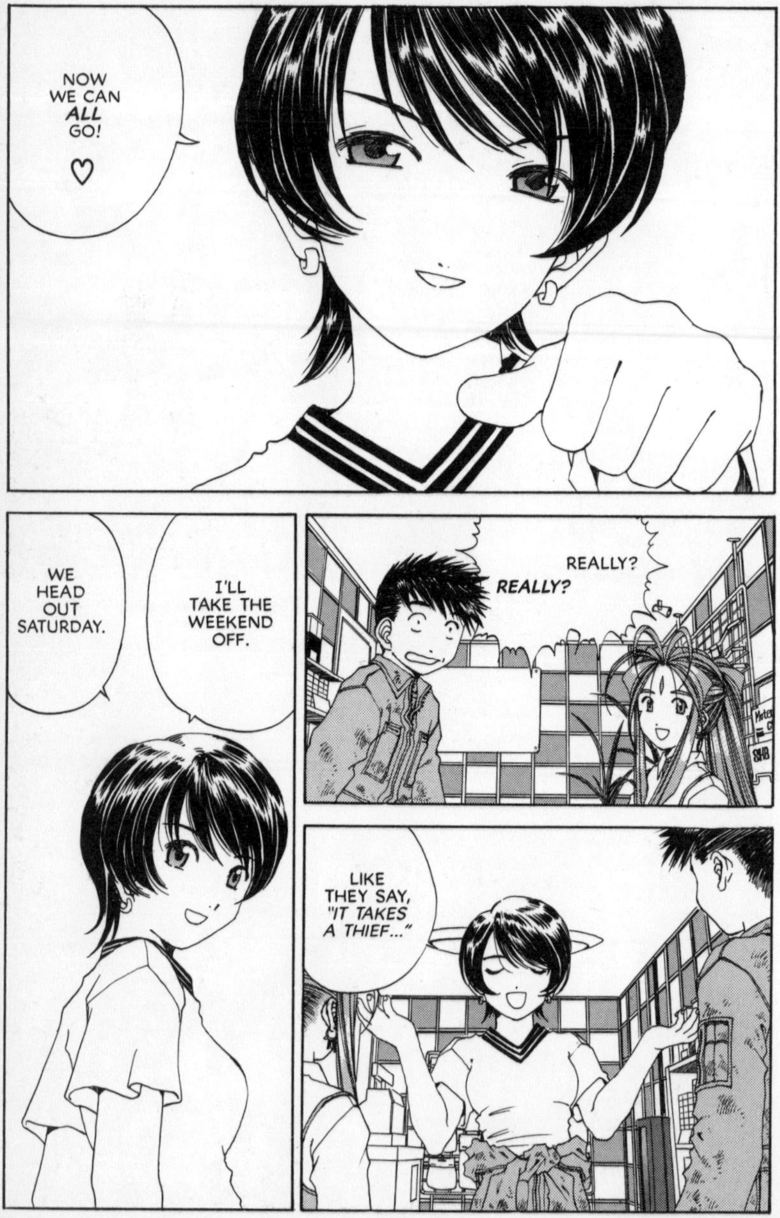
NOW WE CAN ***ALL*** GO! ♡
REALLY?
REALLY?
LIKE THEY SAY, *"IT TAKES A THIEF..."*
I'LL TAKE THE WEEKEND OFF.
WE HEAD OUT SATURDAY.

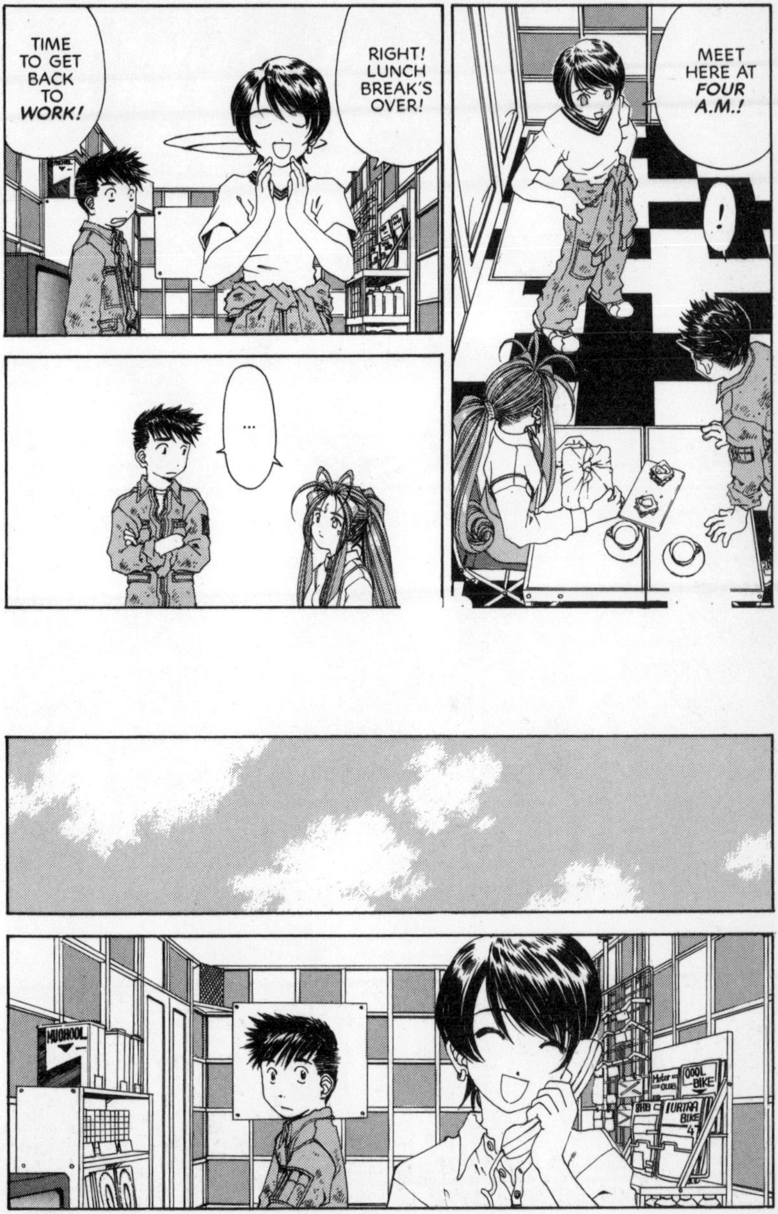
MEET HERE AT FOUR A.M.!
!
RIGHT! LUNCH BREAK'S OVER!
TIME TO GET BACK TO WORK!
...

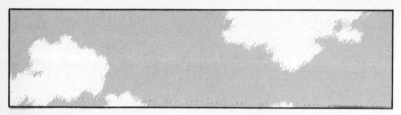

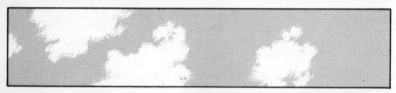

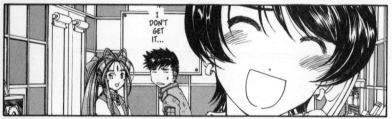

I
DON'T
GET
IT...

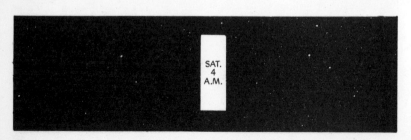

SAT.
4
A.M.

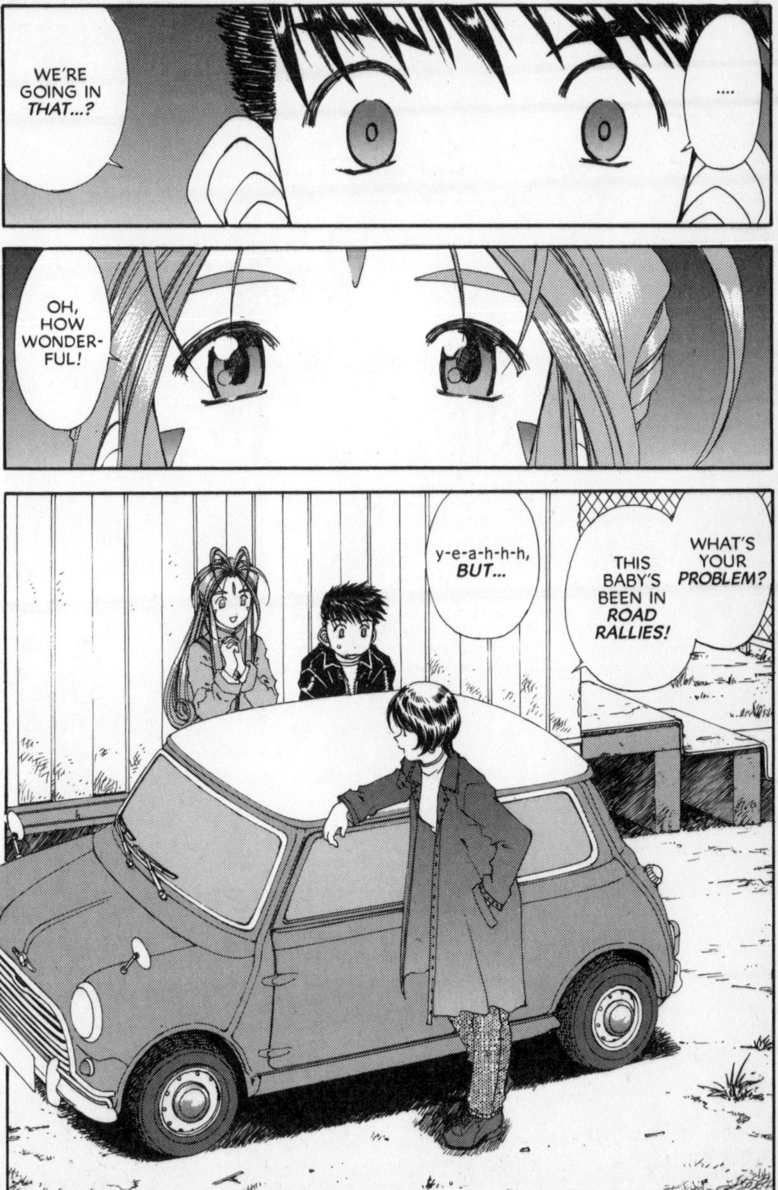
....
WE'RE GOING IN *THAT...?*
OH, HOW WONDER-FUL!
WHAT'S YOUR *PROBLEM?*
THIS BABY'S BEEN IN *ROAD RALLIES!*
y-e-a-h-h-h, *BUT...*

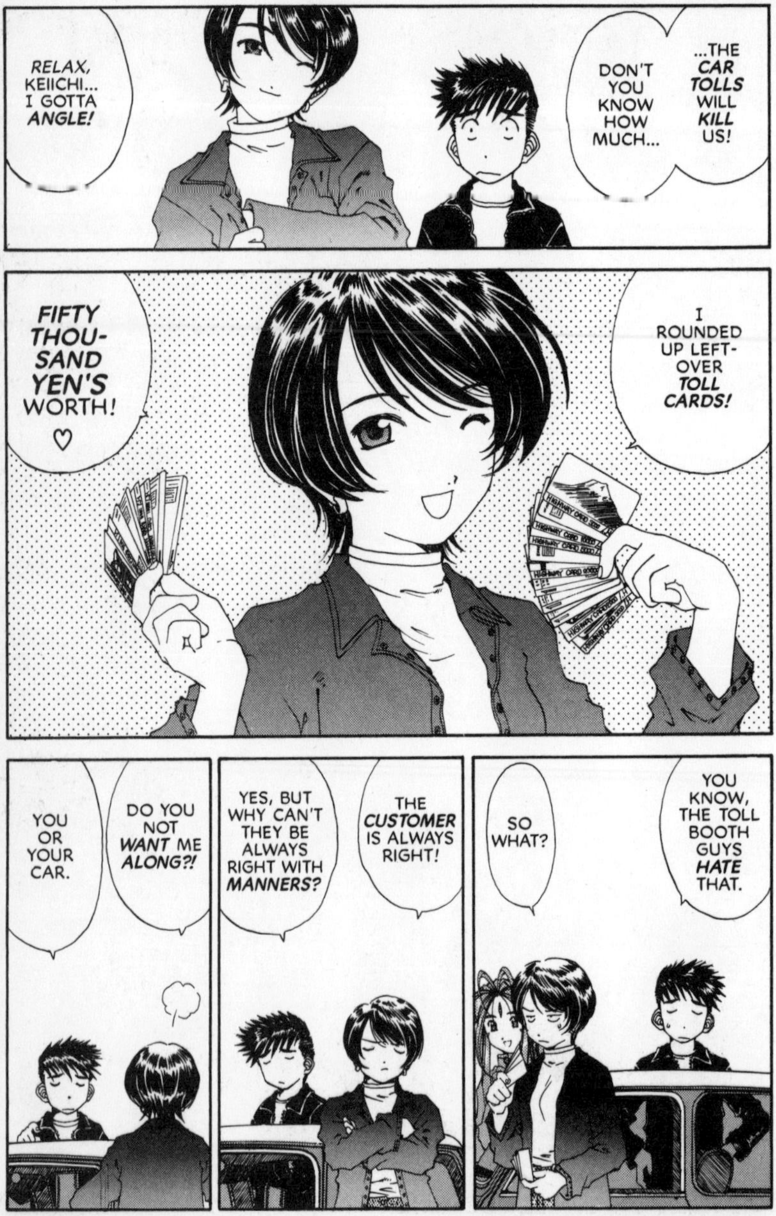
...THE CAR TOLLS WILL KILL US!
DON'T YOU KNOW HOW MUCH...
RELAX, KEIICHI... I GOTTA ANGLE!
I ROUNDED UP LEFT-OVER TOLL CARDS!
FIFTY THOU-SAND YEN'S WORTH! ♡
YOU KNOW, THE TOLL BOOTH GUYS HATE THAT.
SO WHAT?
THE CUSTOMER IS ALWAYS RIGHT!
YES, BUT WHY CAN'T THEY BE ALWAYS RIGHT WITH MANNERS?
DO YOU NOT WANT ME ALONG?!
YOU OR YOUR CAR.

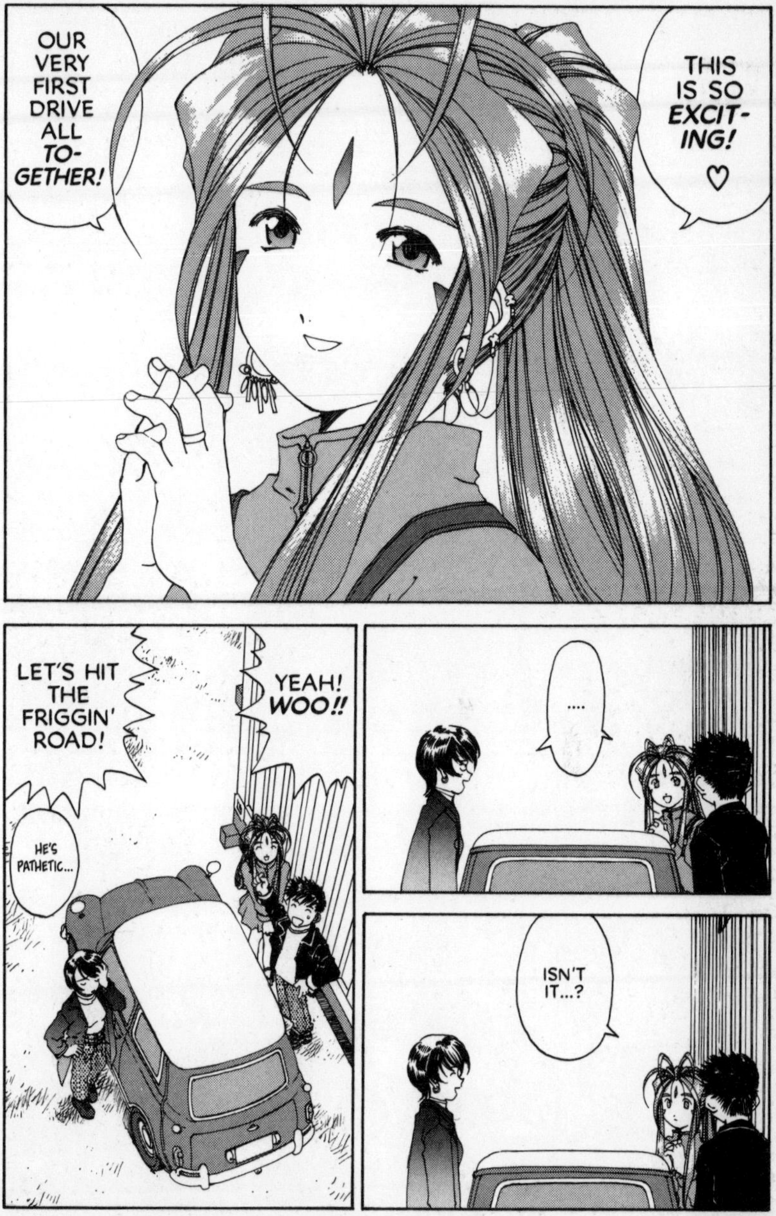
THIS IS SO EXCIT- ING! ♡
OUR VERY FIRST DRIVE ALL TO- GETHER!
....
ISN'T IT...?
YEAH! WOO!!
LET'S HIT THE FRIGGIN' ROAD!
HE'S PATHETIC...

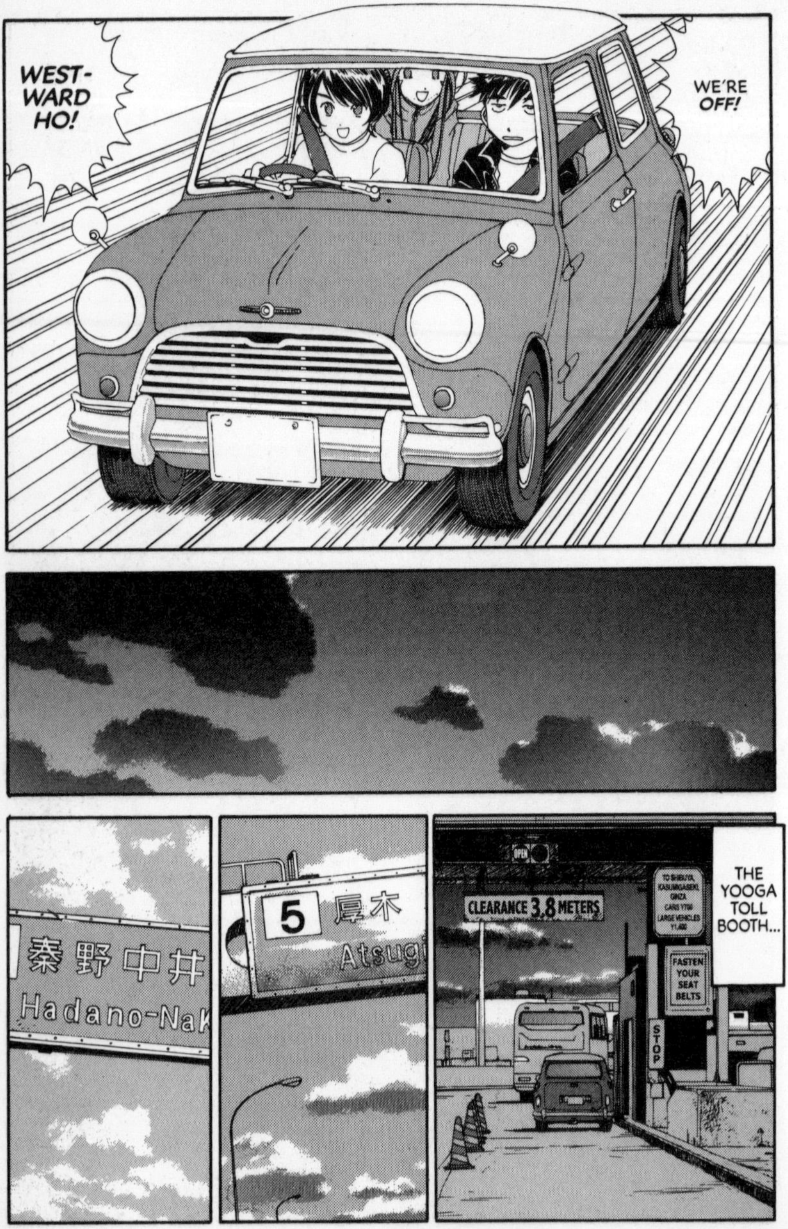
WE'RE OFF!
WEST-WARD HO!
THE YOOGA TOLL BOOTH...
OPEN
CLEARANCE 3.8 METERS
TO SHIBUYA
GINZA
LARGE VEHICLES
FASTEN YOUR SEAT BELTS
STOP
5 厚木
Atsugi
秦野中井
Hadano-Nak

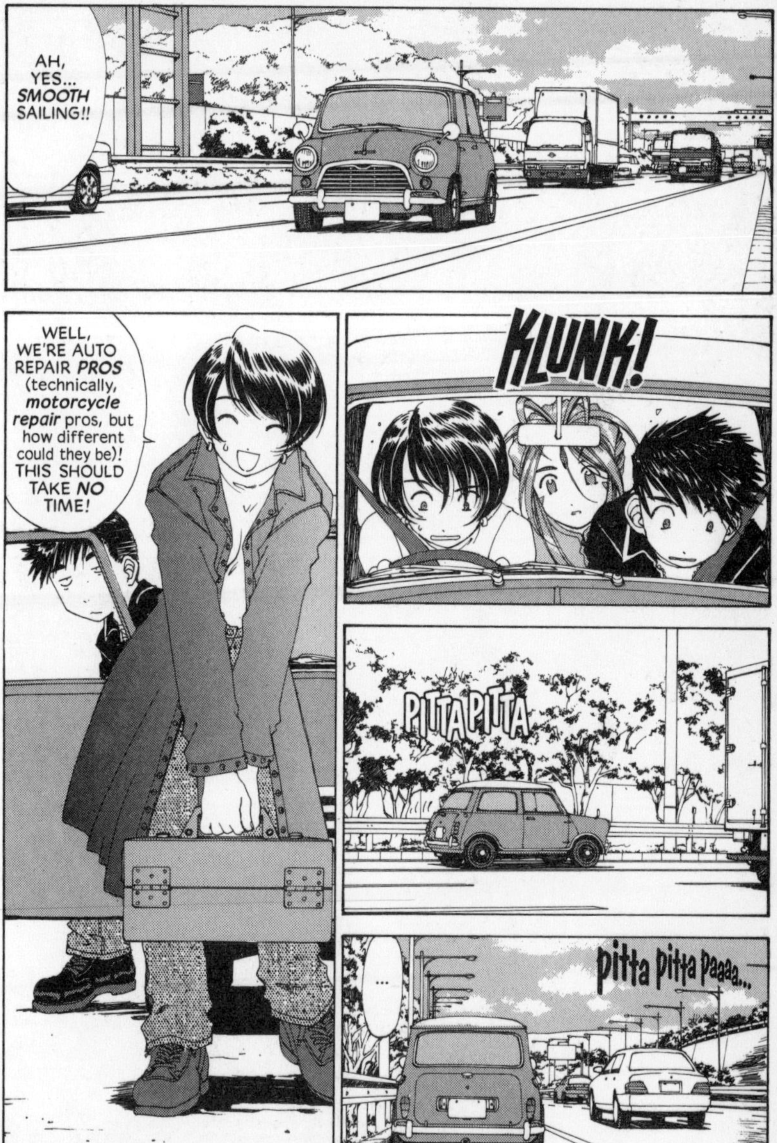
AH, YES... SMOOTH SAILING!!
KLUNK!
PITTA PITTA
pitta pitta paaa...
...
WELL, WE'RE AUTO REPAIR PROS (technically, motorcycle repair pros, but how different could they be)! THIS SHOULD TAKE NO TIME!

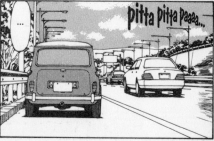

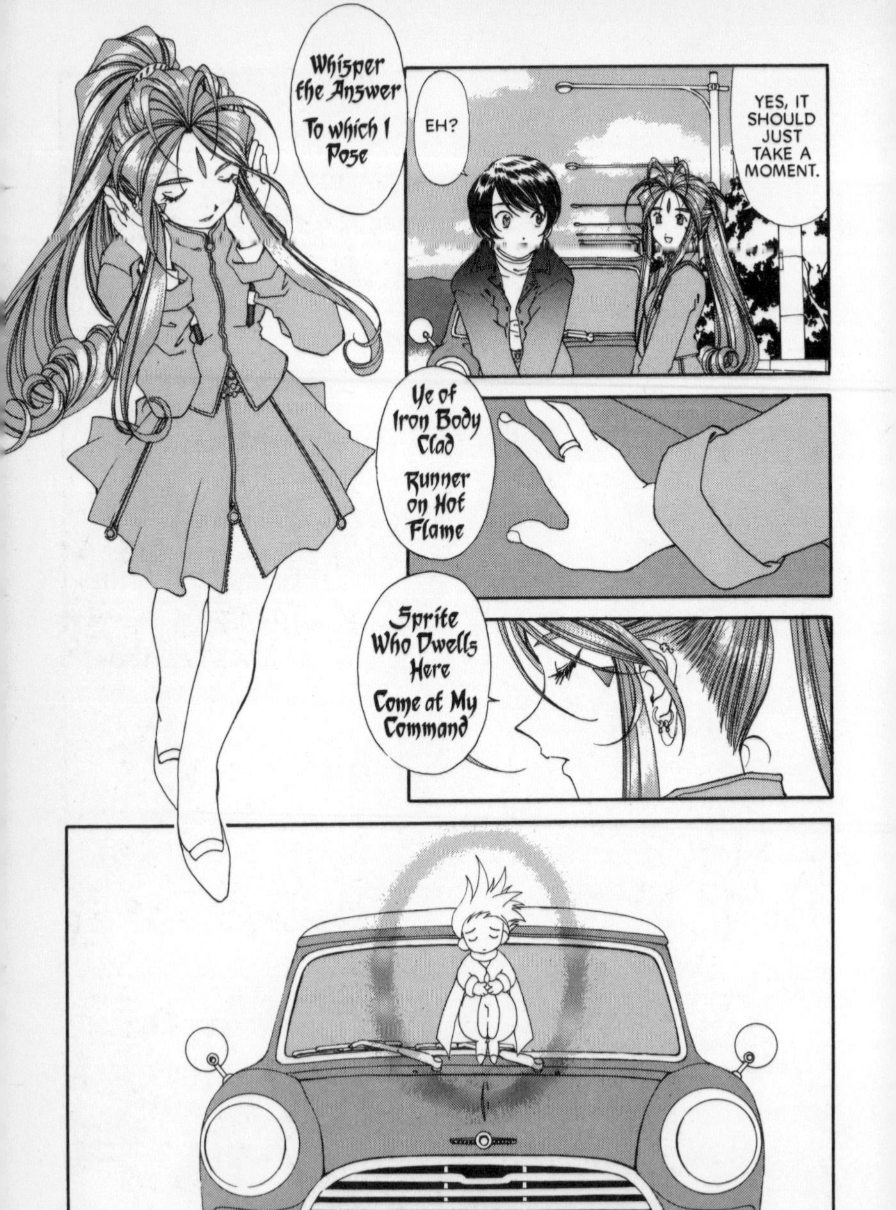
YES, IT SHOULD JUST TAKE A MOMENT.
EH?
Whisper the Answer To which I Pose
Ye of Iron Body Clad Runner on Hot Flame
Sprite Who Dwells Here Come at My Command

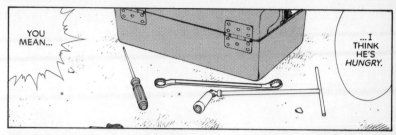

...I THINK HE'S *HUNGRY.*
YOU MEAN...
shff
slishh
WE'RE OUT OF GAS.
NUH-*UH!* WE'RE *THREE-QUARTERS* FULL!
SEE?!
I ***SEE*** A BROKEN ***GAUGE.***
431394
OIL
IGN
FUEL
E 1/2 F
harumph
SHALL I CALL THE JAPAN AUTO FEDERATION?

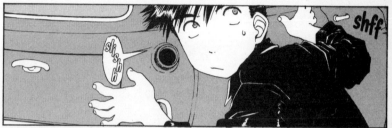

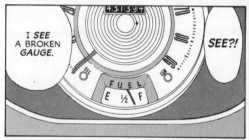

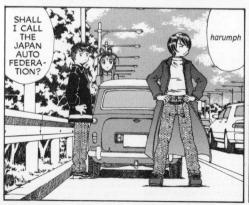

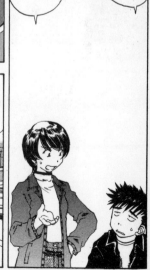

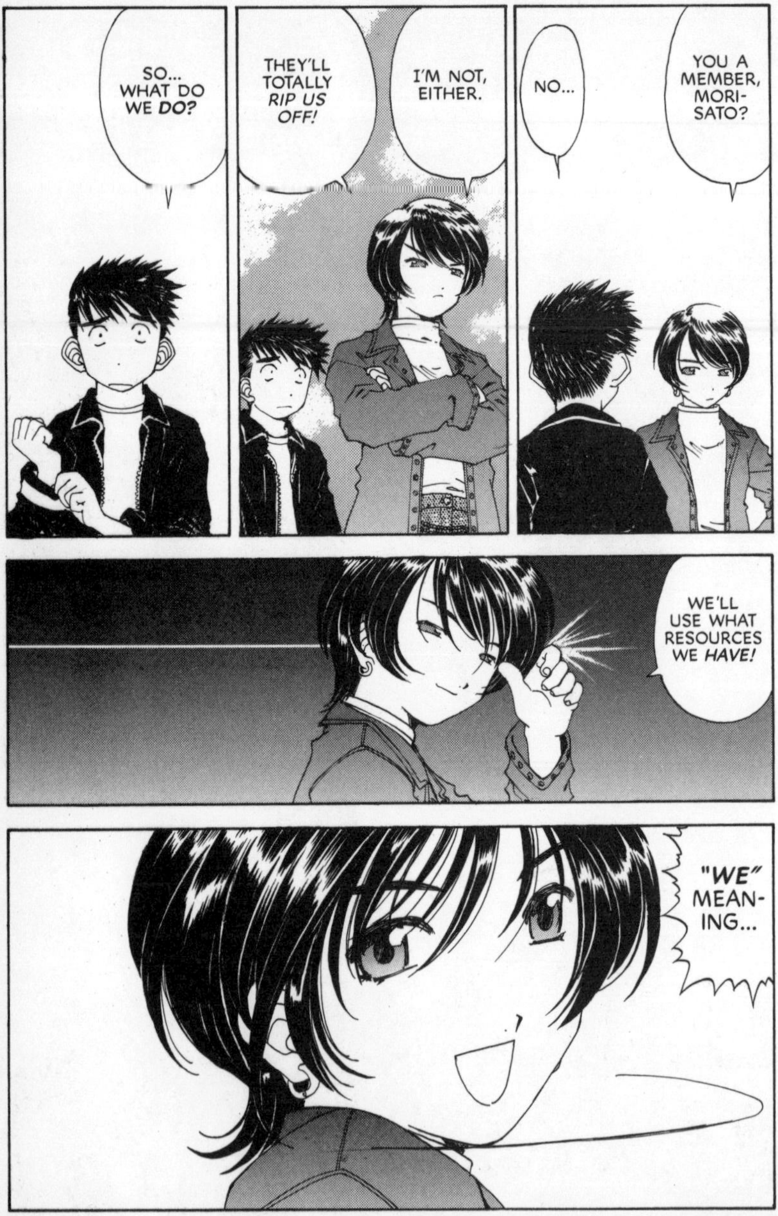
YOU A MEMBER, MORI-SATO?
NO...
I'M NOT, EITHER.
THEY'LL TOTALLY RIP US OFF!
SO... WHAT DO WE DO?
WE'LL USE WHAT RESOURCES WE HAVE!
"WE" MEAN-ING...

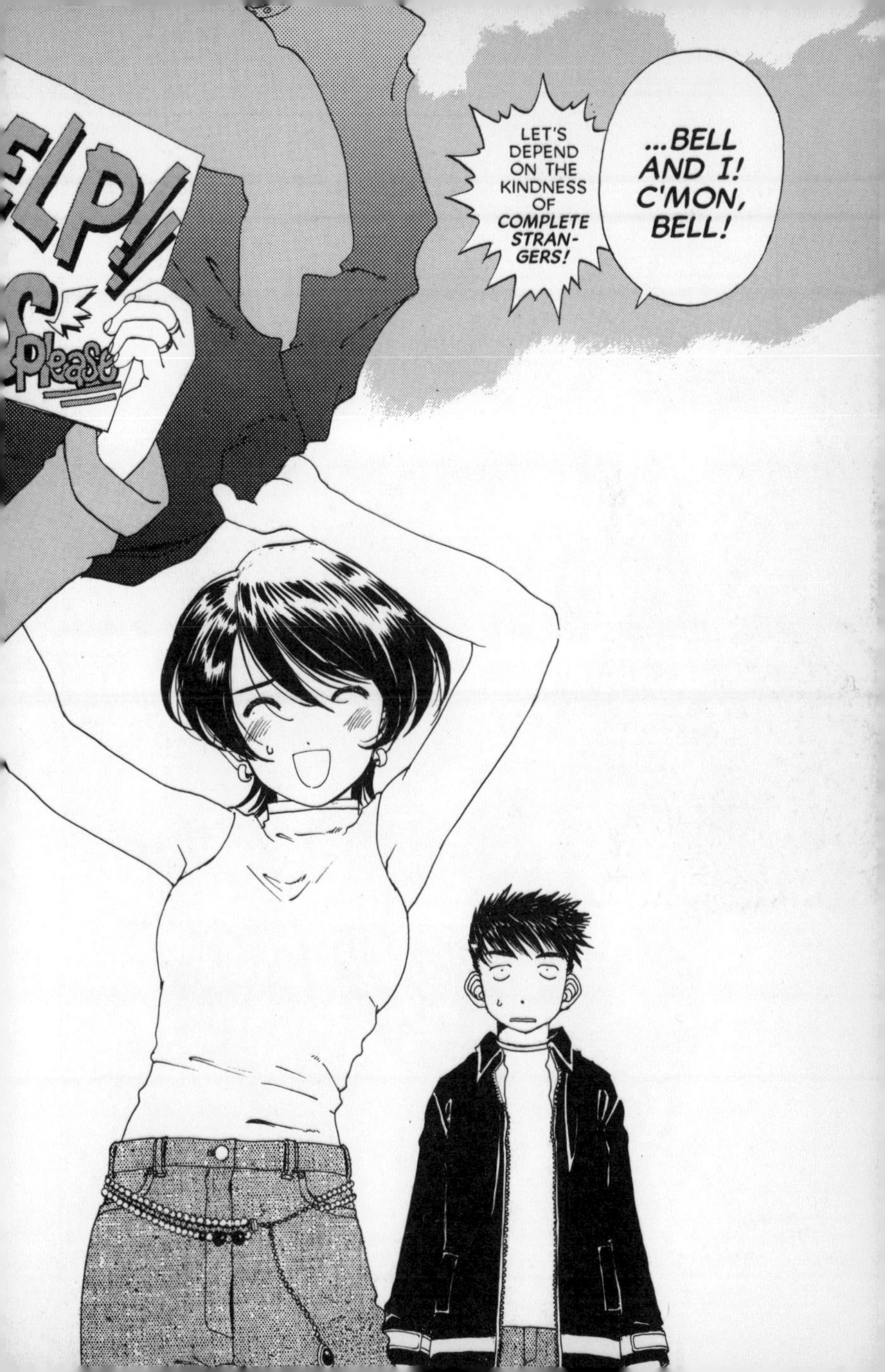
...BELL AND I! C'MON, BELL!
LET'S DEPEND ON THE KINDNESS OF COMPLETE STRAN-GERS!
Please

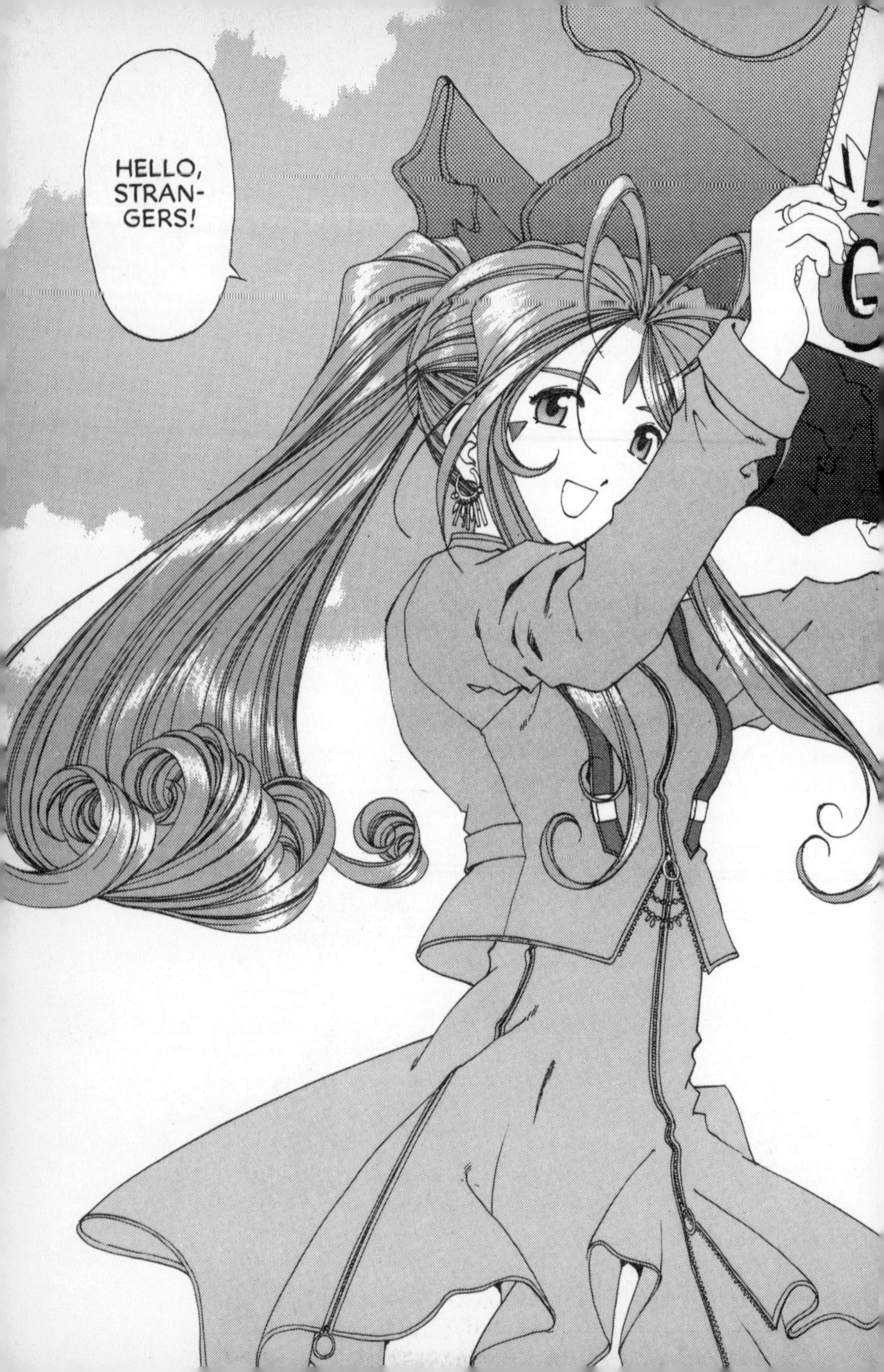
HELLO, STRANGERS!

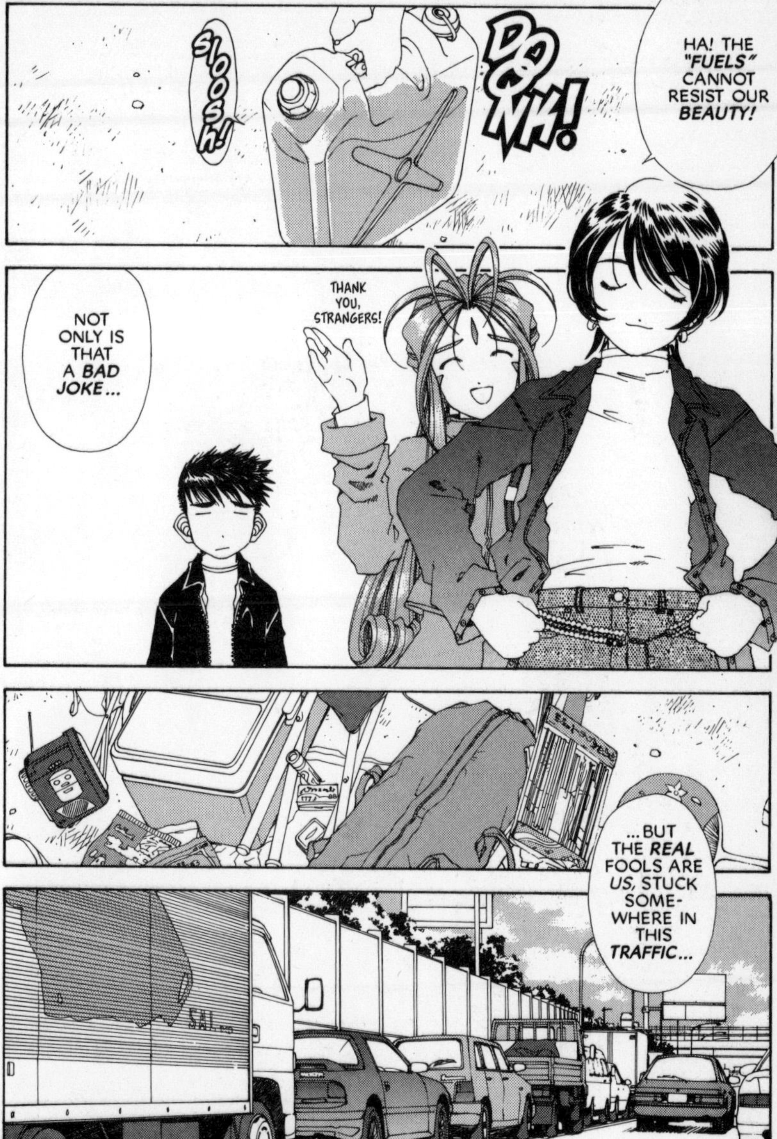
HA! THE "FUELS" CANNOT RESIST OUR BEAUTY!
DOGONK!
sloosh!
THANK YOU, STRANGERS!
NOT ONLY IS THAT A BAD JOKE...
...BUT THE REAL FOOLS ARE US, STUCK SOME-WHERE IN THIS TRAFFIC...

CHAPTER 154

I Dub Thee, Yuufuin

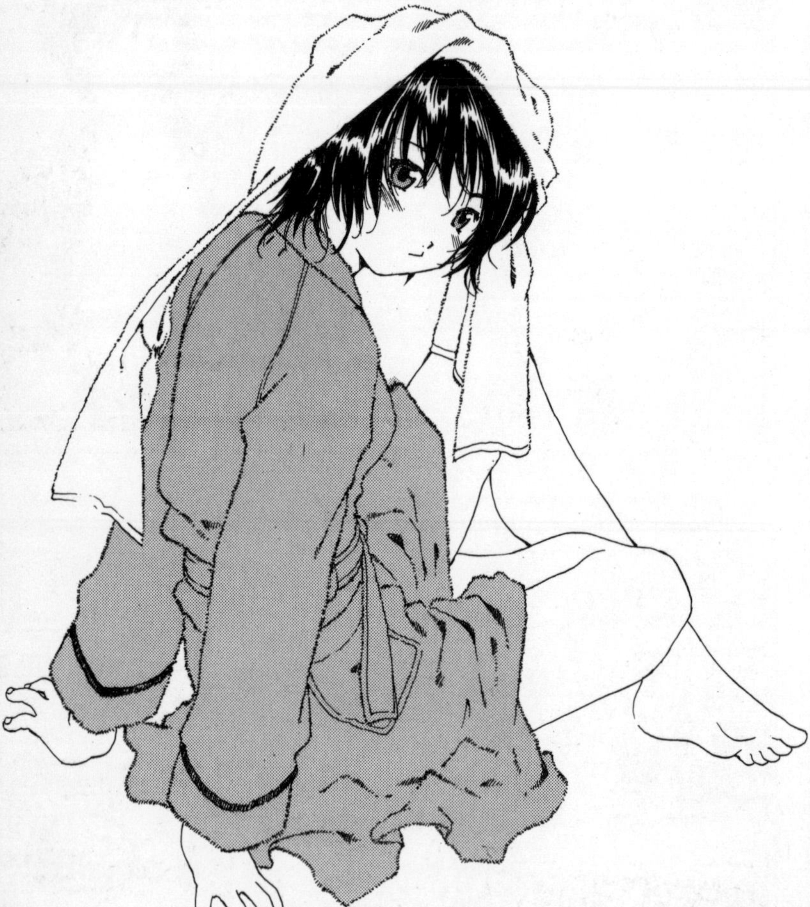

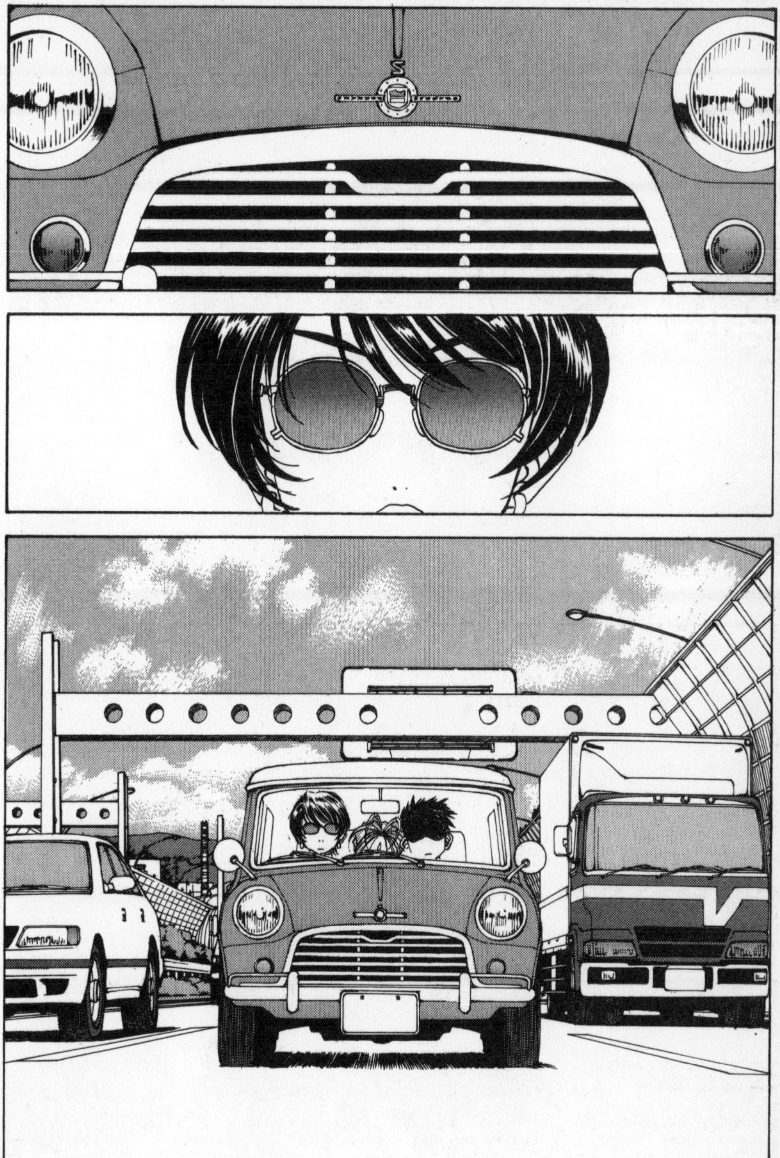

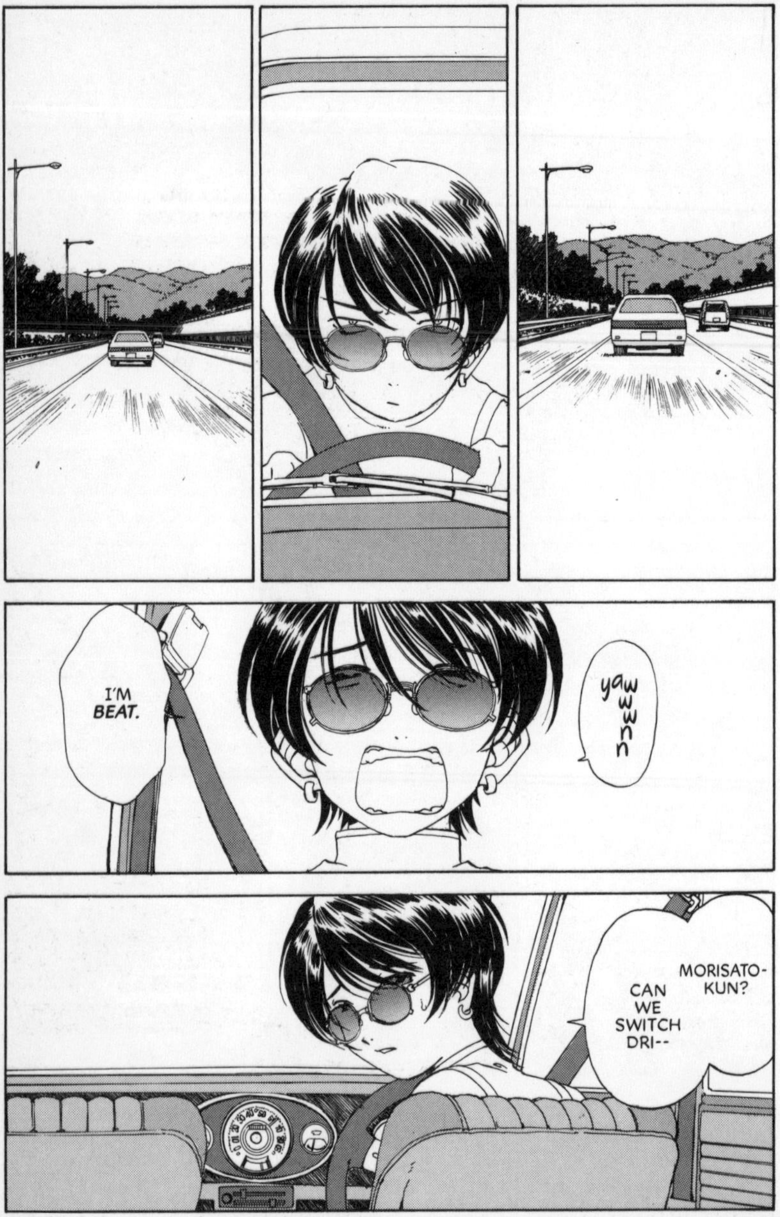
yawwwnn
I'M BEAT.
MORISATO-KUN?
CAN WE SWITCH DRI--

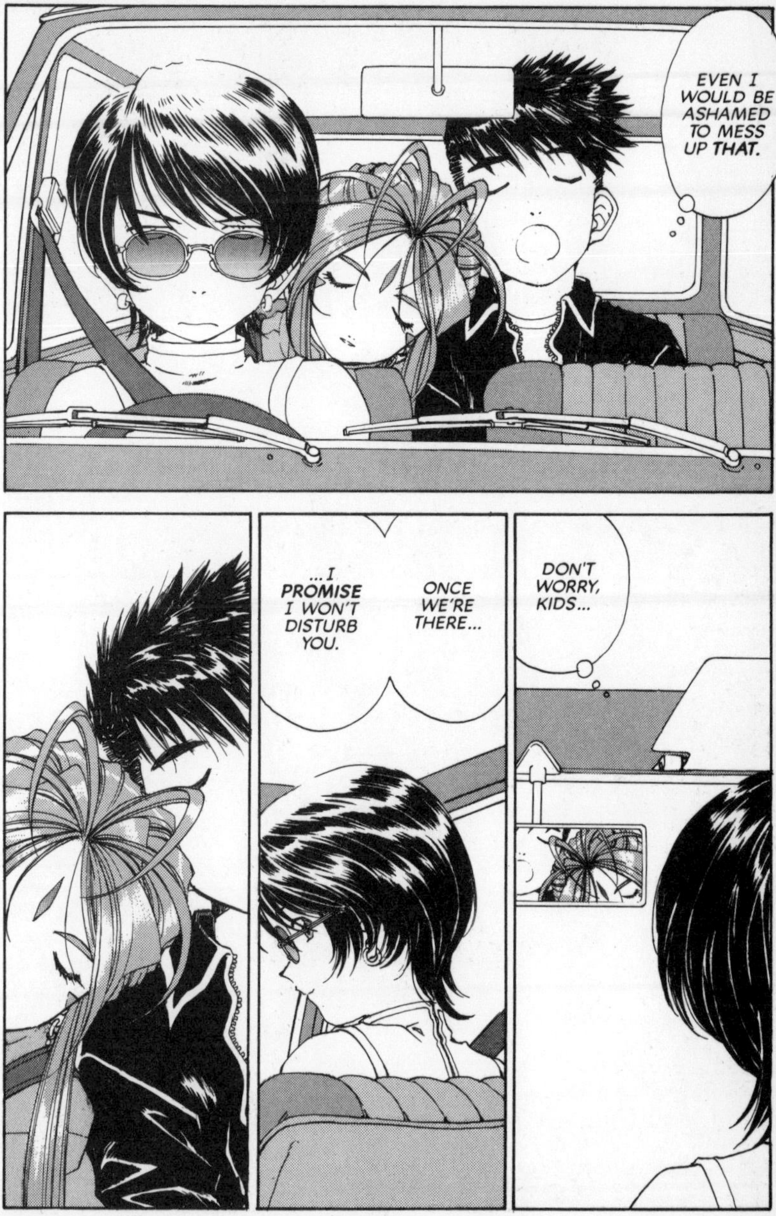
EVEN I WOULD BE ASHAMED TO MESS UP THAT.
DON'T WORRY, KIDS...
ONCE WE'RE THERE...
...I PROMISE I WON'T DISTURB YOU.

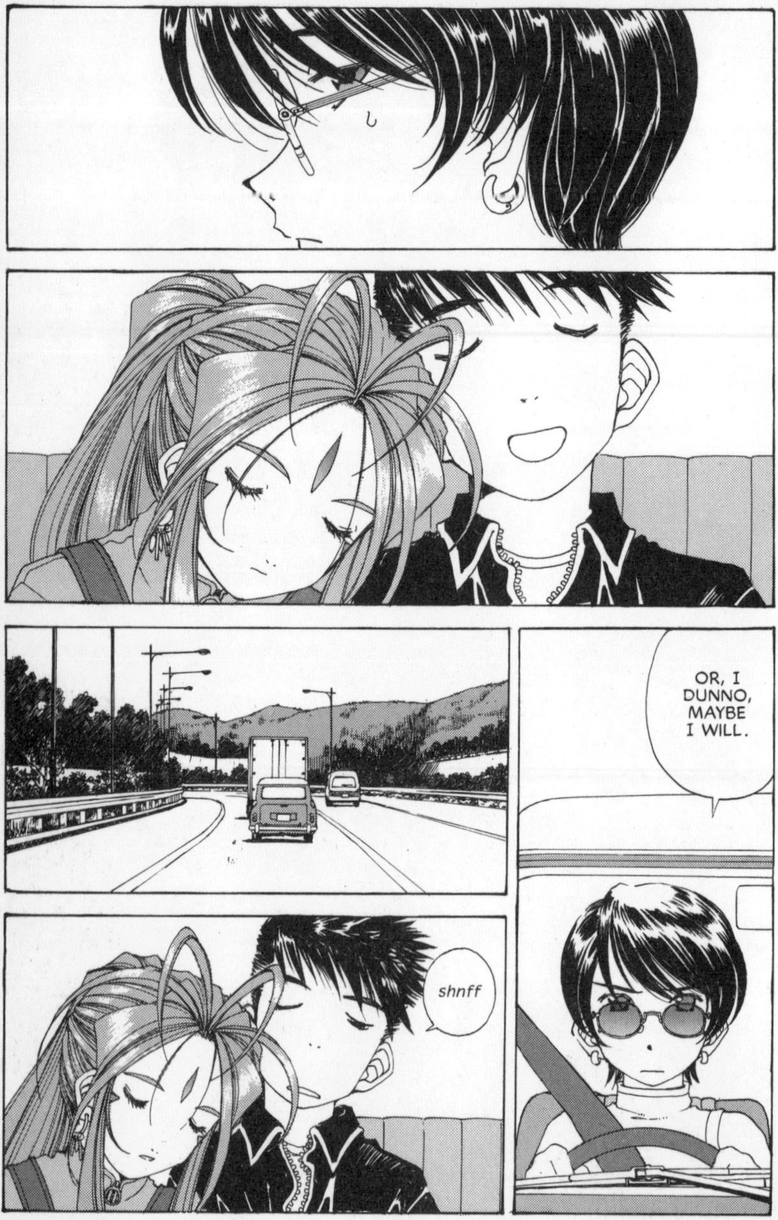
OR, I DUNNO, MAYBE I WILL.
shnff

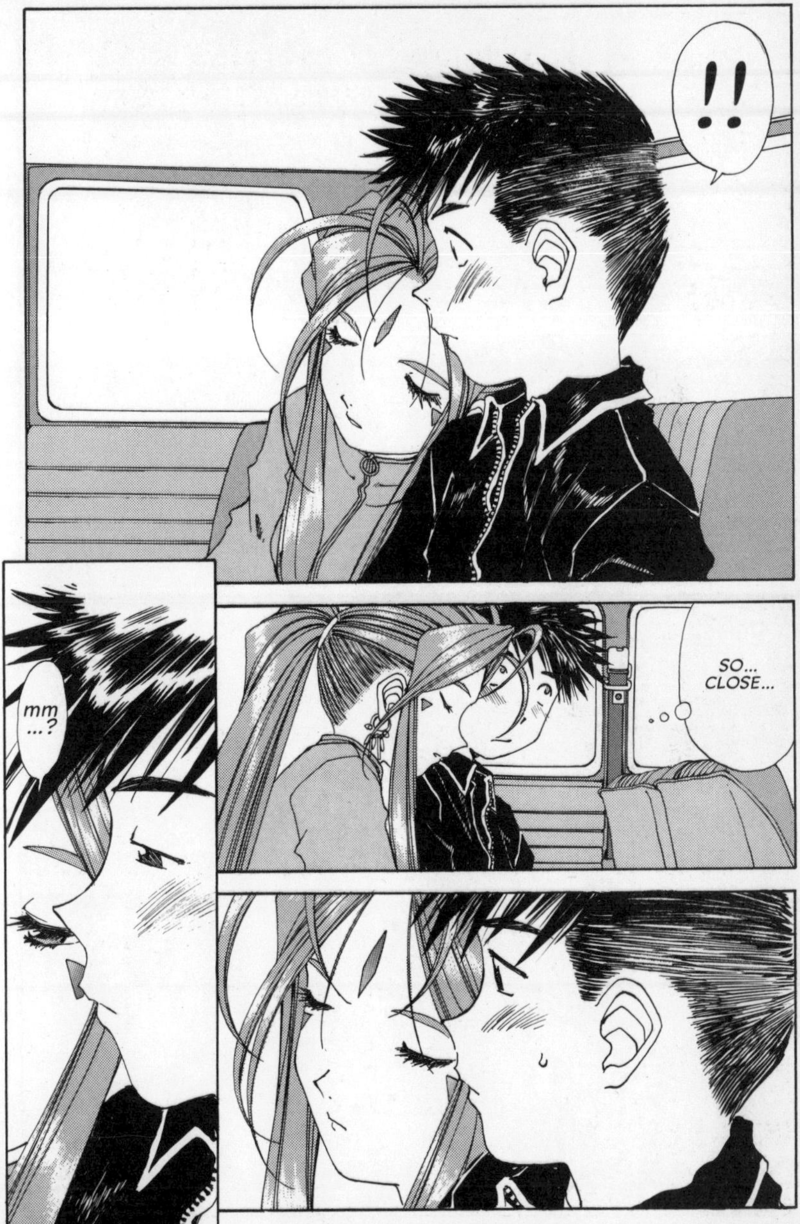
!!
SO... CLOSE...
mm ...?

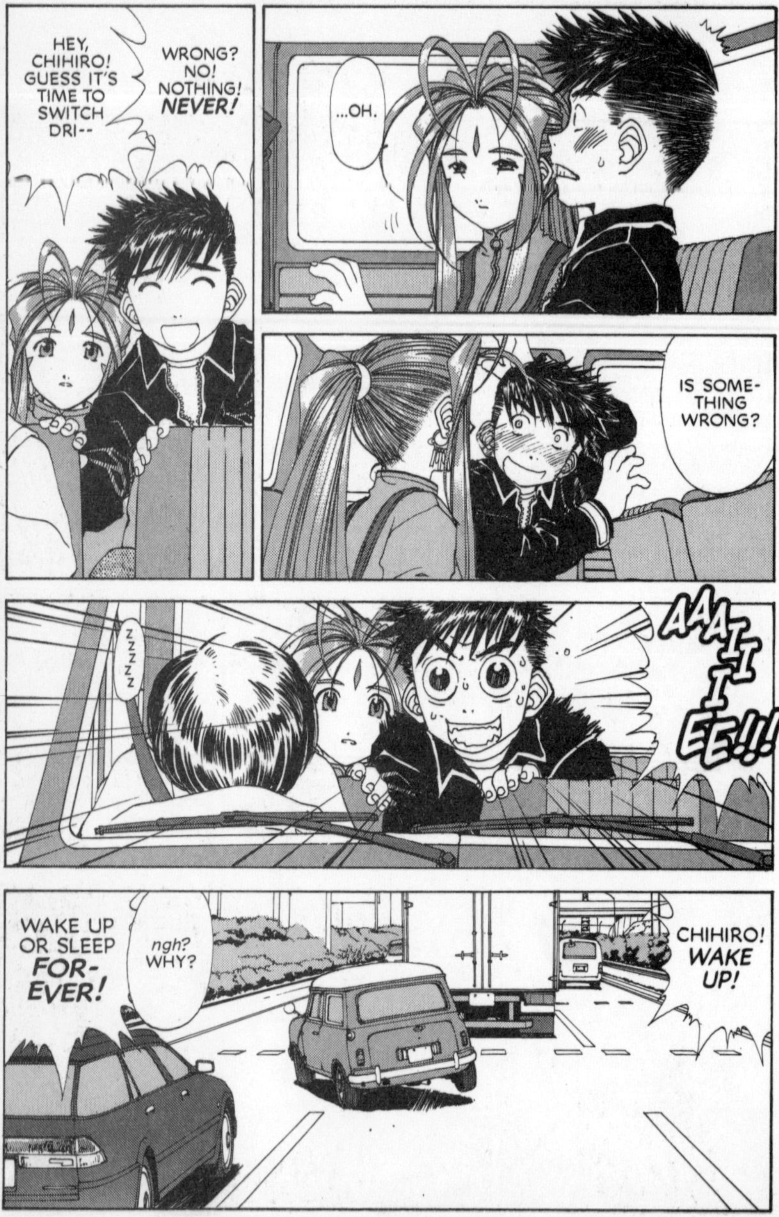
...OH.
IS SOME-THING WRONG?
WRONG? NO! NOTHING! NEVER!
HEY, CHIHIRO! GUESS IT'S TIME TO SWITCH DRI--
AAAIIEE!!!
ZZZZ
CHIHIRO! WAKE UP!
ngh? WHY?
WAKE UP OR SLEEP FOR-EVER!

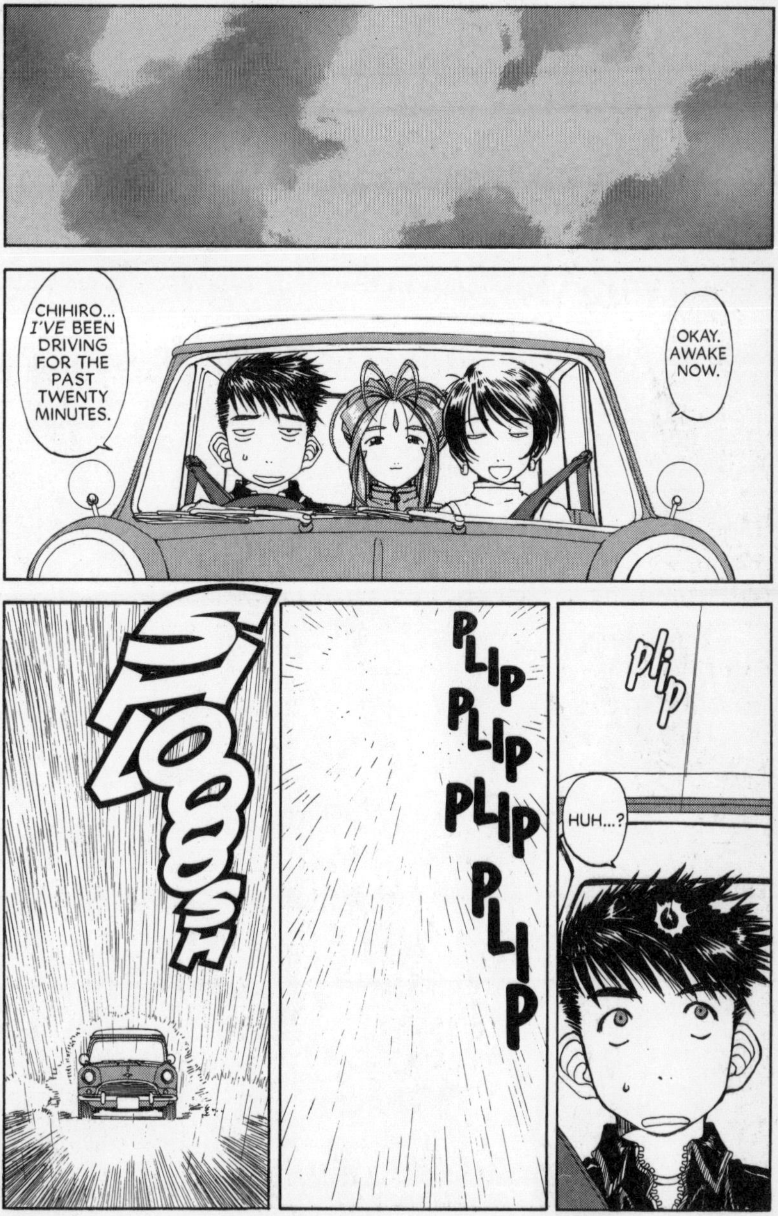
OKAY. AWAKE NOW.
CHIHIRO... *I'VE* BEEN DRIVING FOR THE PAST TWENTY MINUTES.
plip
HUH...?
PLIP PLIP PLIP PLIP
SPLOOOSH

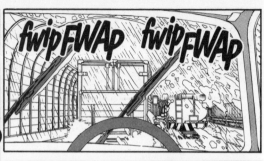

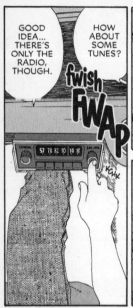

GOOD IDEA... THERE'S ONLY THE RADIO, THOUGH.

HOW ABOUT SOME TUNES?

fwish FWAP

57 78 82 10 14 16

KLIK

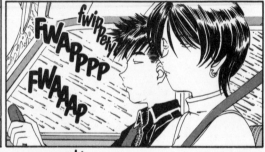

fwippety FWAPPPP FWAAAAP

fwappety FWAP

TURN IT OFF!

death...

KLIK

57 78 82 10 14 16

fwappety FWAP

...angels have no thought of ever returning you...

IT'S STUCK?

KLIK KLIK

57 78 82 10 14 16

ffwappety FWAP

CHANGE IT!

...not where the black coach of sorrow has taken you...

KLIK

57 78 82 10 14 16

KICKIN' OFF A GLOOMY SATURDAY WITH... "GLOOMY SUNDAY"!

YOU'RE LISTENIN' TO J-SAD... WHERE IT'S NOTHING BUT SAD SONGS!

fwrRSSH FWAP FWAP FWAP

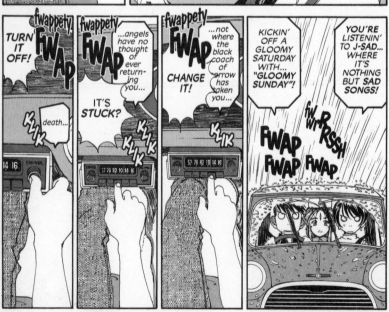

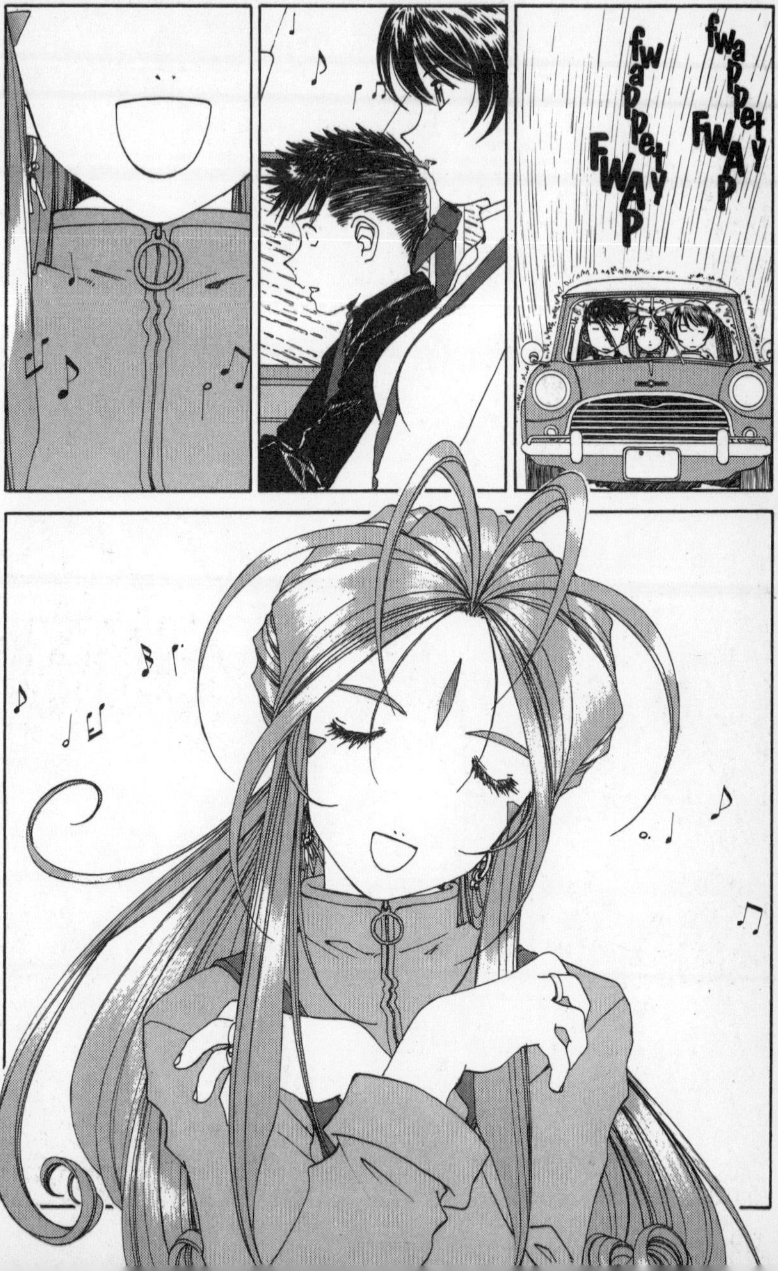
fwappety FWAP
fwappety FWAP

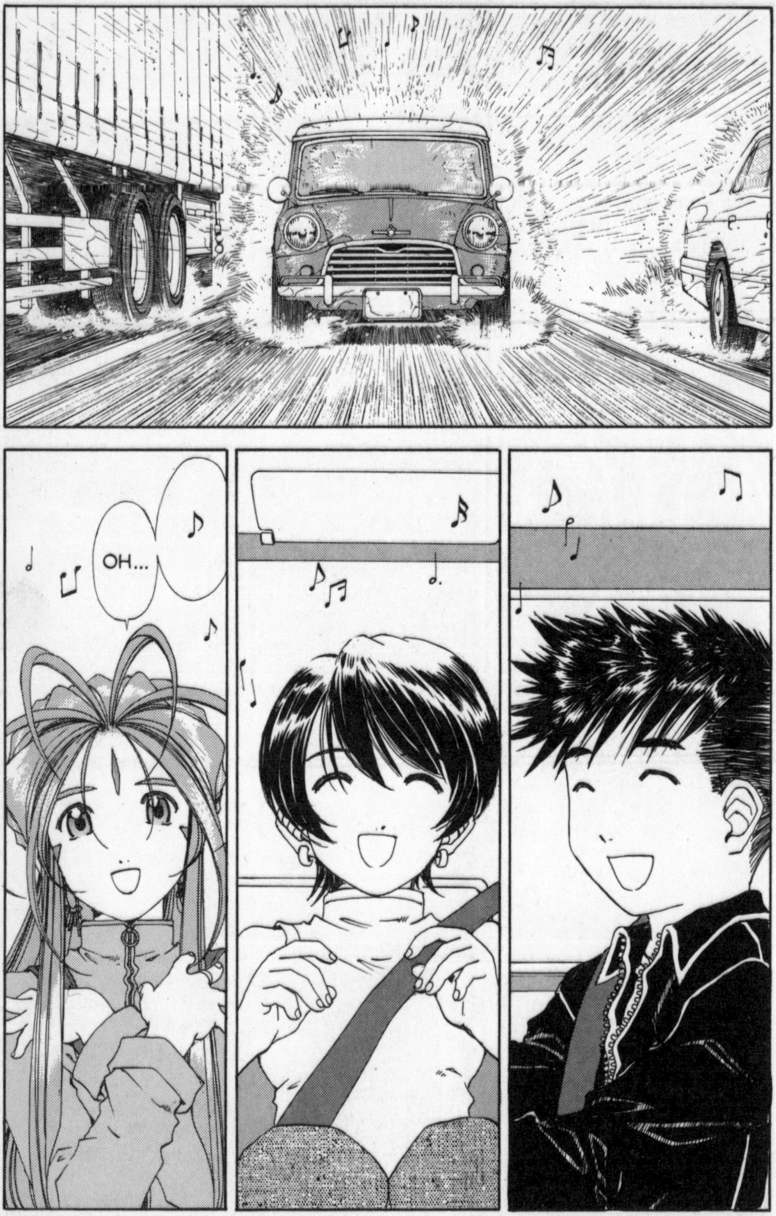
OH...

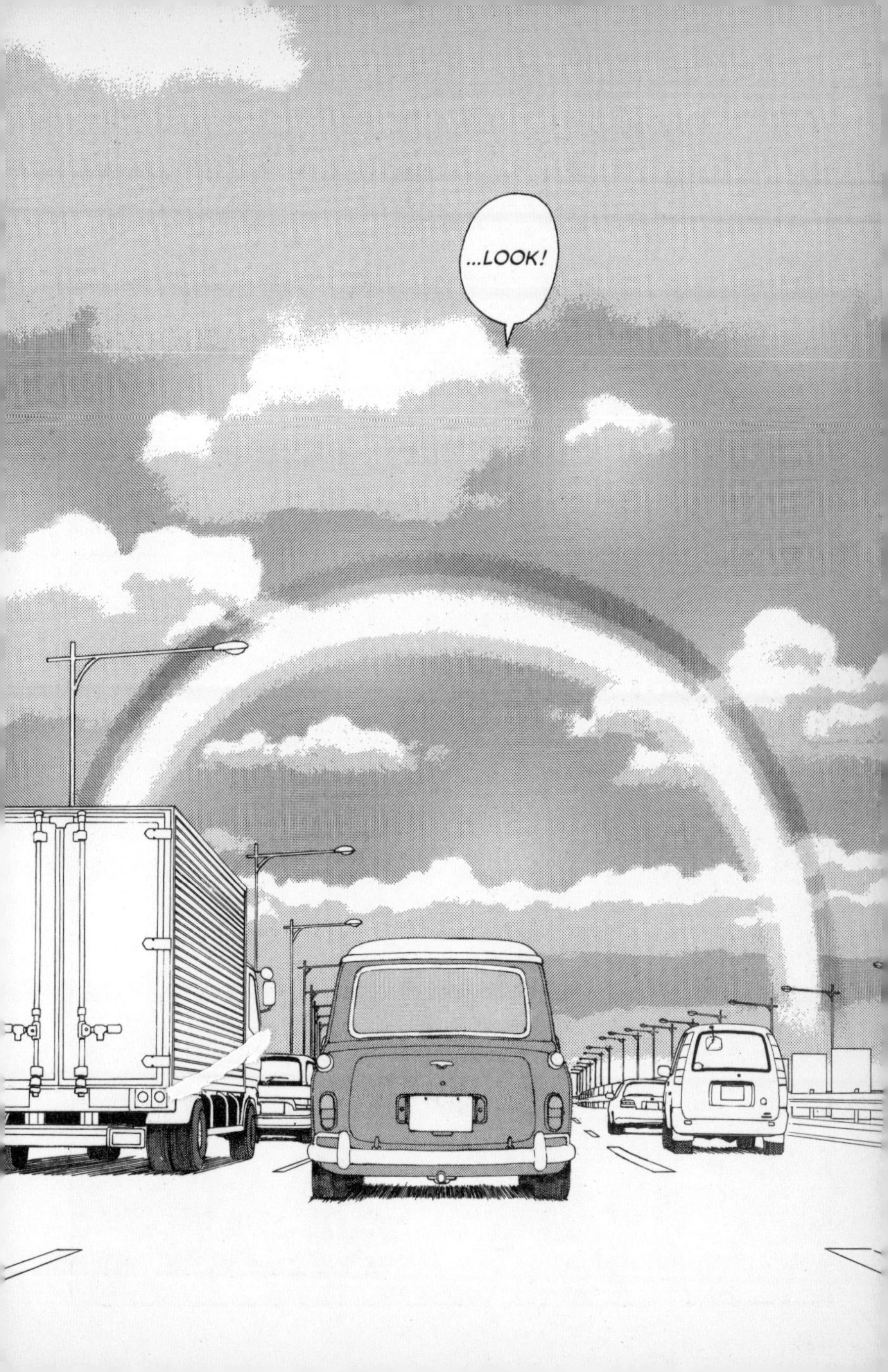
...LOOK!

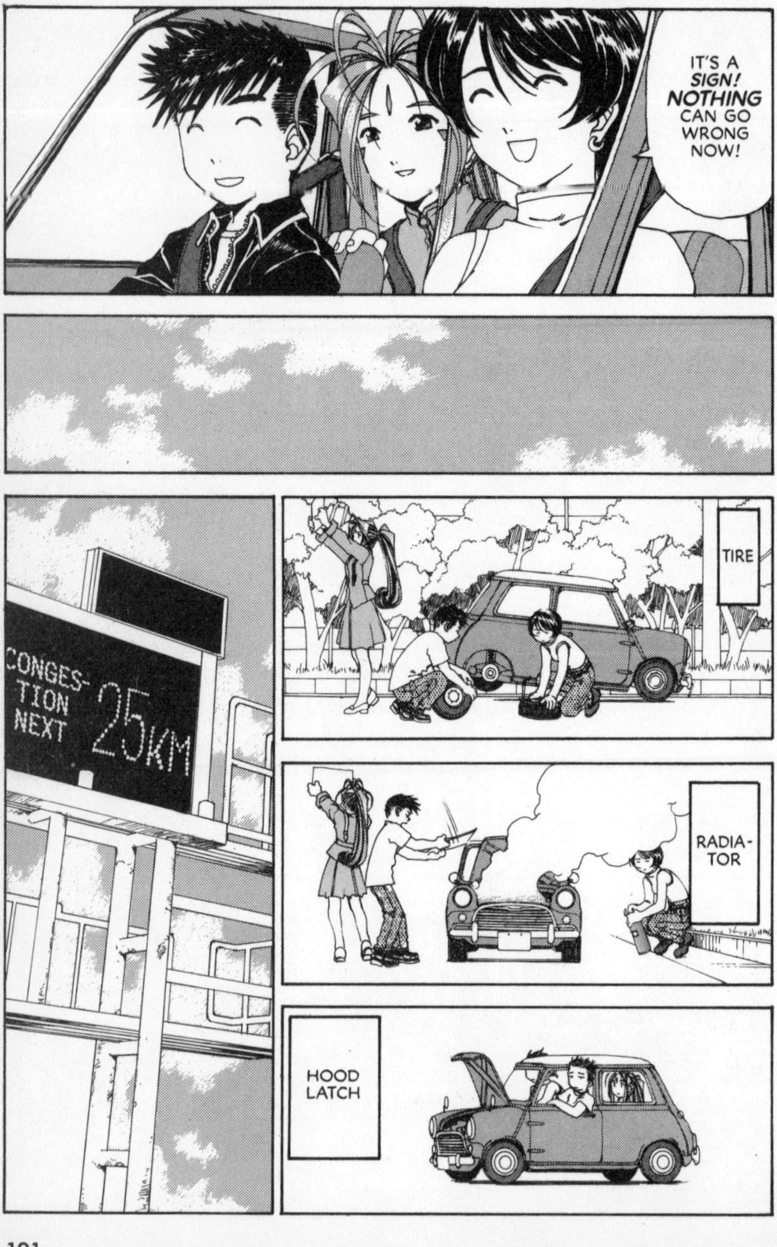
IT'S A SIGN! NOTHING CAN GO WRONG NOW!
TIRE
RADIA-TOR
HOOD LATCH
CONGES-TION NEXT 25KM

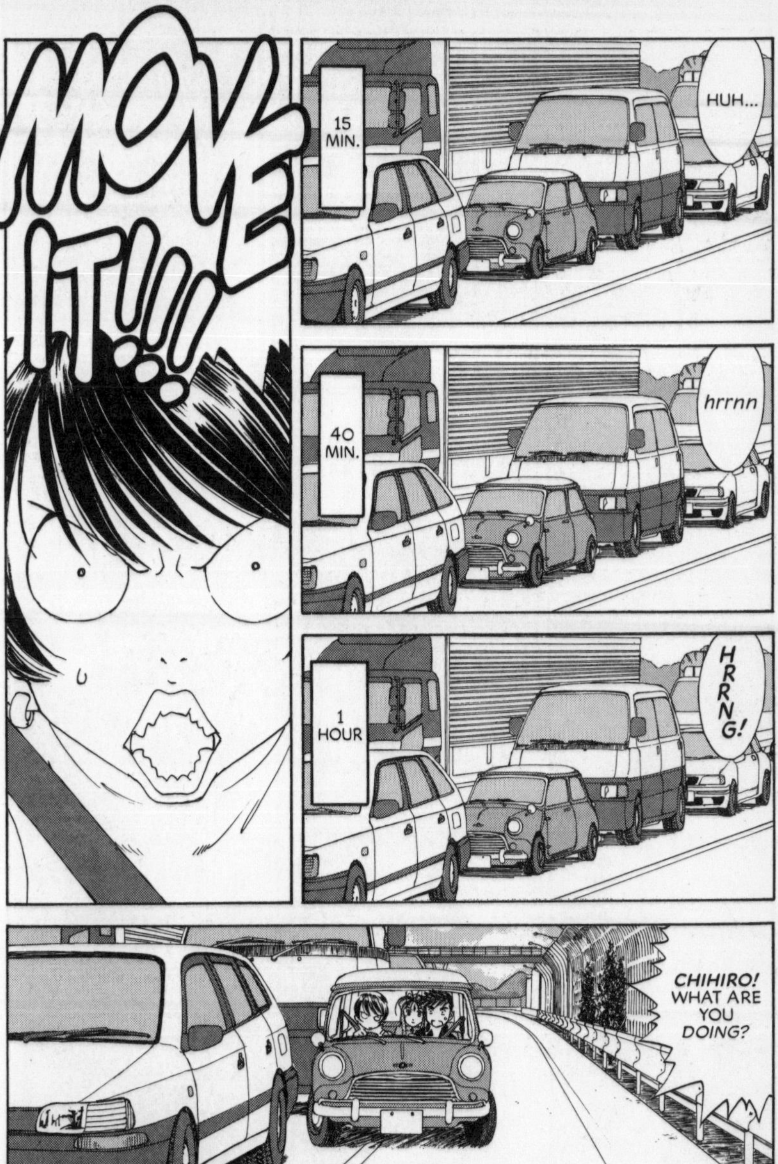

HUH...
15 MIN.
hrrnn
40 MIN.
HRRNG!
1 HOUR
MOVE IT!!!!
CHIHIRO! WHAT ARE YOU DOING?

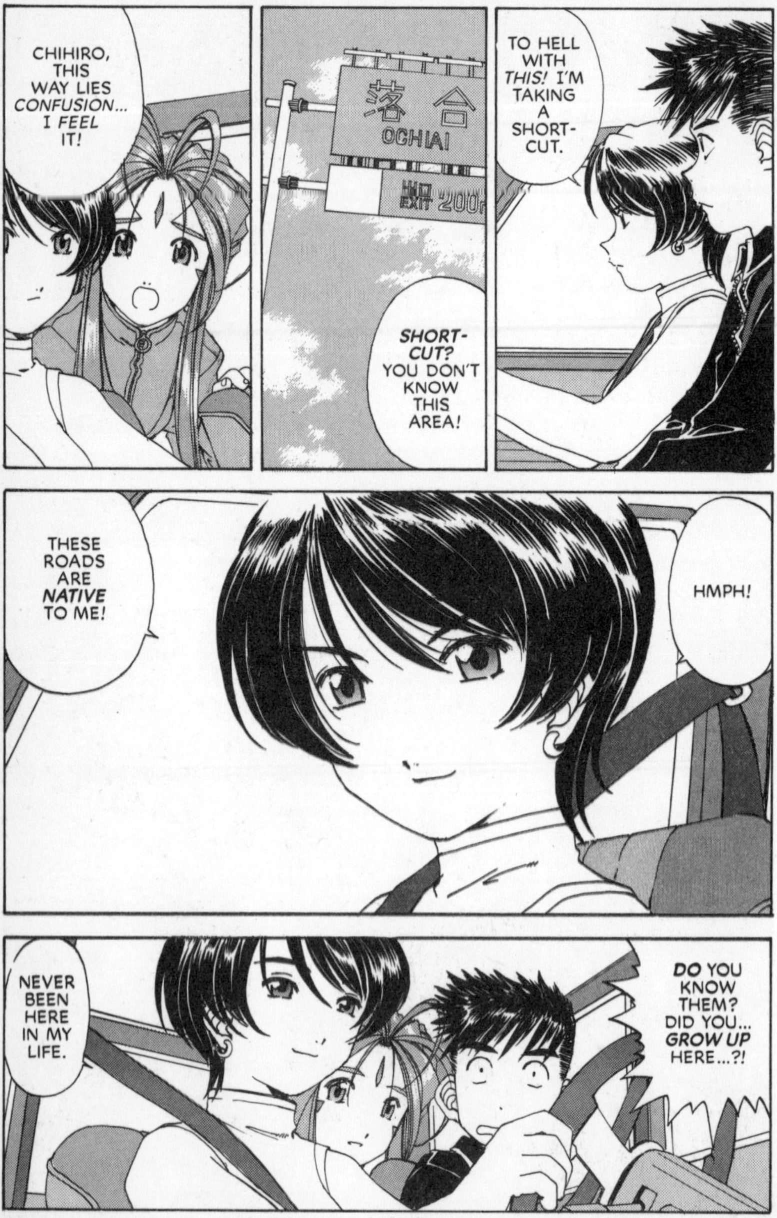
TO HELL WITH *THIS!* I'M TAKING A SHORT-CUT.
落合
OCHIAI
SHORT-CUT? YOU DON'T KNOW THIS *AREA!*
CHIHIRO, THIS WAY LIES *CONFUSION...* I *FEEL* IT!
HMPH!
THESE ROADS ARE ***NATIVE*** TO ME!
DO YOU KNOW THEM? DID YOU... ***GROW UP*** HERE...?!
NEVER BEEN HERE IN MY LIFE.

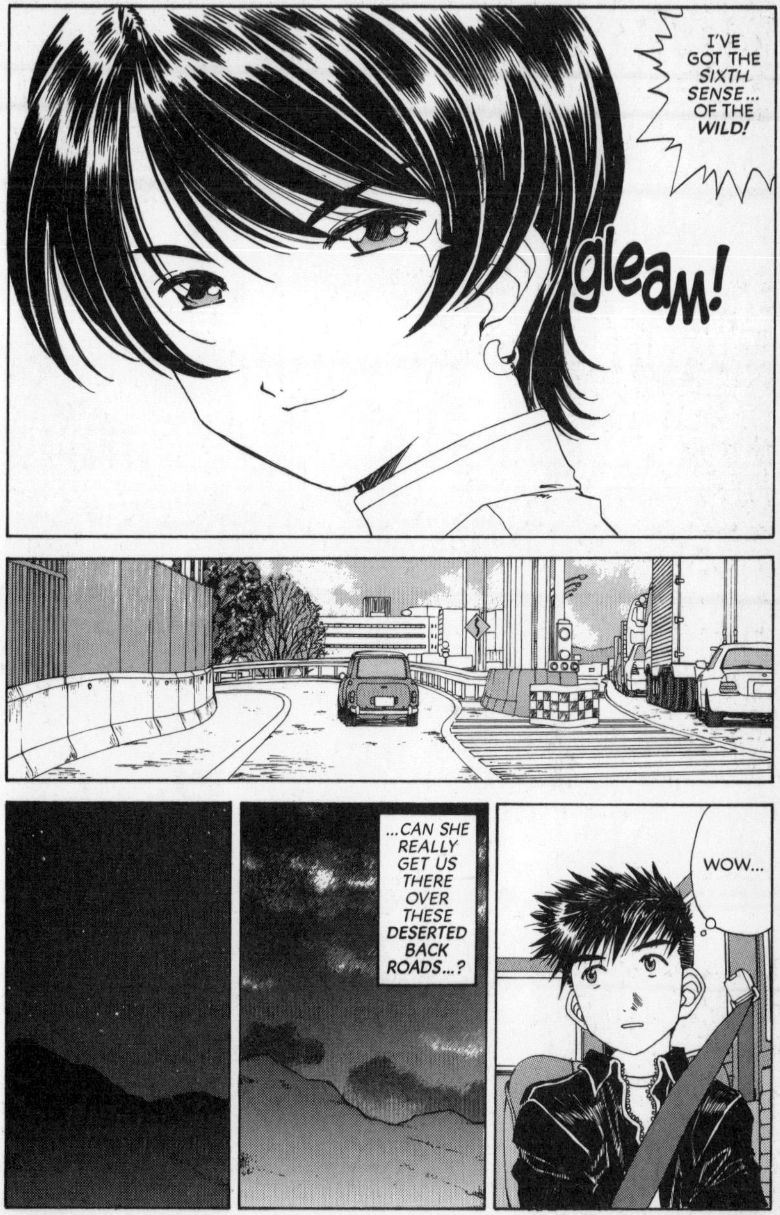
I'VE GOT THE *SIXTH SENSE*... OF THE *WILD!*
gleam!
WOW...
...CAN SHE REALLY GET US THERE OVER THESE DESERTED BACK ROADS...?

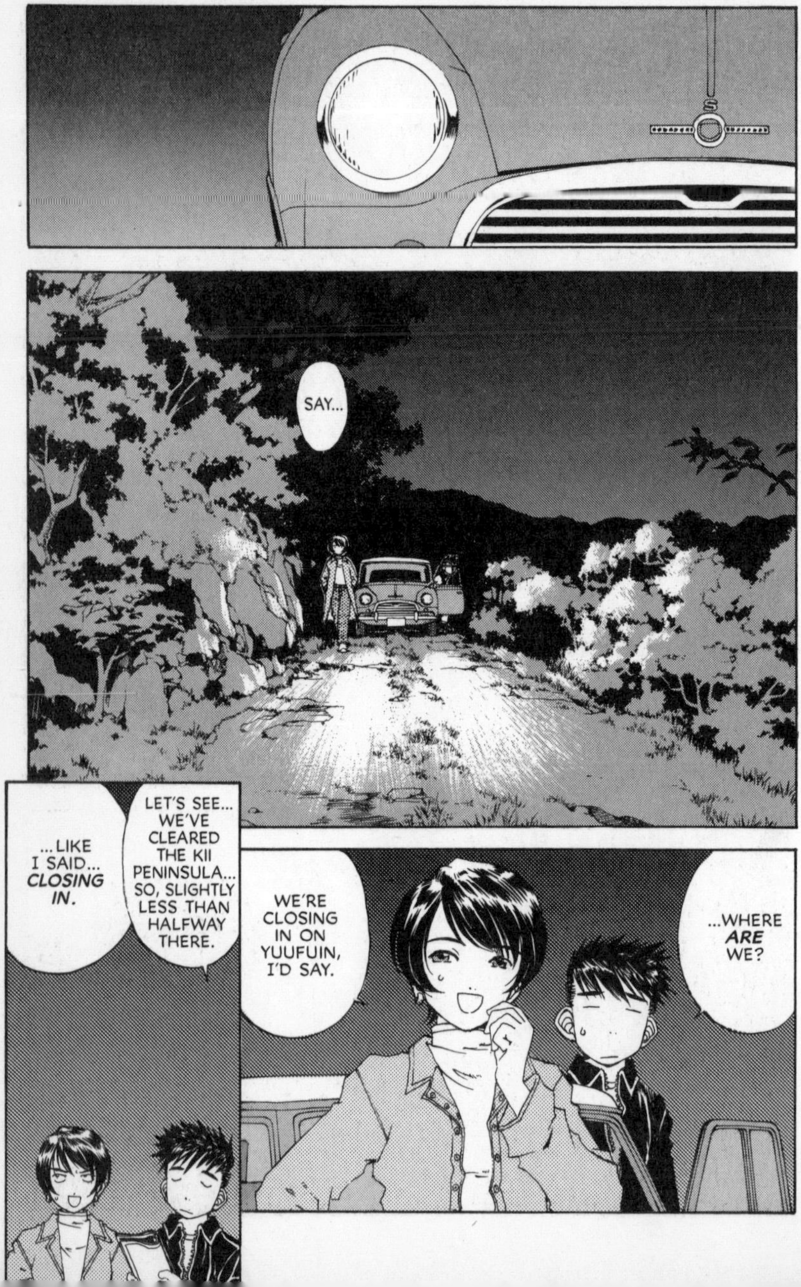
SAY...
...WHERE *ARE* WE?
WE'RE CLOSING IN ON YUUFUIN, I'D SAY.
LET'S SEE... WE'VE CLEARED THE KII PENINSULA... SO, SLIGHTLY LESS THAN HALFWAY THERE.
...LIKE I SAID... ***CLOSING IN***.

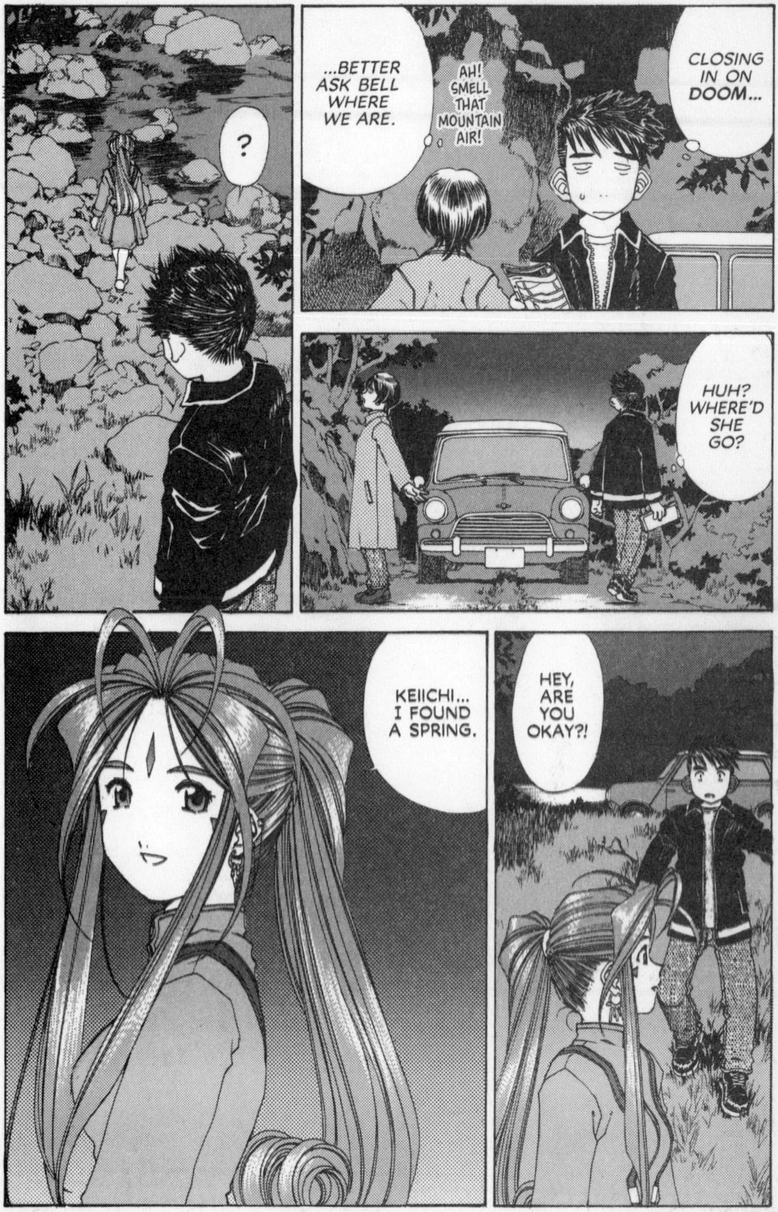
CLOSING IN ON DOOM...
AH! SMELL THAT MOUNTAIN AIR!
...BETTER ASK BELL WHERE WE ARE.
HUH? WHERE'D SHE GO?
?
HEY, ARE YOU OKAY?!
KEIICHI... I FOUND A SPRING.

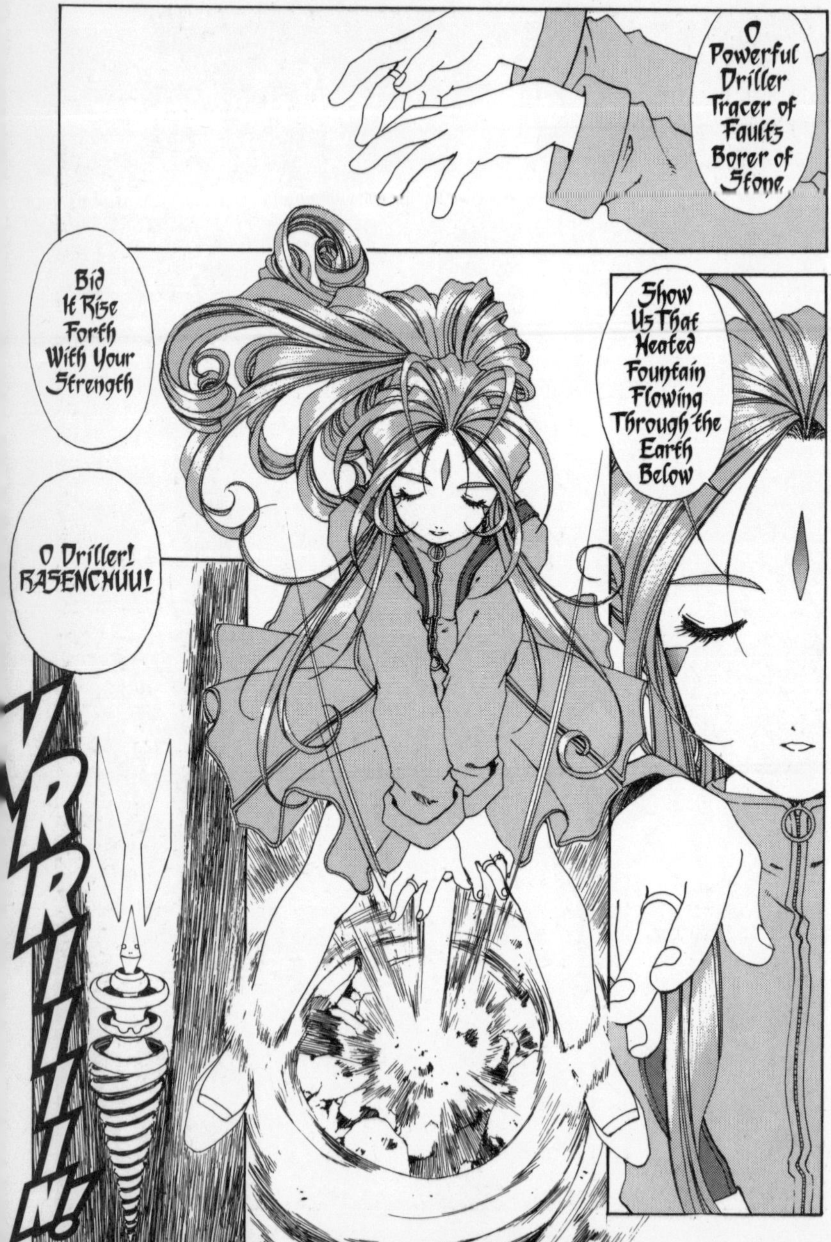
O Powerful Driller Tracer of Faults Borer of Stone
Show Us That Heated Fountain Flowing Through the Earth Below
Bid It Rise Forth With Your Strength
O Driller! RASENCHUU!
VRRIIIN!

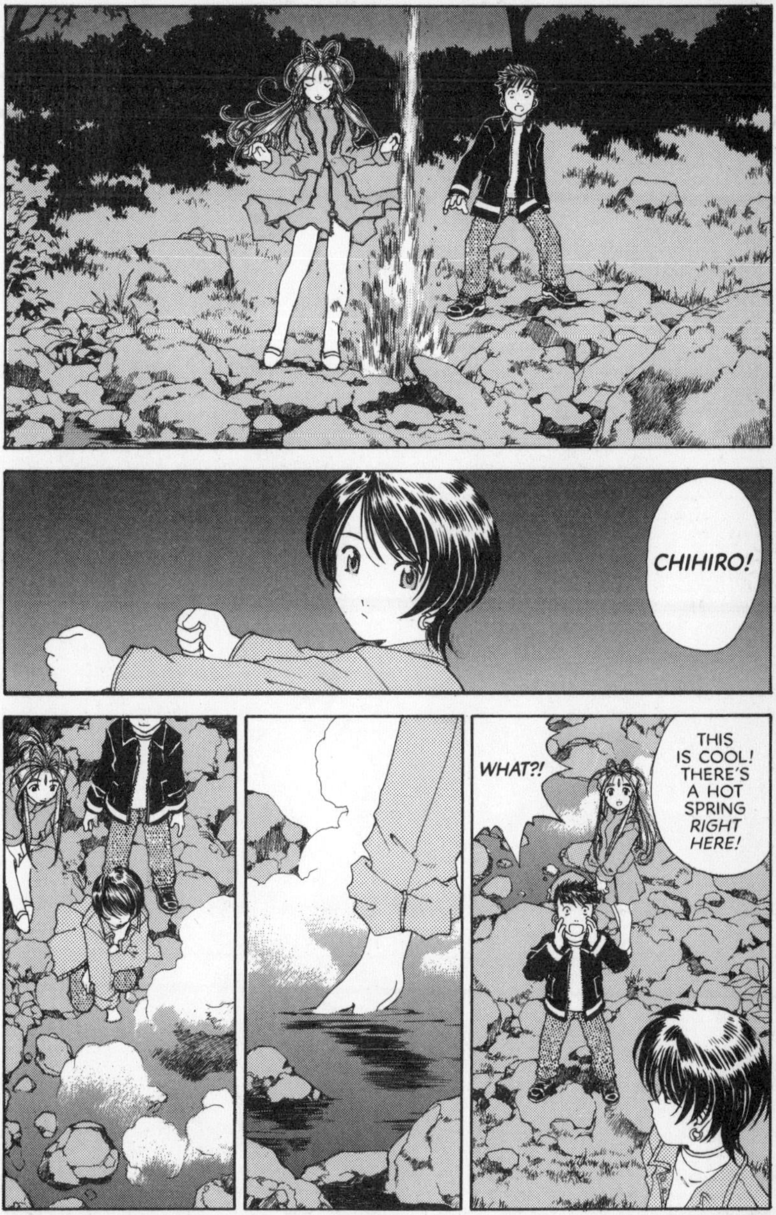
CHIHIRO!
THIS IS COOL! THERE'S A HOT SPRING *RIGHT HERE!*
WHAT?!

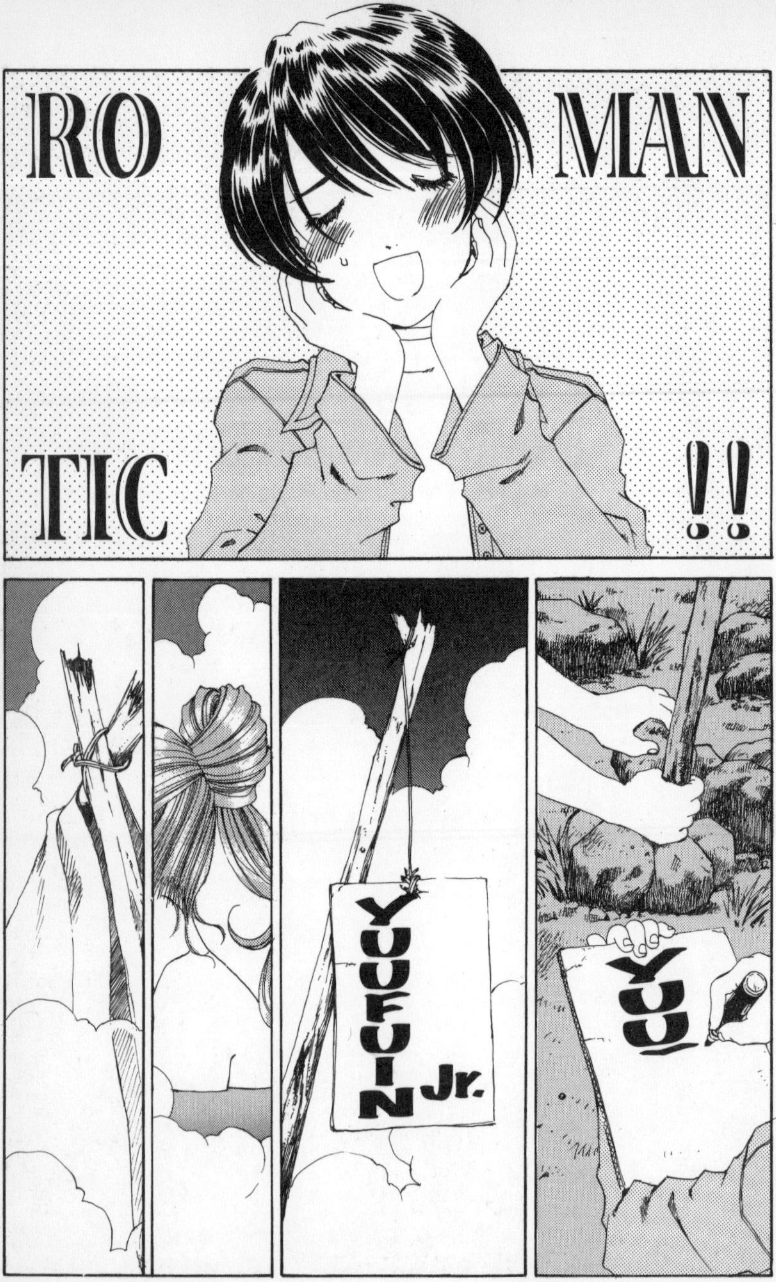
RO MAN TIC !!
YUU
YUUFUIN Jr.

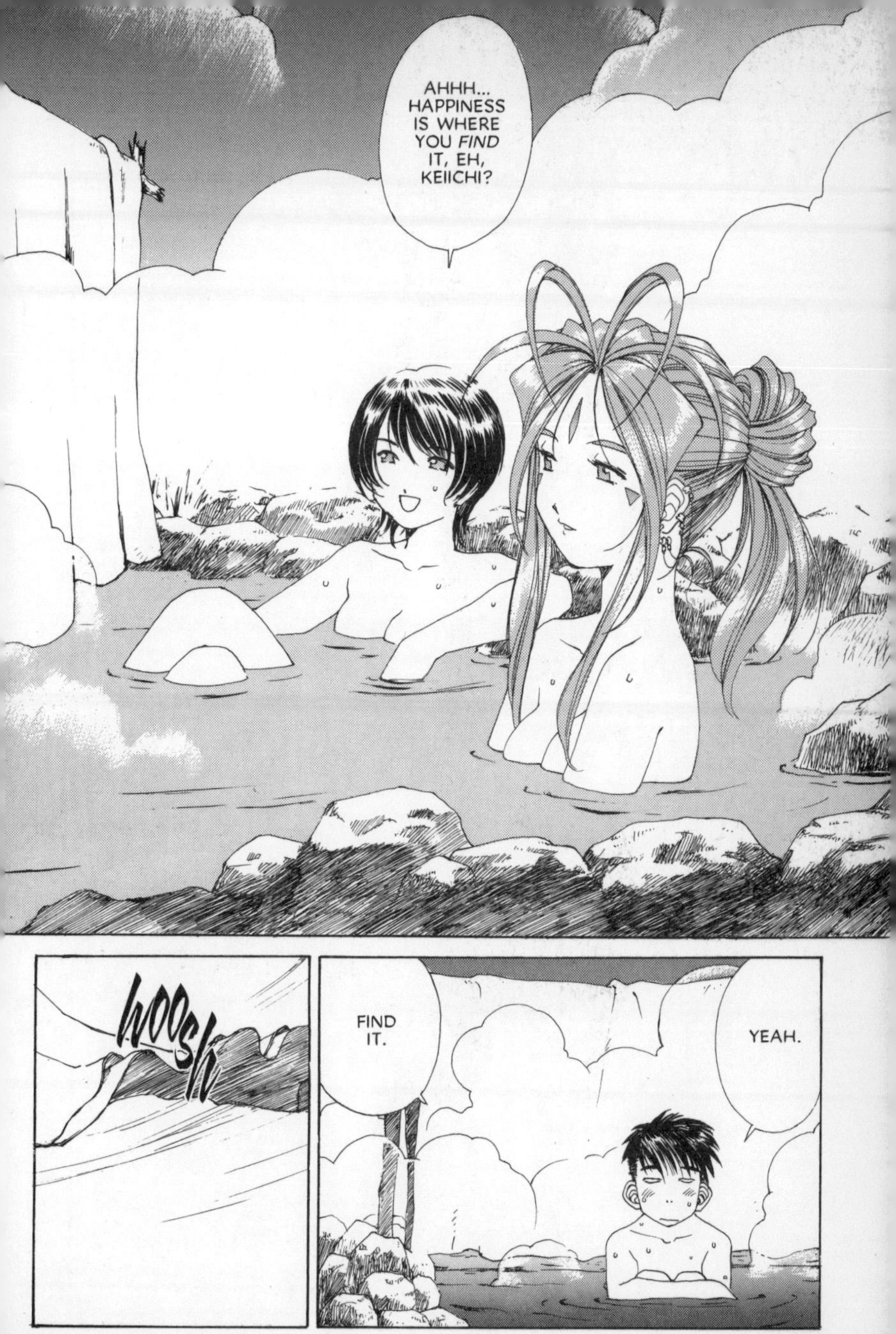
AHHH... HAPPINESS IS WHERE YOU *FIND* IT, EH, KEIICHI?
YEAH.
FIND IT.
WOOSH

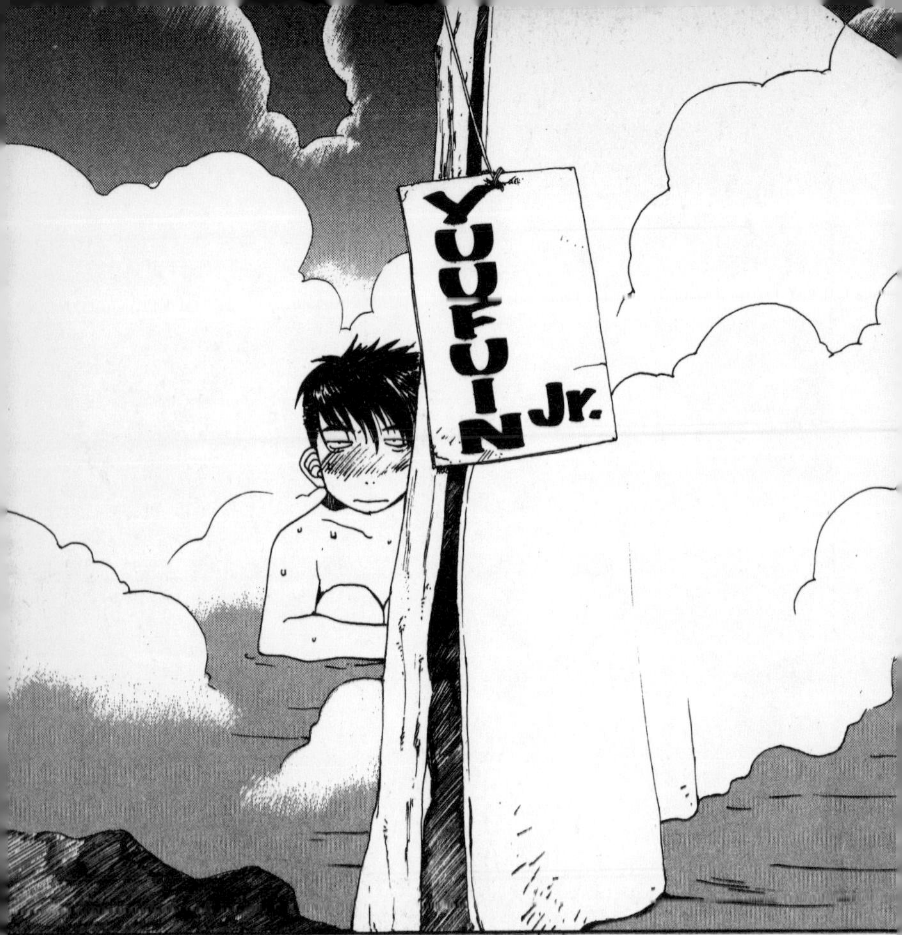
YUUFUIN Jr.

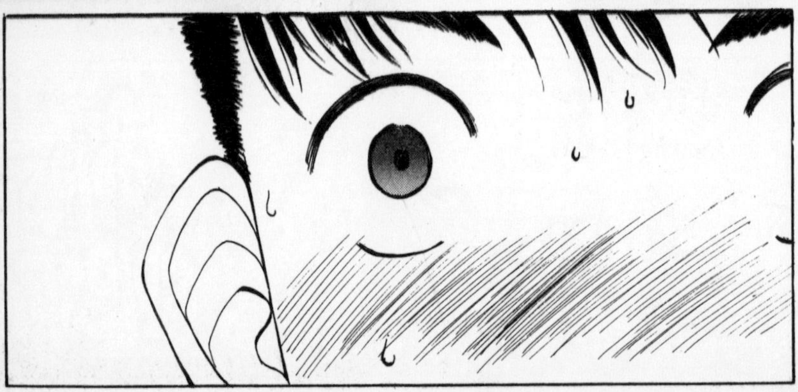

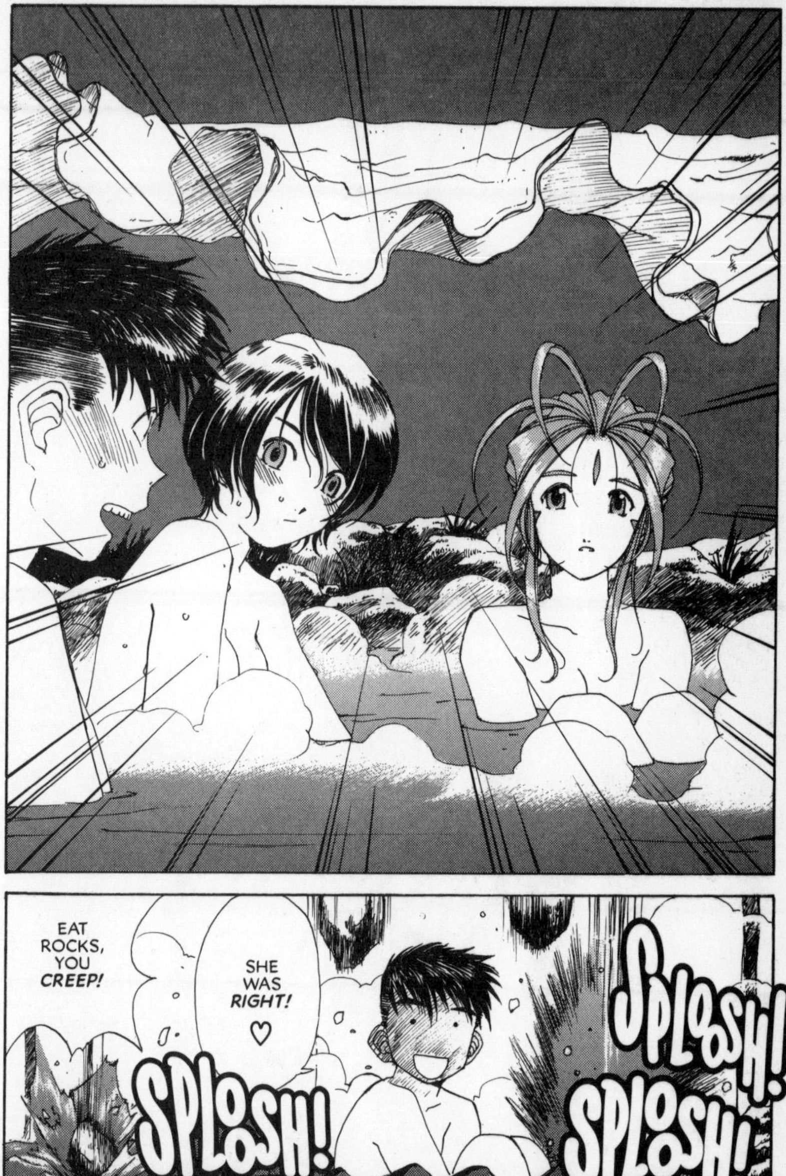
SPLOSH!
SPLOSH!
SHE WAS RIGHT! ♥
EAT ROCKS, YOU CREEP!
SPLOSH!

CHAPTER 155

Fighting Wings

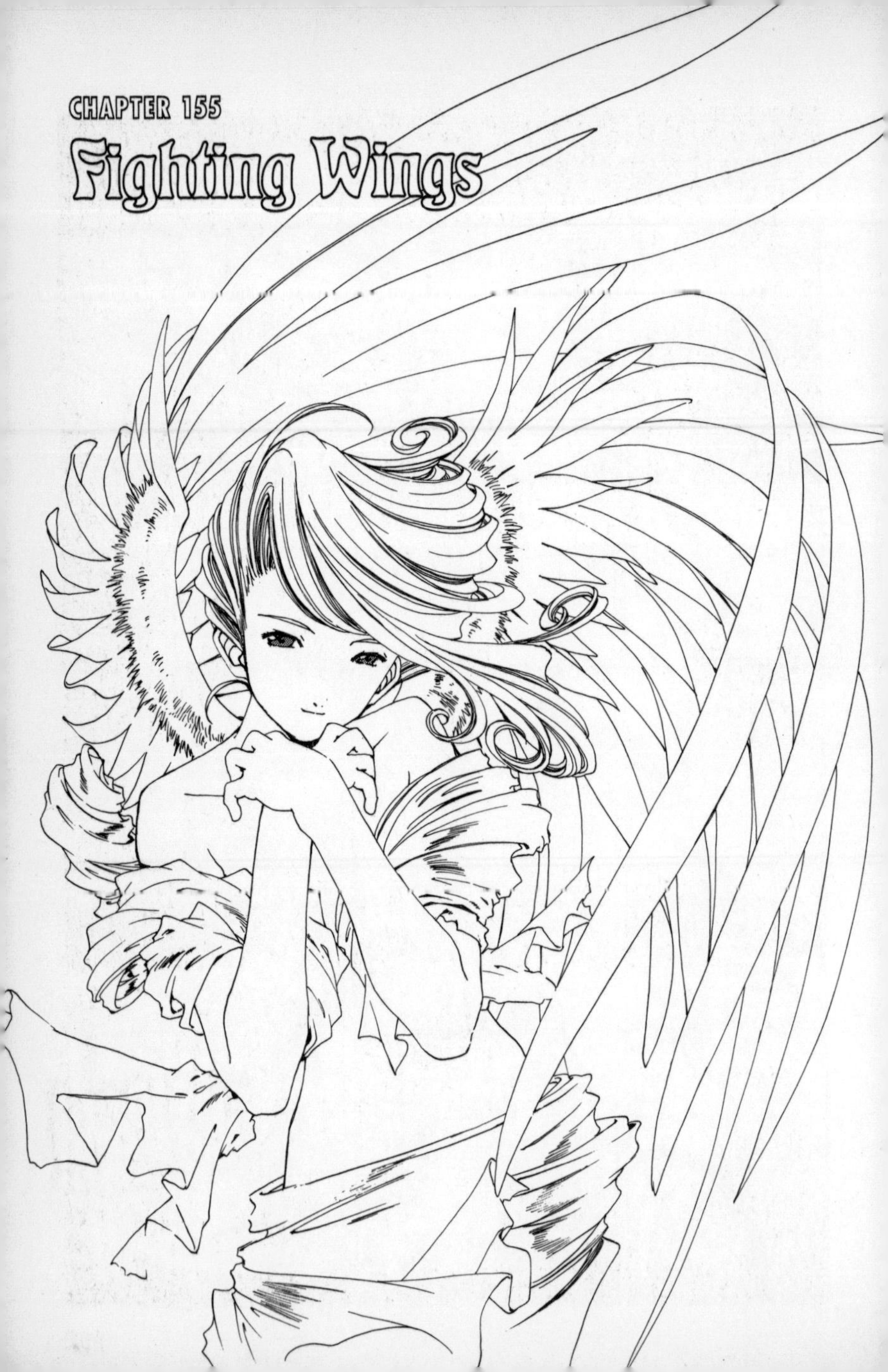

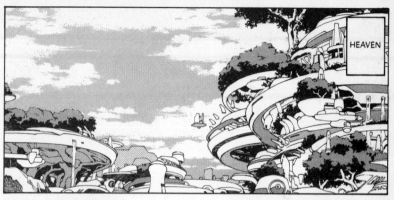

HEAVEN

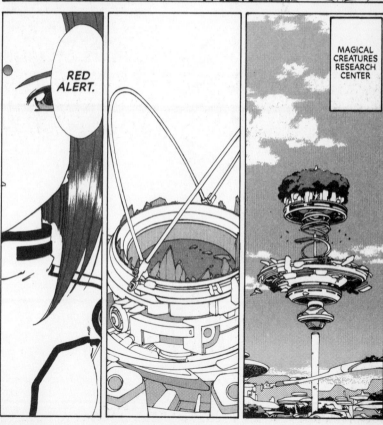

RED ALERT.

MAGICAL CREATURES RESEARCH CENTER

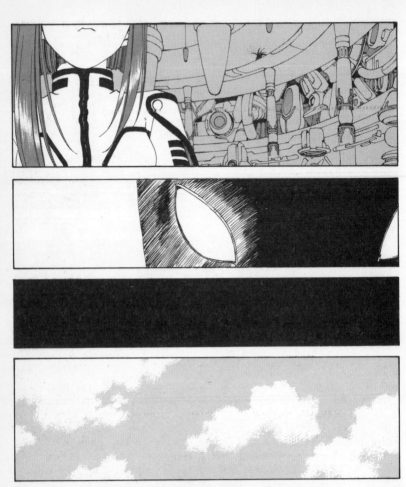

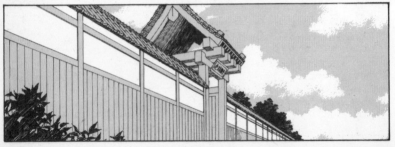

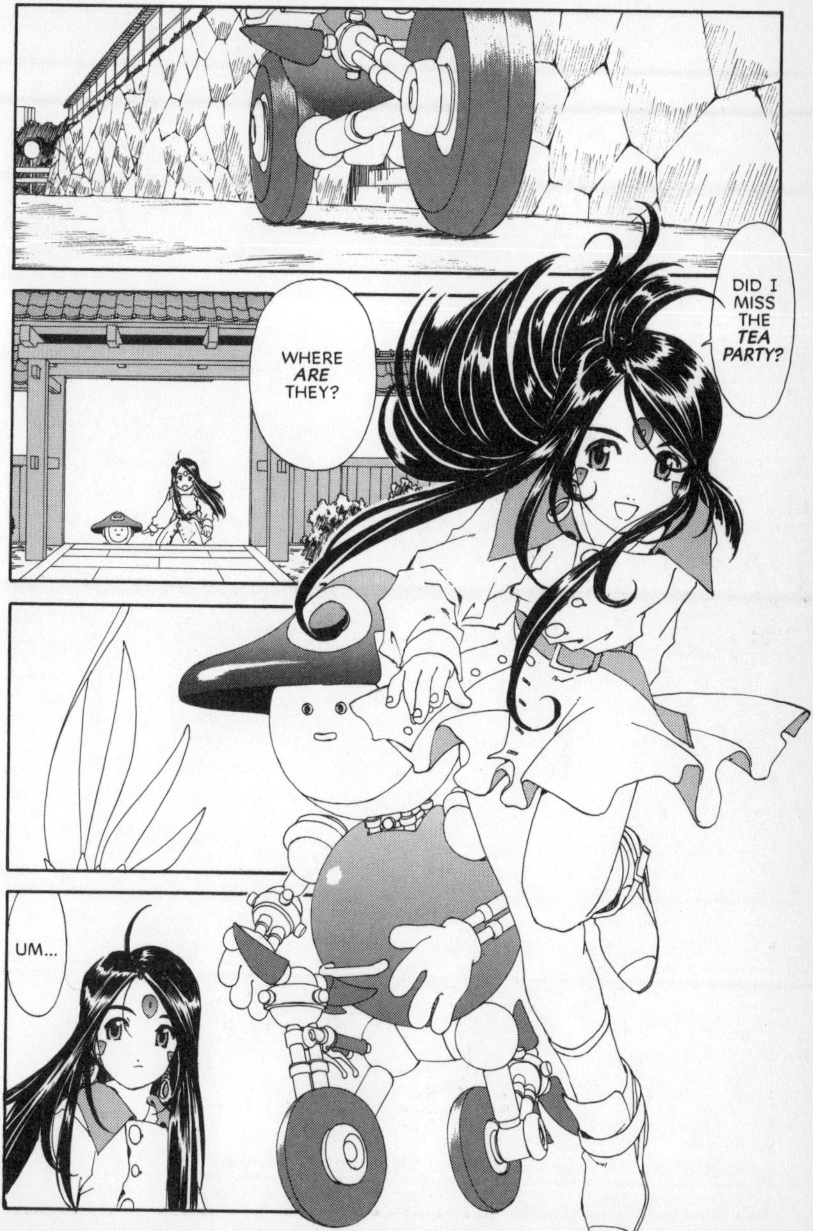
DID I MISS THE *TEA PARTY?*
WHERE *ARE* THEY?
UM...

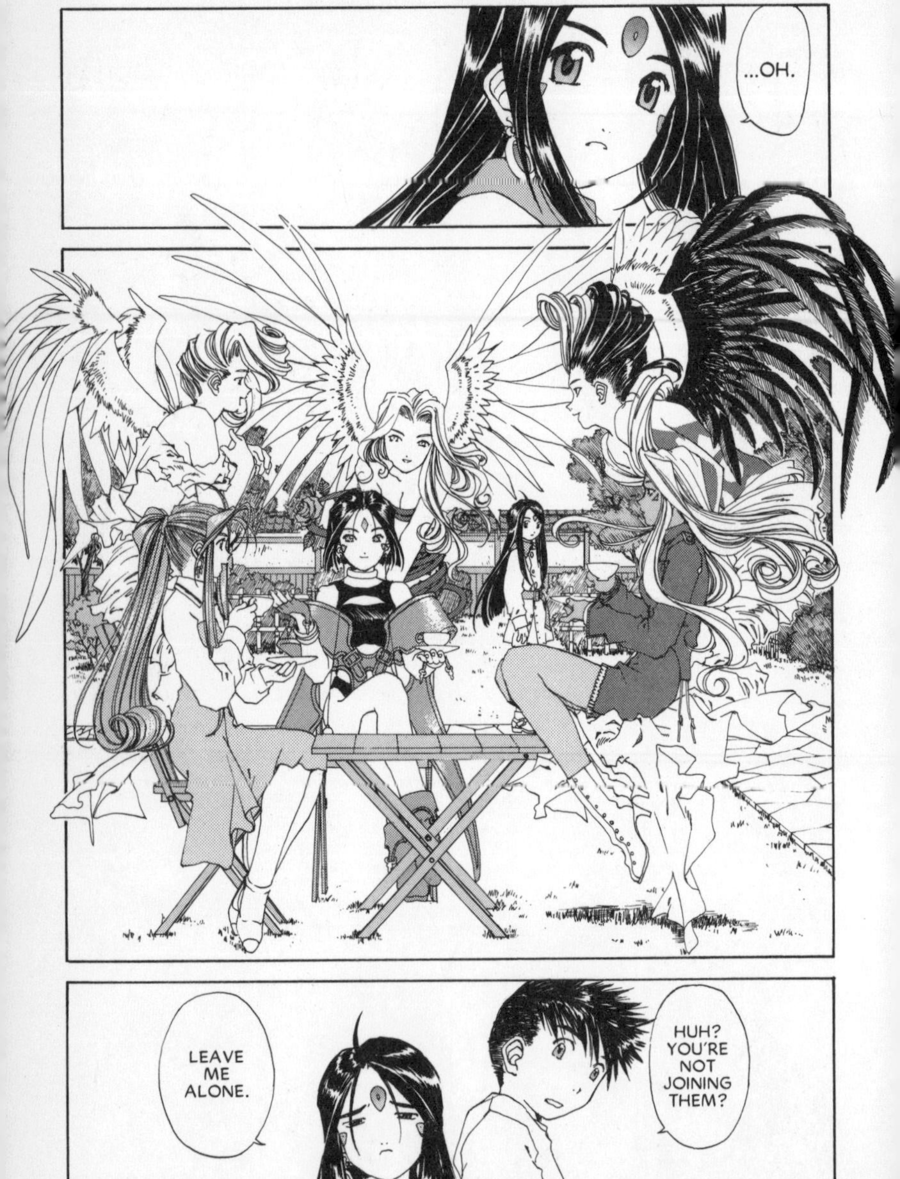
...OH.
HUH? YOU'RE NOT JOINING THEM?
LEAVE ME ALONE.

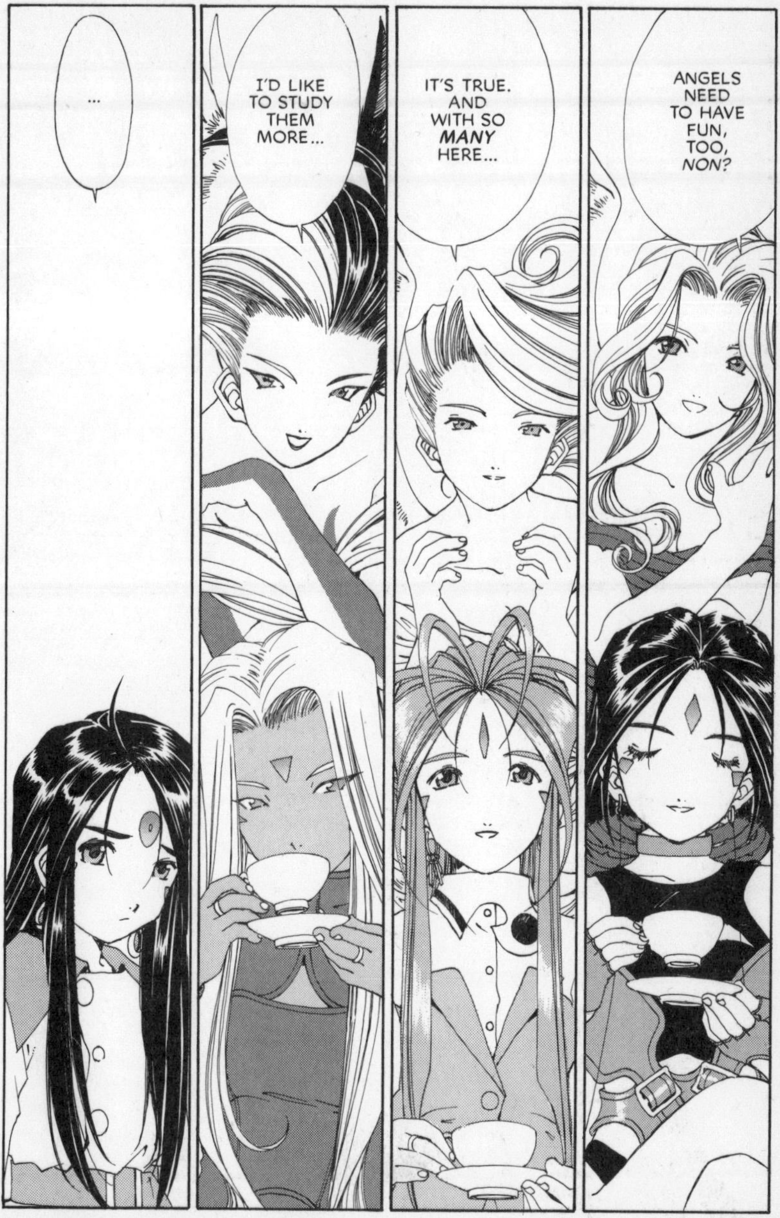
ANGELS NEED TO HAVE FUN, TOO, *NON?*
IT'S TRUE. AND WITH SO *MANY* HERE...
I'D LIKE TO STUDY THEM MORE...
...

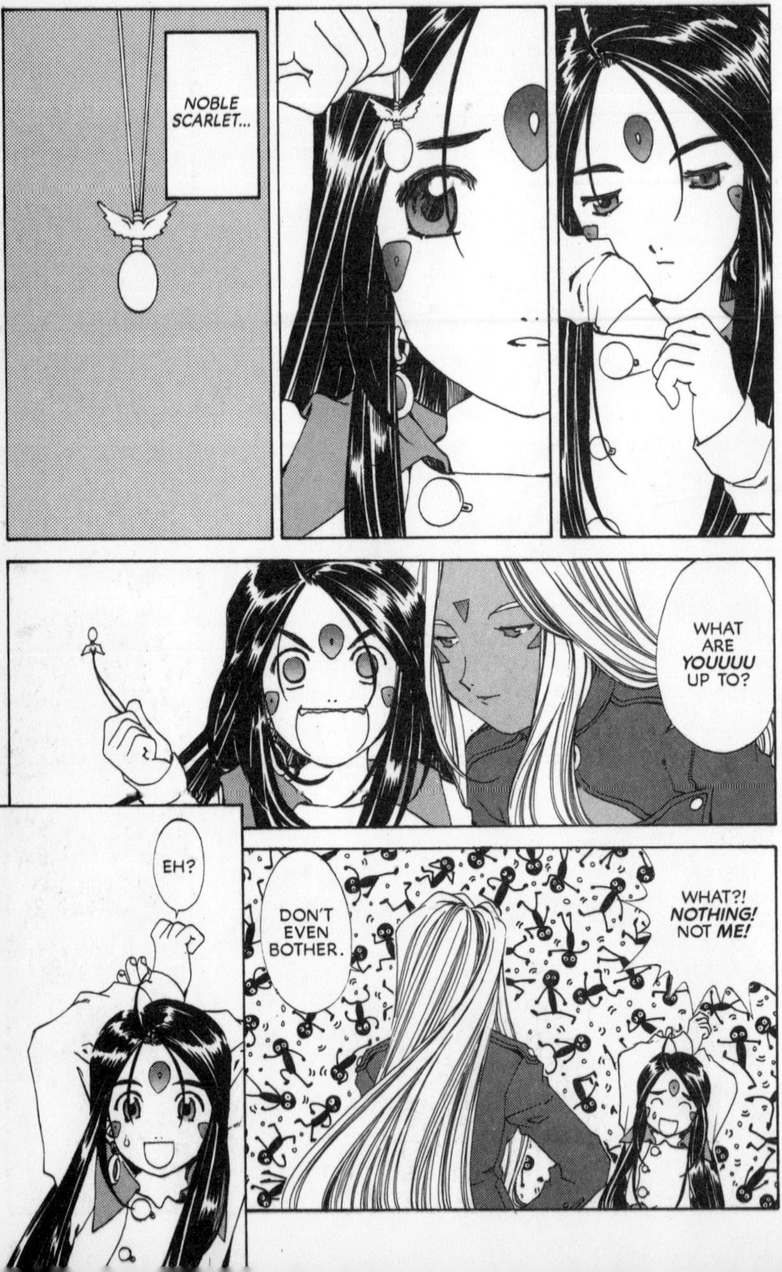
NOBLE SCARLET...
WHAT ARE *YOUUUU* UP TO?
WHAT?! *NOTHING!* NOT *ME!*
DON'T EVEN BOTHER.
EH?

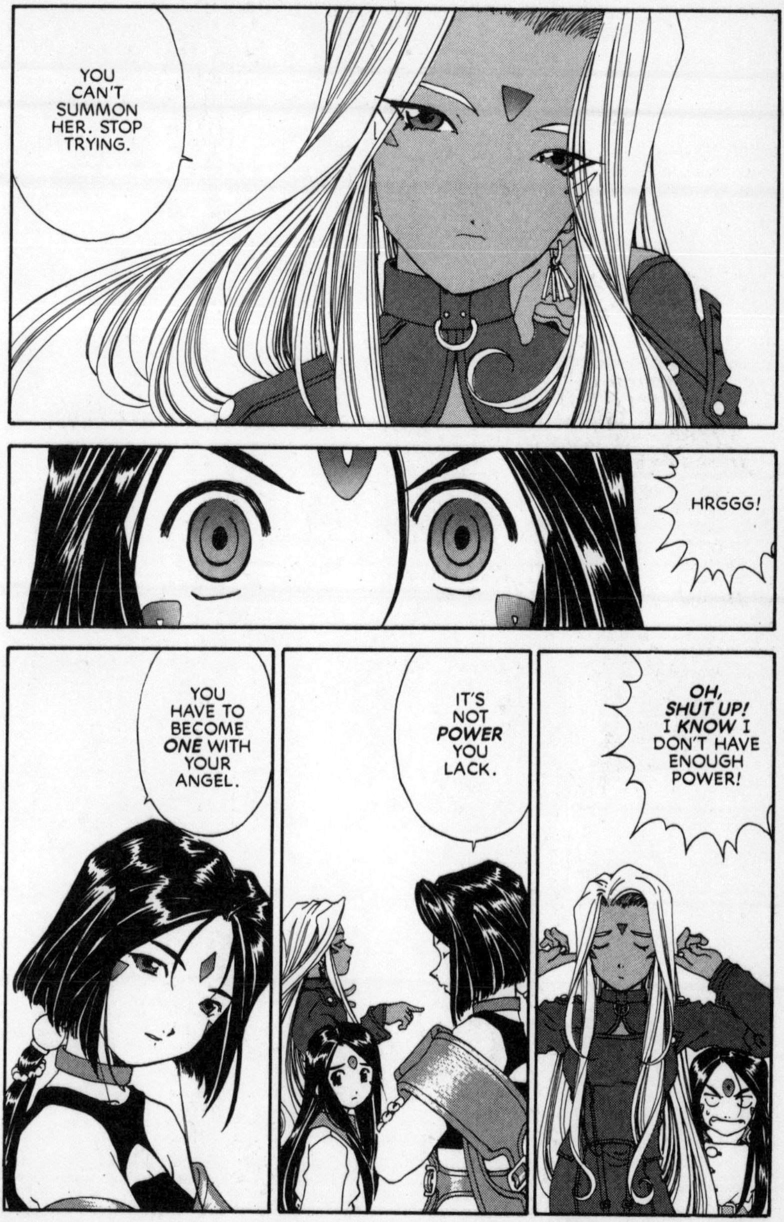
YOU CAN'T SUMMON HER. STOP TRYING.
HRGGG!
OH, SHUT UP! I ***KNOW*** I DON'T HAVE ENOUGH POWER!
IT'S NOT ***POWER*** YOU LACK.
YOU HAVE TO BECOME ***ONE*** WITH YOUR ANGEL.

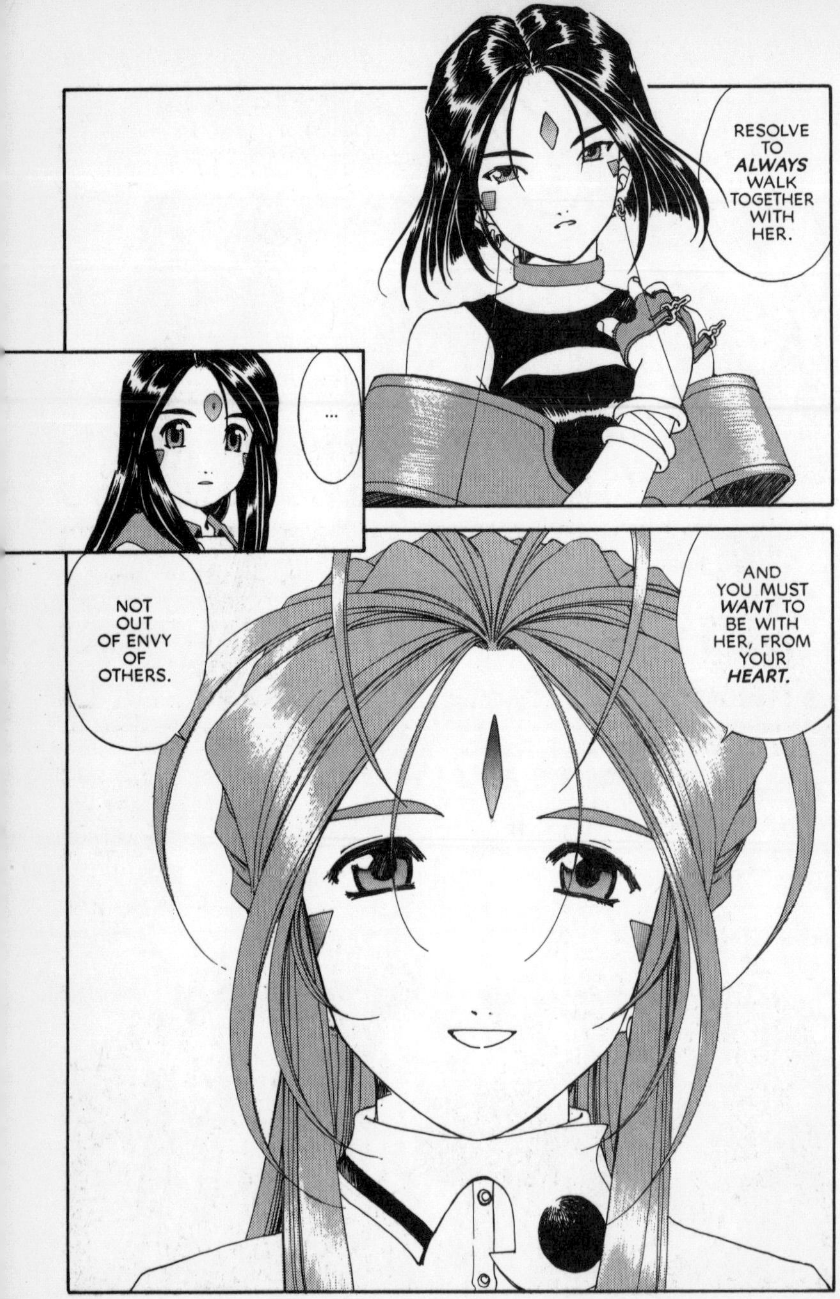
RESOLVE TO ***ALWAYS*** WALK TOGETHER WITH HER.
...
AND YOU MUST *WANT* TO BE WITH HER, FROM YOUR ***HEART.***
NOT OUT OF ENVY OF OTHERS.

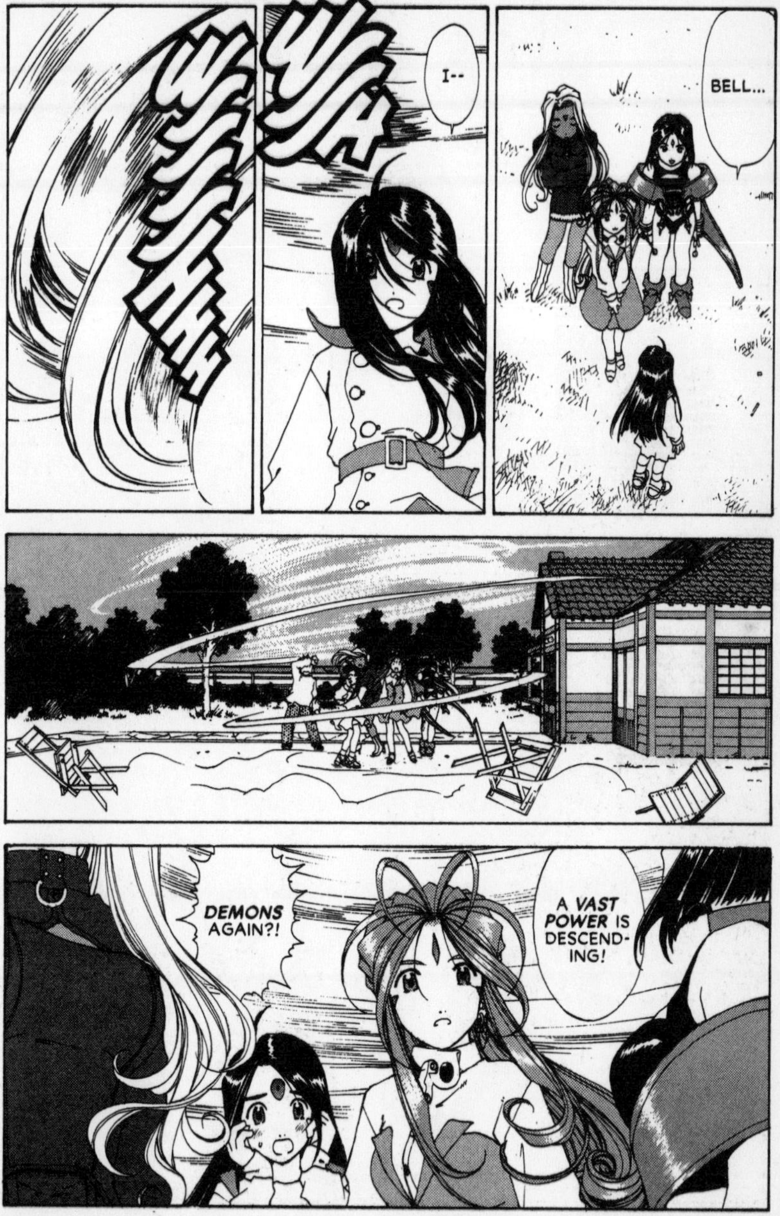
BELL...
I--
A *VAST POWER* IS DESCENDING!
DEMONS AGAIN?!

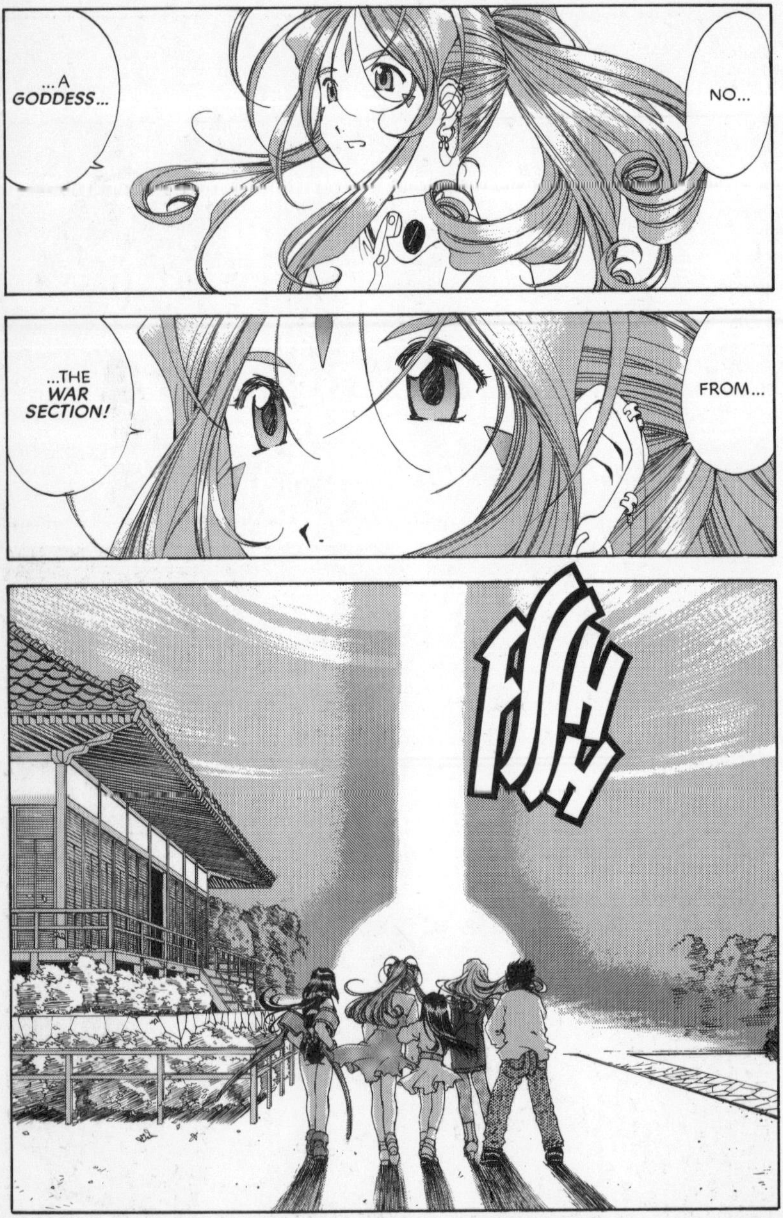
NO...
...A GODDESS...
FROM...
...THE WAR SECTION!

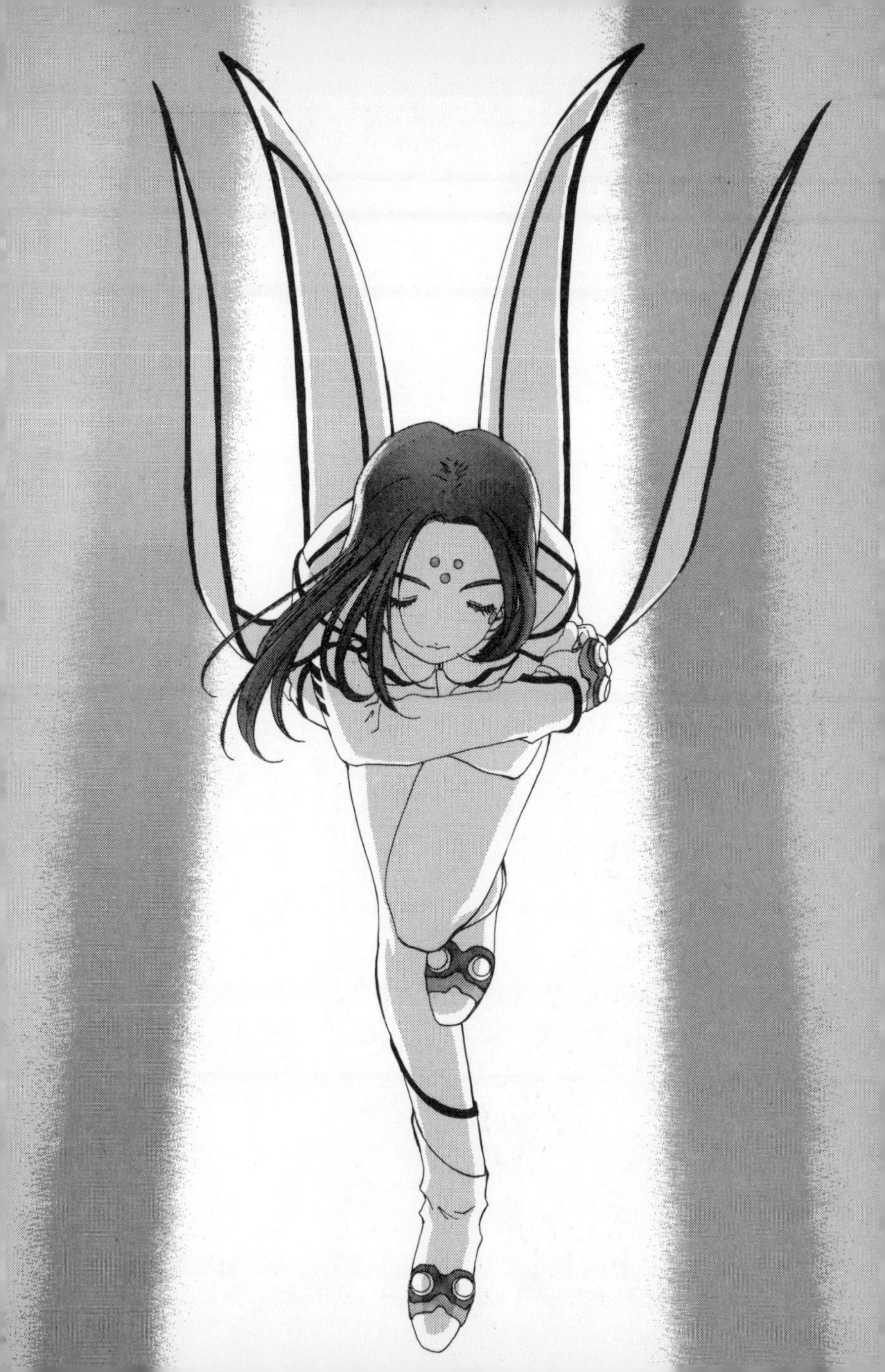

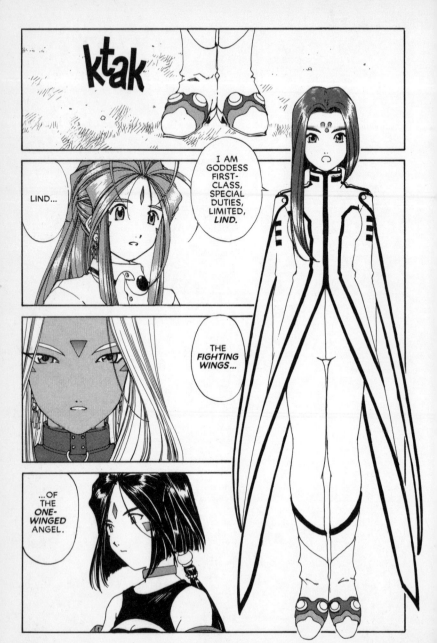

ktak

I AM
GODDESS
FIRST-
CLASS,
SPECIAL
DUTIES,
LIMITED,
LIND.

LIND...

THE
*FIGHTING
WINGS*...

...OF
THE
*ONE-
WINGED*
ANGEL.

145

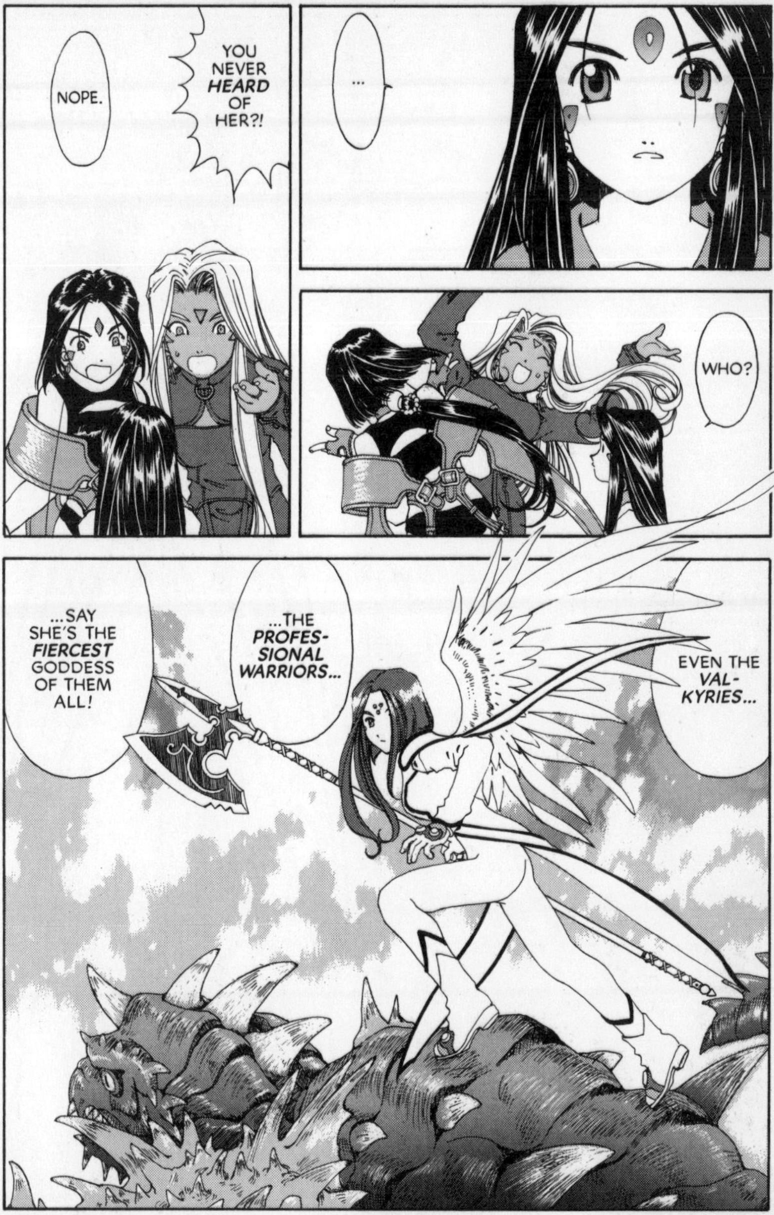
...
YOU NEVER HEARD OF HER?!
NOPE.
WHO?
EVEN THE VAL-KYRIES...
...THE PROFES-SIONAL WARRIORS...
...SAY SHE'S THE FIERCEST GODDESS OF THEM ALL!

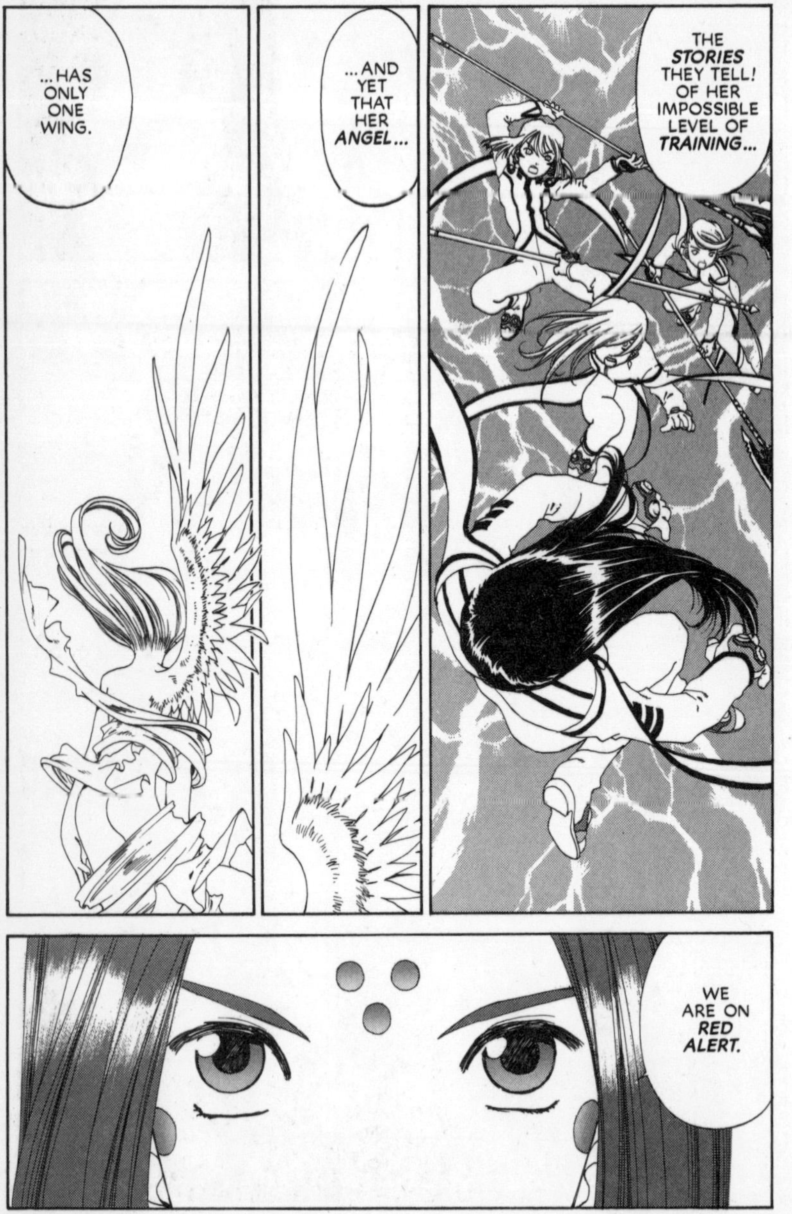
THE STORIES THEY TELL! OF HER IMPOSSIBLE LEVEL OF TRAINING...
...AND YET THAT HER ANGEL...
...HAS ONLY ONE WING.
WE ARE ON RED ALERT.

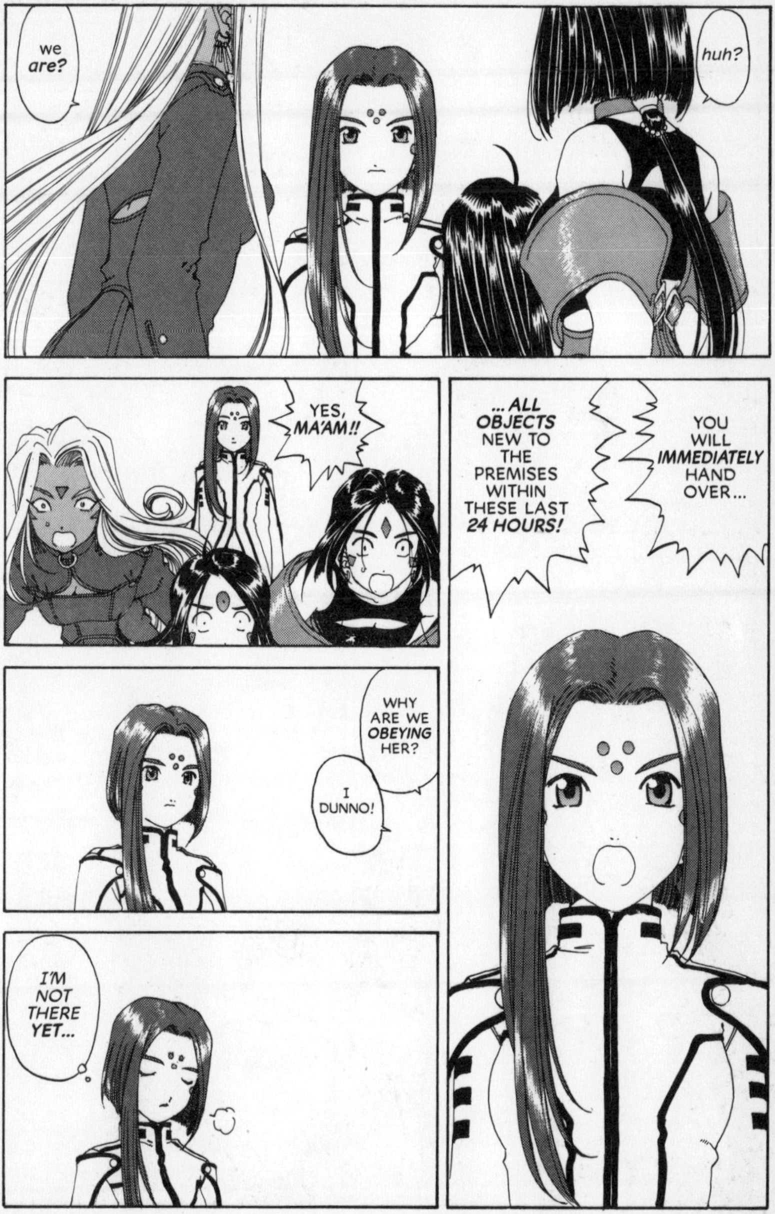
huh?
we are?
YOU WILL IMMEDIATELY HAND OVER...
...ALL OBJECTS NEW TO THE PREMISES WITHIN THESE LAST 24 HOURS!
YES, MA'AM!!
WHY ARE WE OBEYING HER?
I DUNNO!
I'M NOT THERE YET...

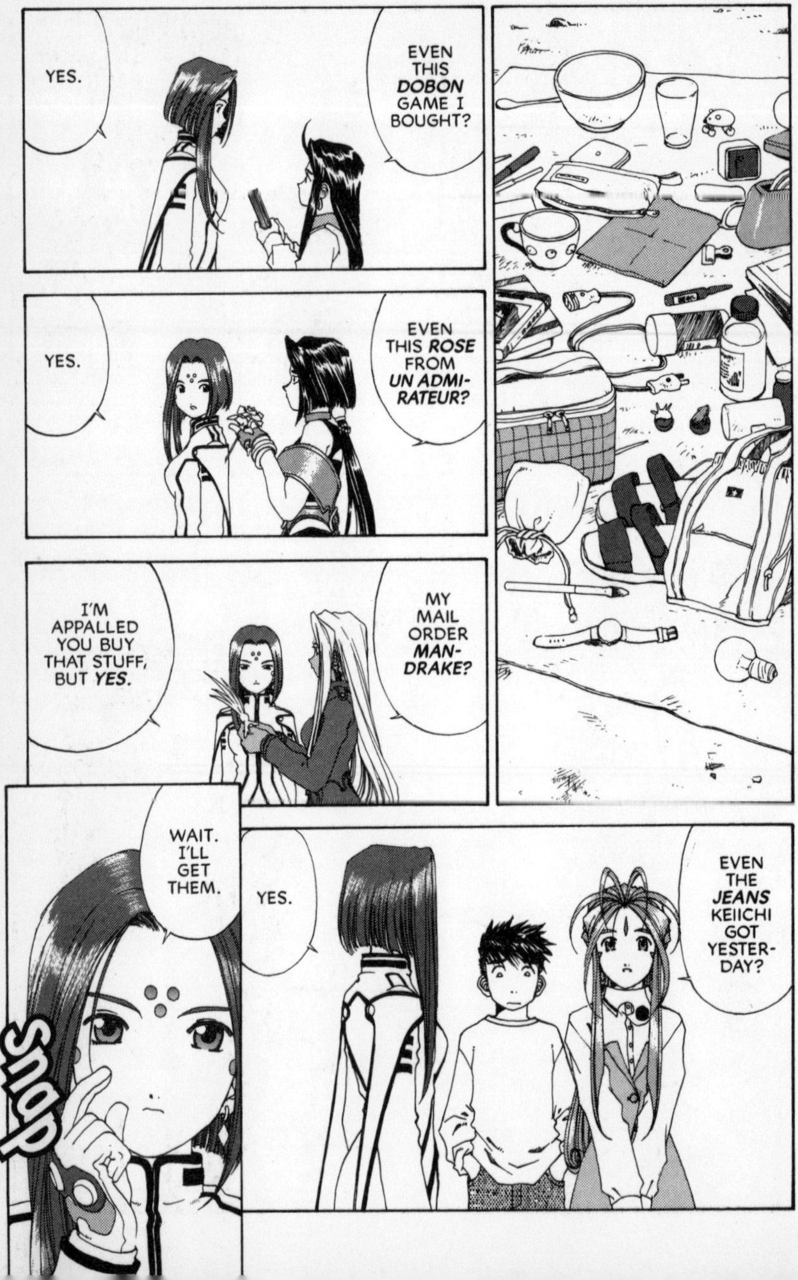
EVEN THIS *DOBON* GAME I BOUGHT?
YES.
EVEN THIS *ROSE* FROM *UN ADMIRATEUR?*
YES.
MY MAIL ORDER *MANDRAKE?*
I'M APPALLED YOU BUY THAT STUFF, BUT *YES.*
EVEN THE *JEANS* KEIICHI GOT YESTERDAY?
YES.
WAIT. I'LL GET THEM.
snap

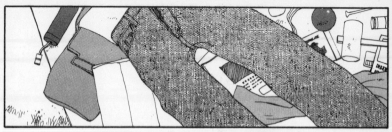

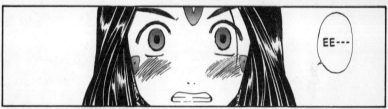

EE---

HRM!

LIND, WHAT ON EARTH...

EEEEK!!

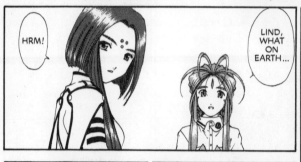

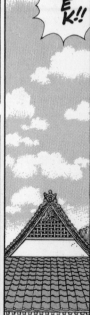

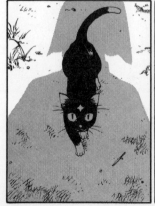

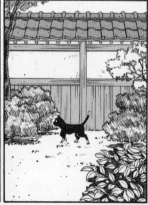

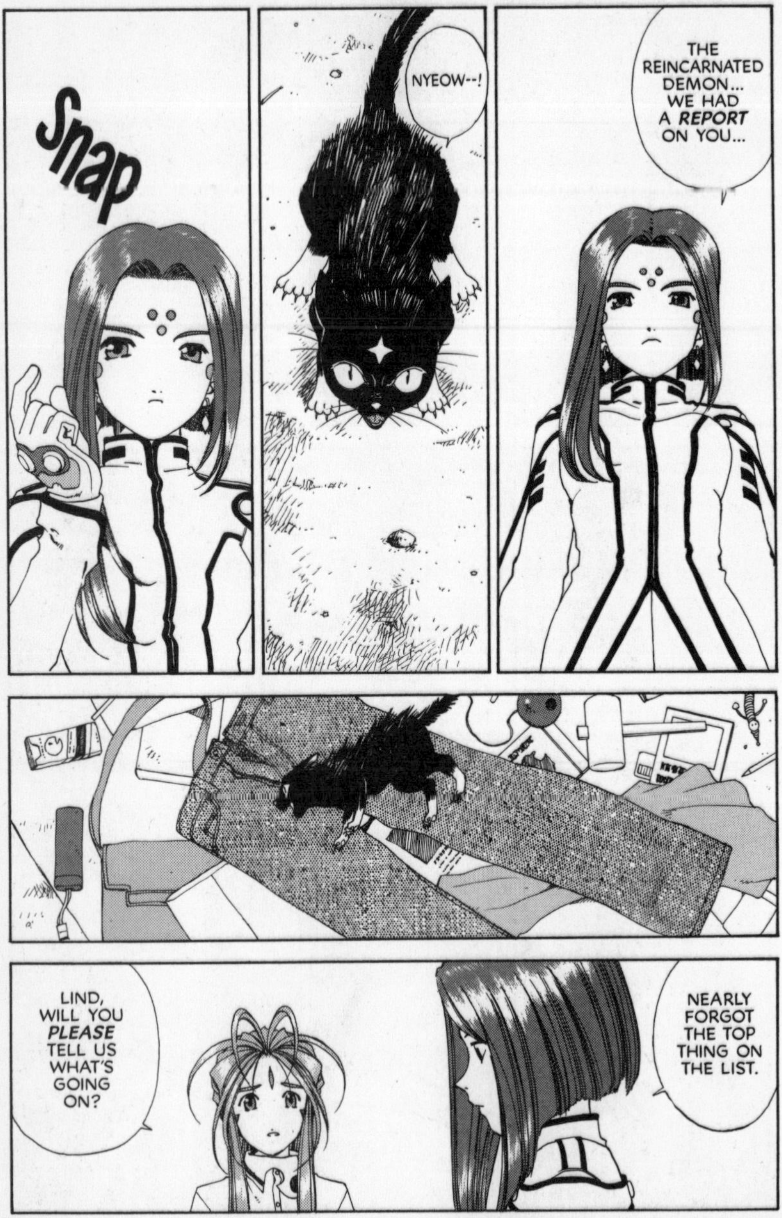
THE REINCARNATED DEMON... WE HAD A REPORT ON YOU...
NYEOW--!
Snap
NEARLY FORGOT THE TOP THING ON THE LIST.
LIND, WILL YOU PLEASE TELL US WHAT'S GOING ON?

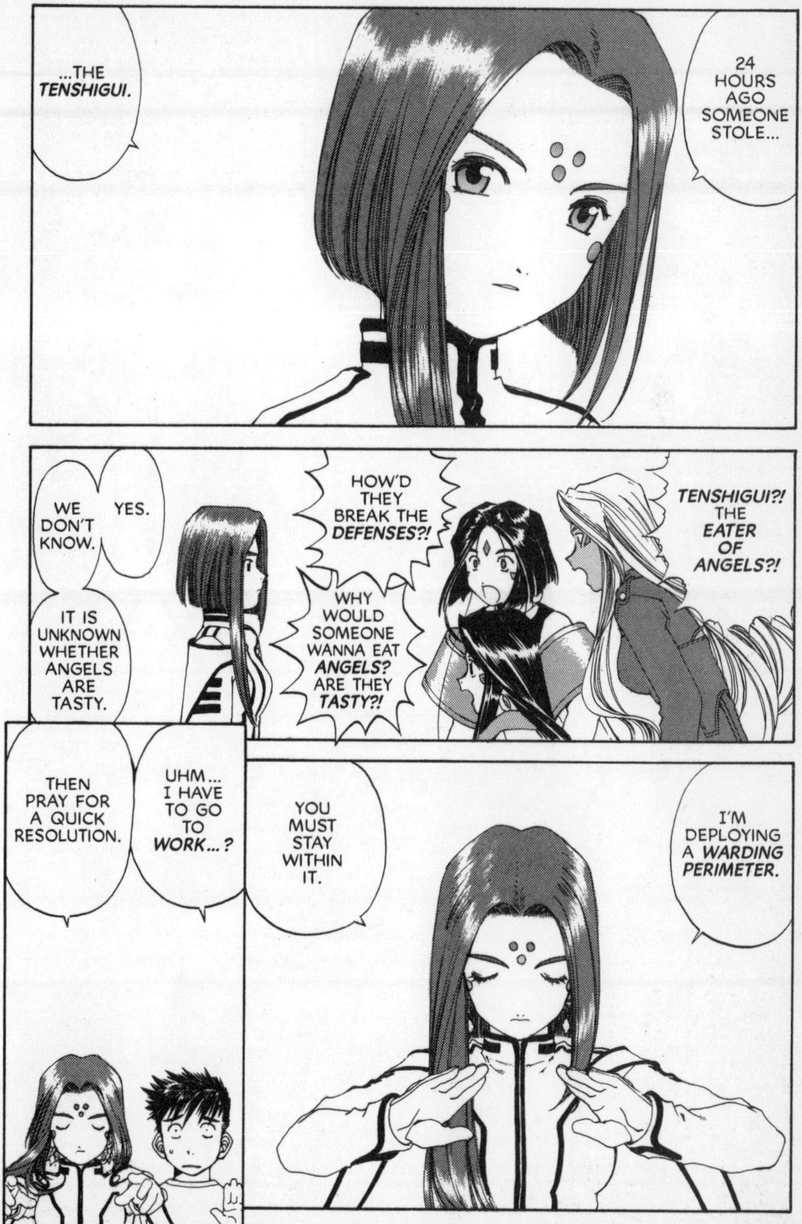
24 HOURS AGO SOMEONE STOLE...
...THE TENSHIGUI.
TENSHIGUI?! THE EATER OF ANGELS?!
HOW'D THEY BREAK THE DEFENSES?!
WHY WOULD SOMEONE WANNA EAT ANGELS? ARE THEY TASTY?!
YES.
WE DON'T KNOW.
IT IS UNKNOWN WHETHER ANGELS ARE TASTY.
I'M DEPLOYING A WARDING PERIMETER.
YOU MUST STAY WITHIN IT.
UHM... I HAVE TO GO TO WORK...?
THEN PRAY FOR A QUICK RESOLUTION.

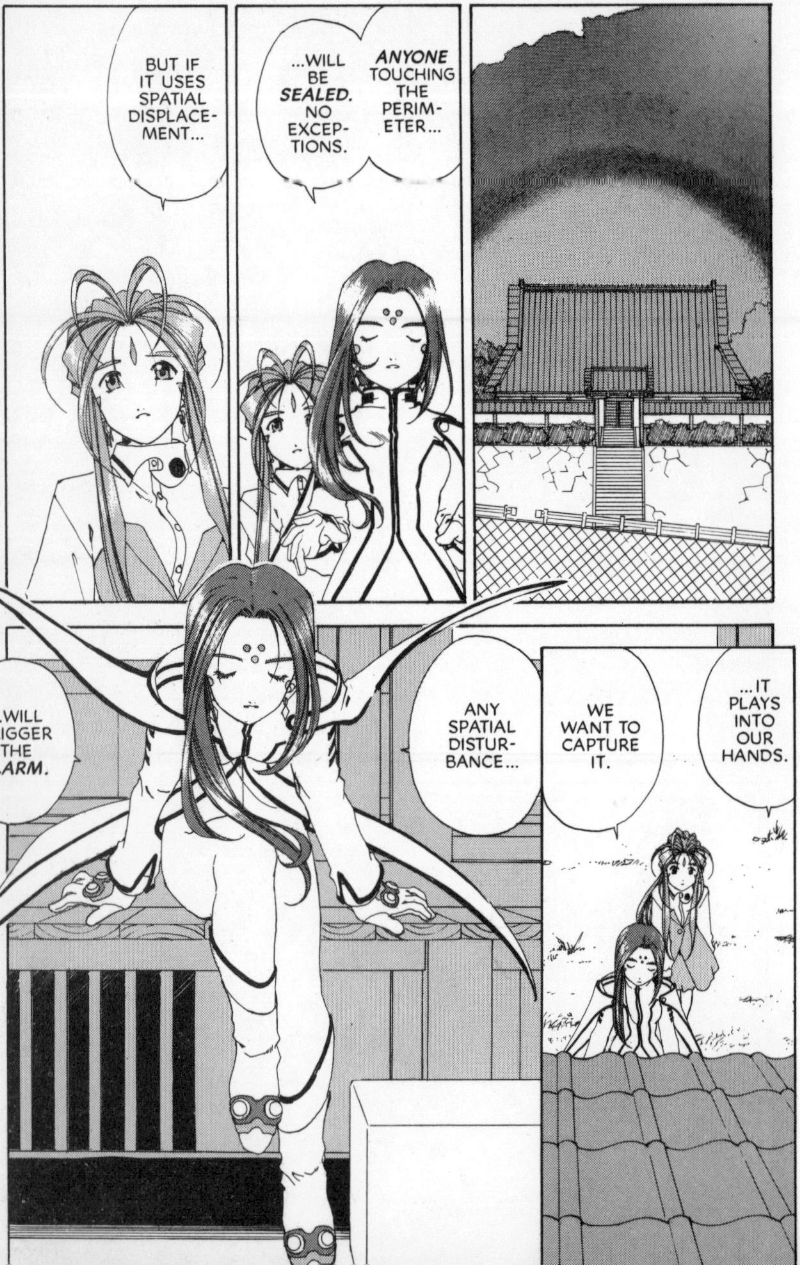
ANYONE TOUCHING THE PERIMETER...
...WILL BE SEALED. NO EXCEPTIONS.
BUT IF IT USES SPATIAL DISPLACEMENT...
...IT PLAYS INTO OUR HANDS.
WE WANT TO CAPTURE IT.
ANY SPATIAL DISTURBANCE...
...WILL TRIGGER THE ALARM.

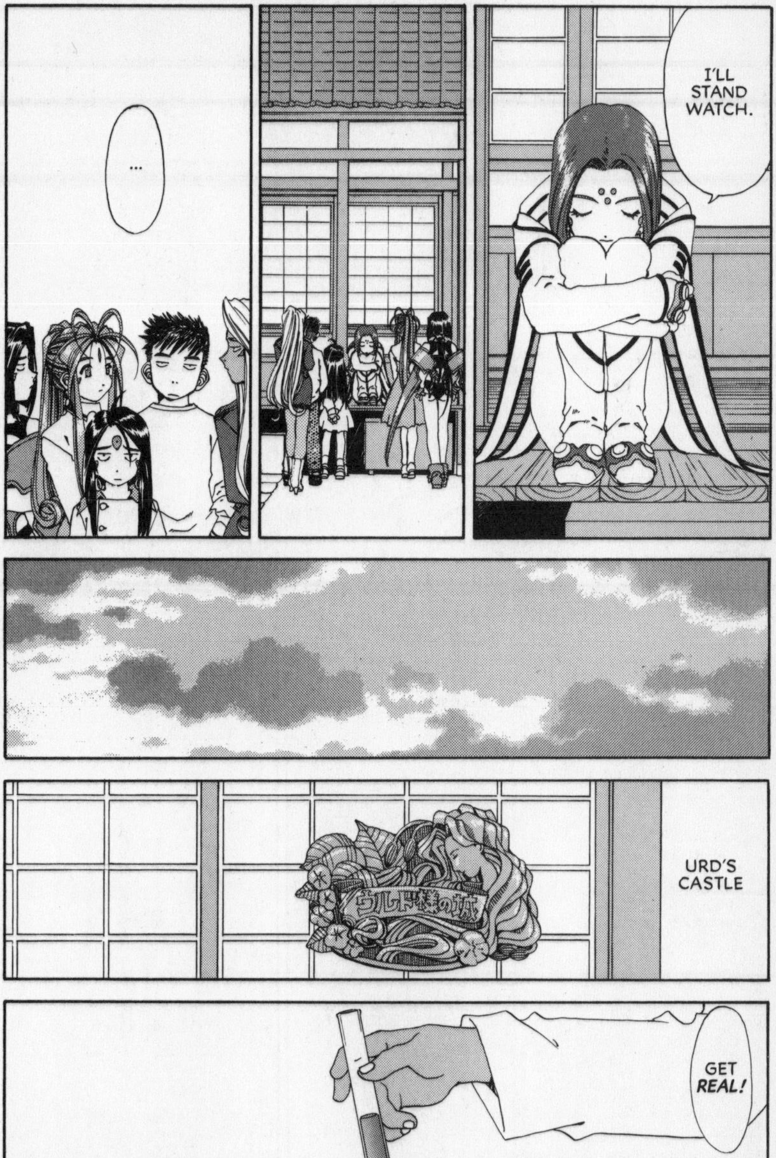
I'LL STAND WATCH.
...
URD'S CASTLE
GET *REAL!*

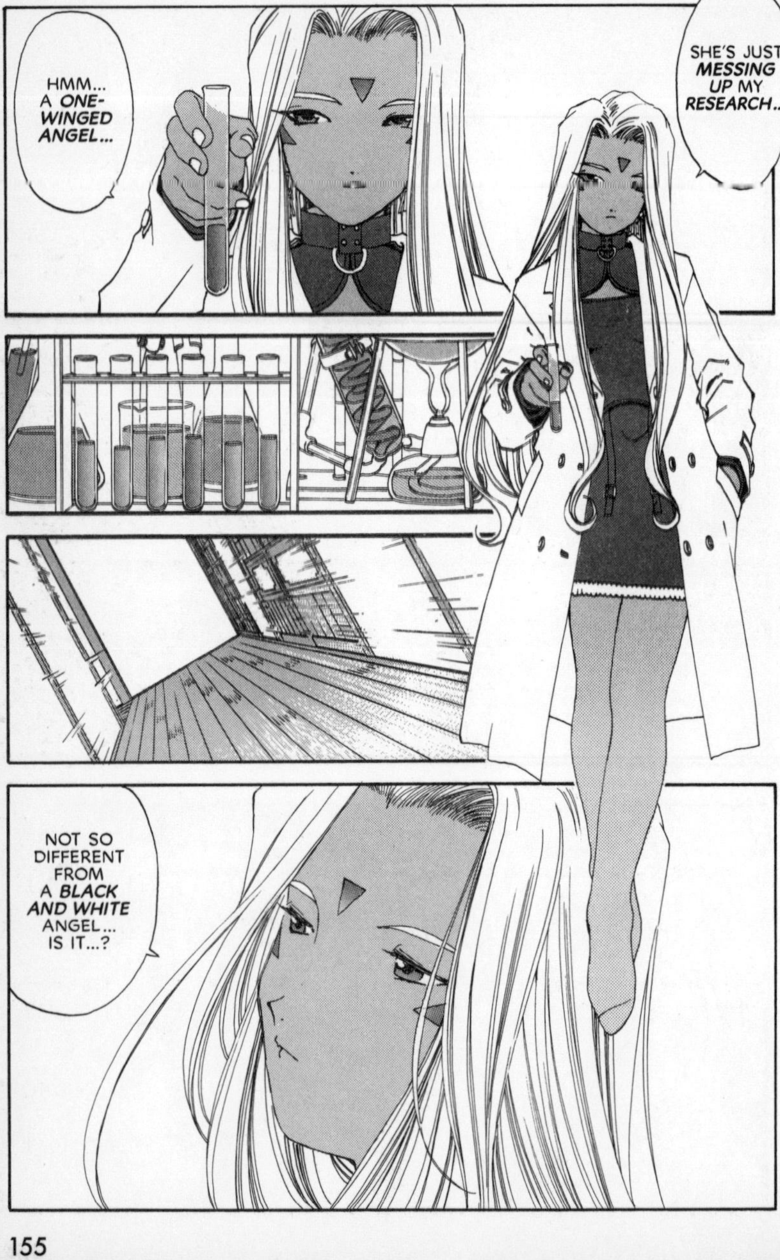
SHE'S JUST *MESSING UP* MY *RESEARCH...*
HMM... A *ONE-WINGED ANGEL...*
NOT SO DIFFERENT FROM A *BLACK AND WHITE* ANGEL... IS IT...?

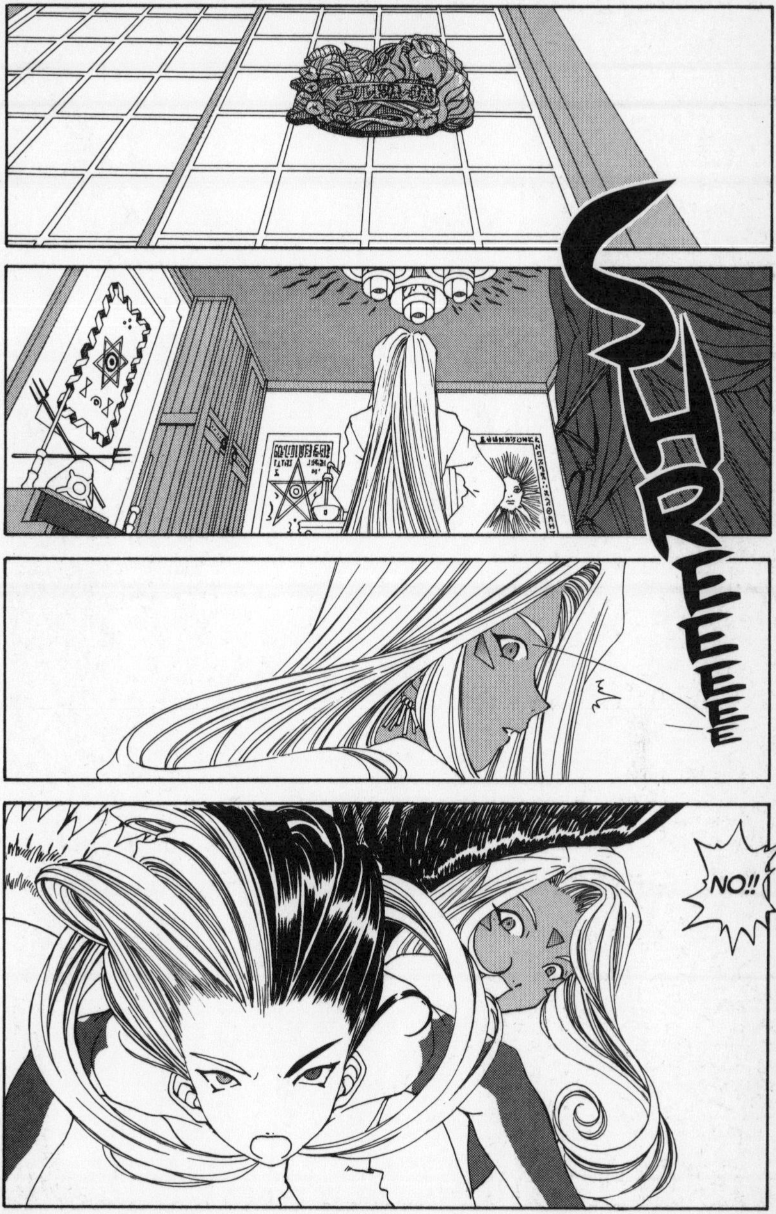
SHREEEEE
NO!!

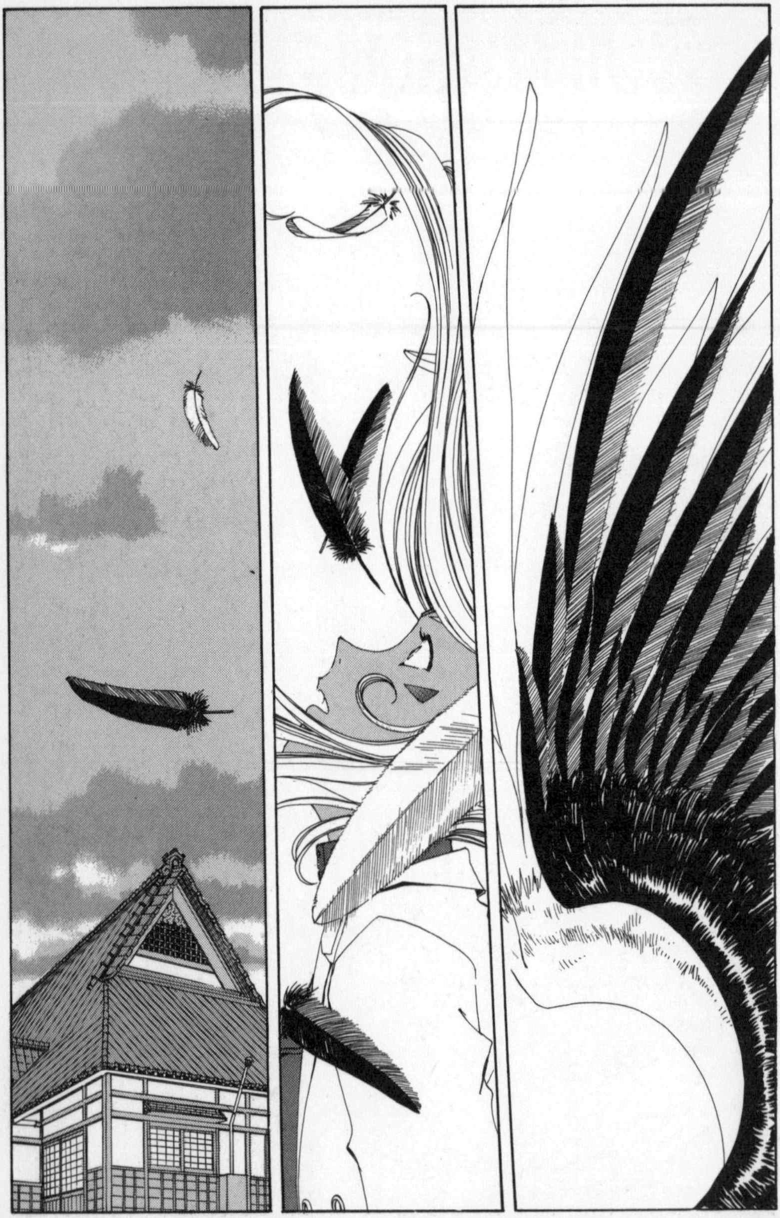

OH MY GODDESS!
L I N D

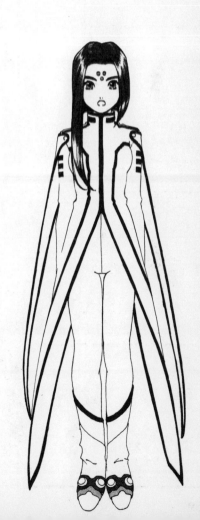

ADVENTURES OF THE MINI-GODDESS SPECIAL: MORE MAGICAL DO MI SO♭ ONLINE!

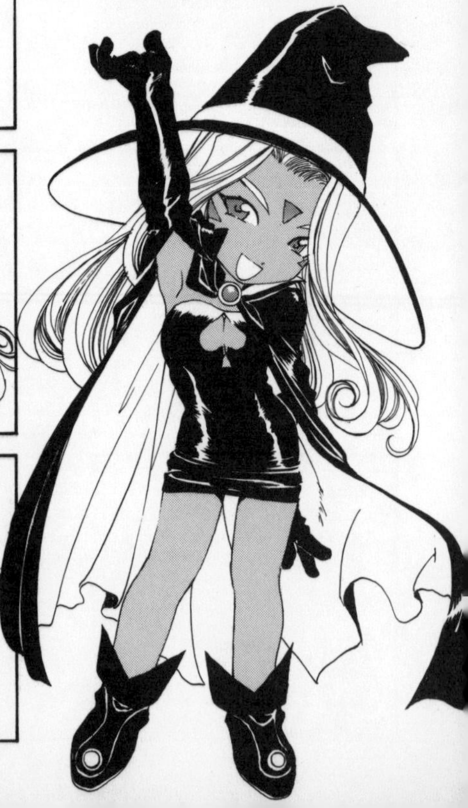

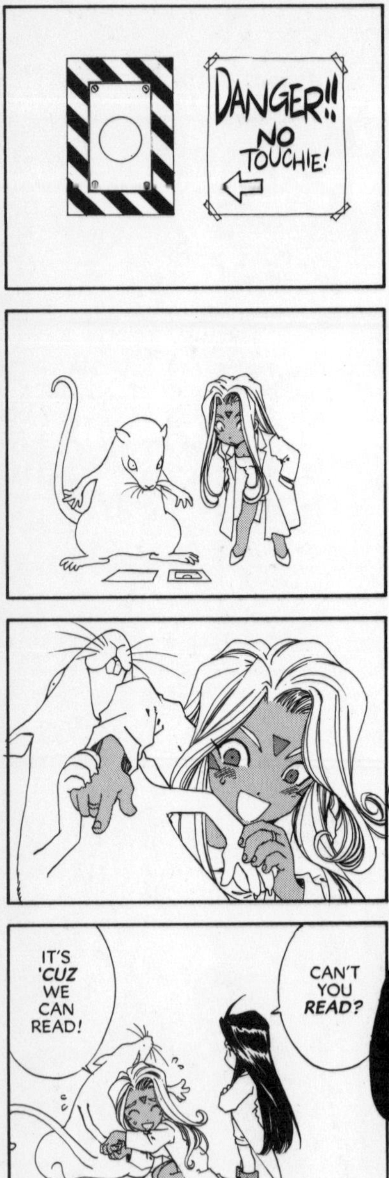
DANGER!! NO TOUCHIE!
CAN'T YOU *READ?*
IT'S '*CUZ* WE CAN READ!

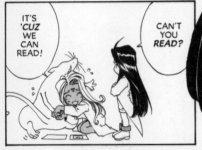

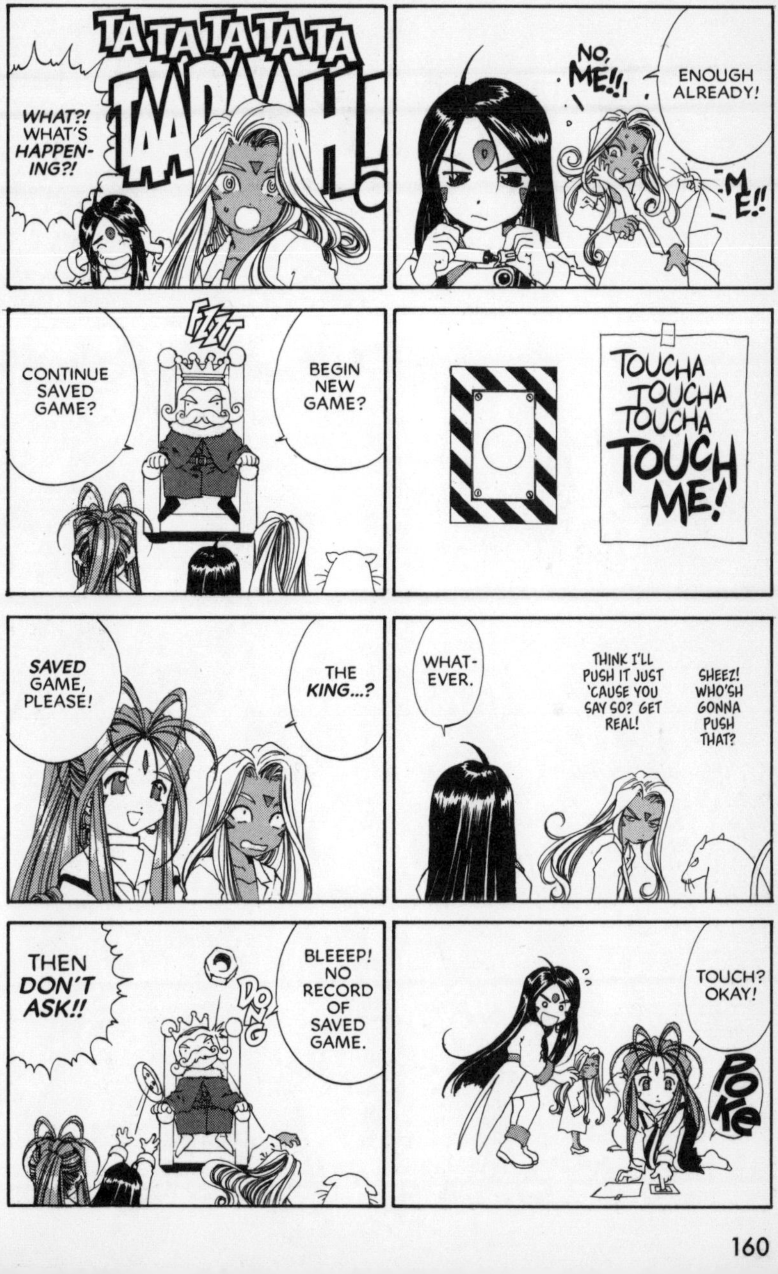
ENOUGH ALREADY!
NO, ME!!
ME!!
TA TA TA TA TA TA
TAADAAH!
WHAT?! WHAT'S HAPPENING?!
TOUCHA TOUCHA TOUCHA TOUCH ME!
BEGIN NEW GAME?
FZZT
CONTINUE SAVED GAME?
SHEEZ! WHO'SH GONNA PUSH THAT?
THINK I'LL PUSH IT JUST 'CAUSE YOU SAY SO? GET REAL!
WHAT-EVER.
THE KING...?
SAVED GAME, PLEASE!
TOUCH? OKAY!
POKE
BLEEEP! NO RECORD OF SAVED GAME.
DONG
THEN DON'T ASK!!

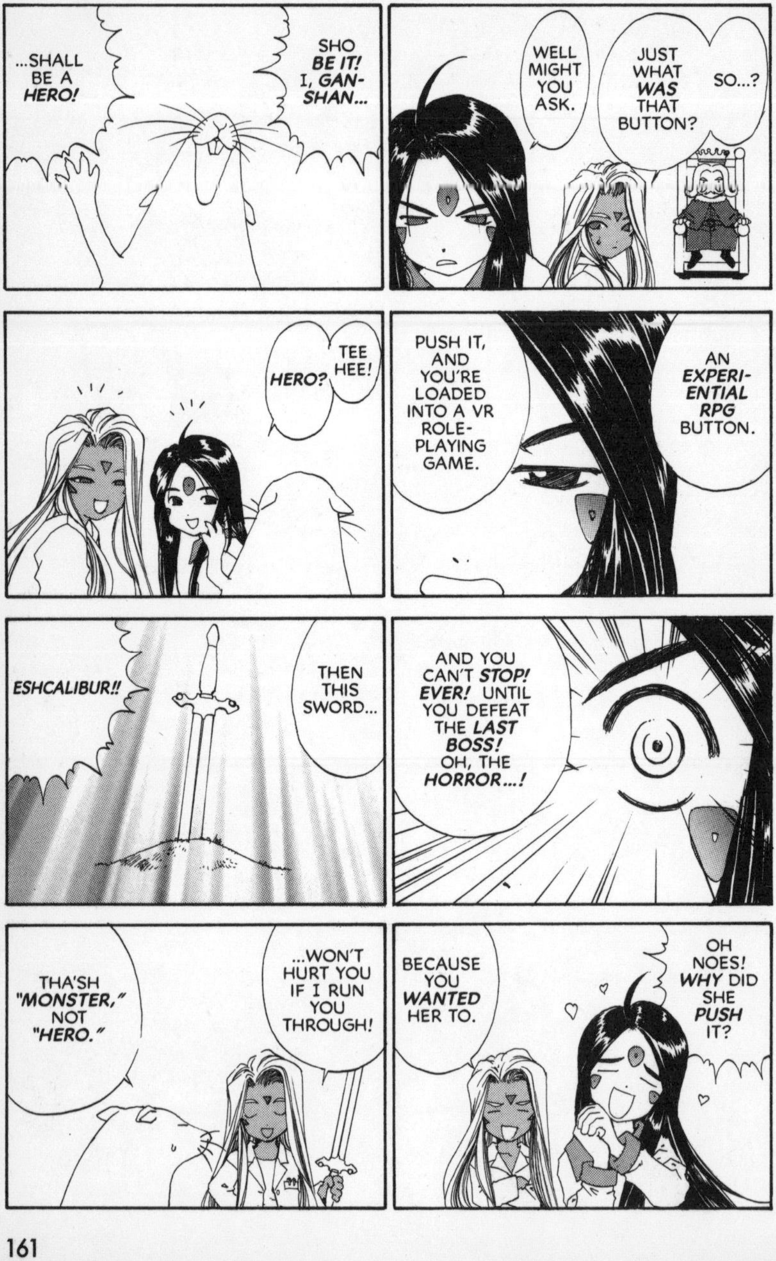
SO...?
JUST WHAT WAS THAT BUTTON?
WELL MIGHT YOU ASK.
SHO BE IT! I, GAN-SHAN...
...SHALL BE A HERO!
AN EXPERIENTIAL RPG BUTTON.
PUSH IT, AND YOU'RE LOADED INTO A VR ROLE-PLAYING GAME.
TEE HEE!
HERO?
AND YOU CAN'T STOP! EVER! UNTIL YOU DEFEAT THE LAST BOSS! OH, THE HORROR...!
THEN THIS SWORD...
ESHCALIBUR!!
OH NOES! WHY DID SHE PUSH IT?
BECAUSE YOU WANTED HER TO.
...WON'T HURT YOU IF I RUN YOU THROUGH!
THA'SH "MONSTER," NOT "HERO."

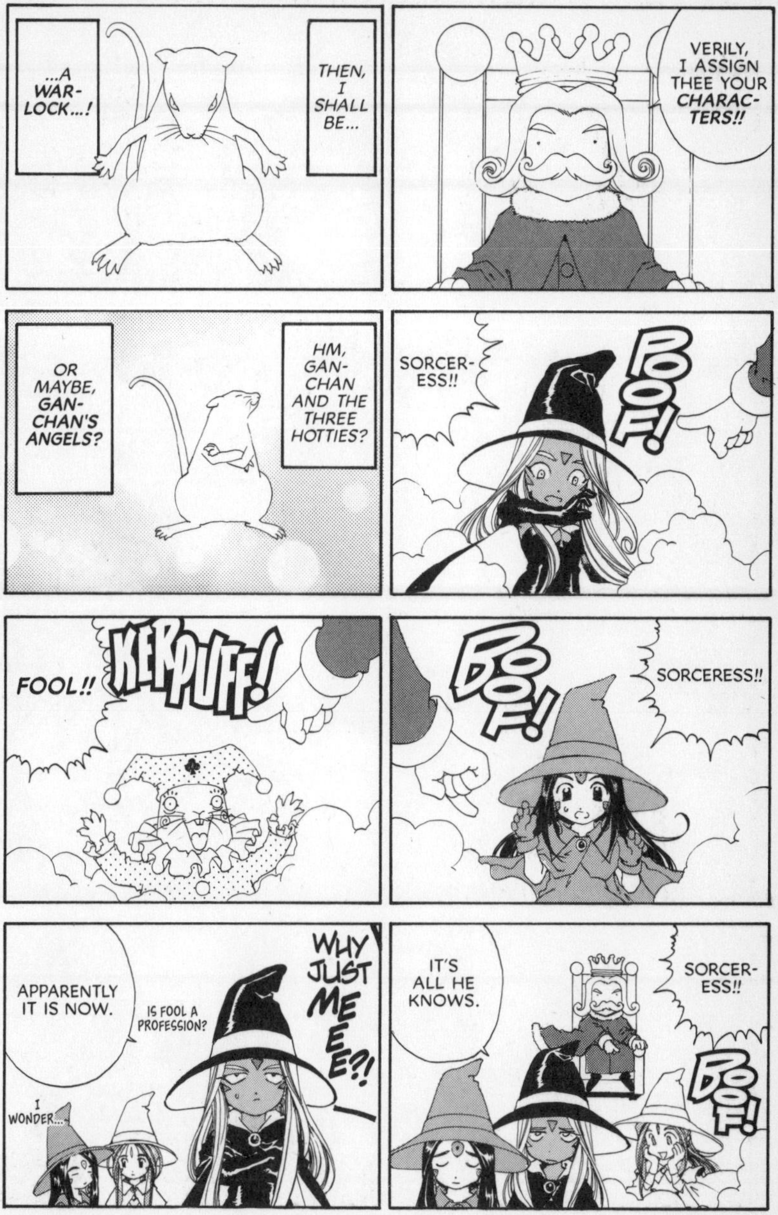
VERILY, I ASSIGN THEE YOUR CHARACTERS!!
THEN, I SHALL BE...
...A WARLOCK...!
BOOF!
SORCERESS!!
HM, GAN-CHAN AND THE THREE HOTTIES?
OR MAYBE, GAN-CHAN'S ANGELS?
SORCERESS!!
BOOF!
KERPUFF!
FOOL!!
SORCERESS!!
BOOF!
IT'S ALL HE KNOWS.
WHY JUST MEEEE?!
IS FOOL A PROFESSION?
APPARENTLY IT IS NOW.
I WONDER...

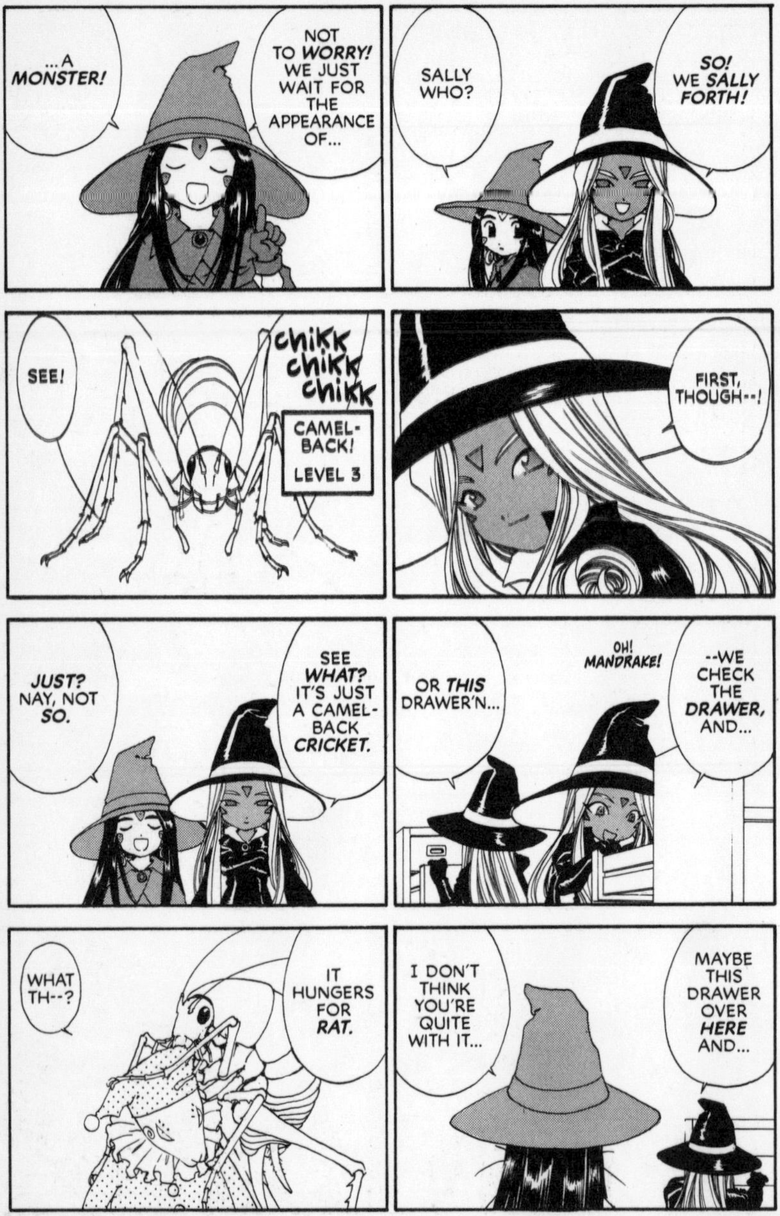
SO! WE SALLY FORTH!
SALLY WHO?
NOT TO WORRY! WE JUST WAIT FOR THE APPEARANCE OF...
...A MONSTER!
FIRST, THOUGH--!
chikk chikk chikk
CAMEL-BACK! LEVEL 3
SEE!
--WE CHECK THE DRAWER, AND...
OH! MANDRAKE!
OR THIS DRAWER'N...
SEE WHAT? IT'S JUST A CAMEL-BACK CRICKET.
JUST? NAY, NOT SO.
MAYBE THIS DRAWER OVER HERE AND...
I DON'T THINK YOU'RE QUITE WITH IT...
IT HUNGERS FOR RAT.
WHAT TH--?

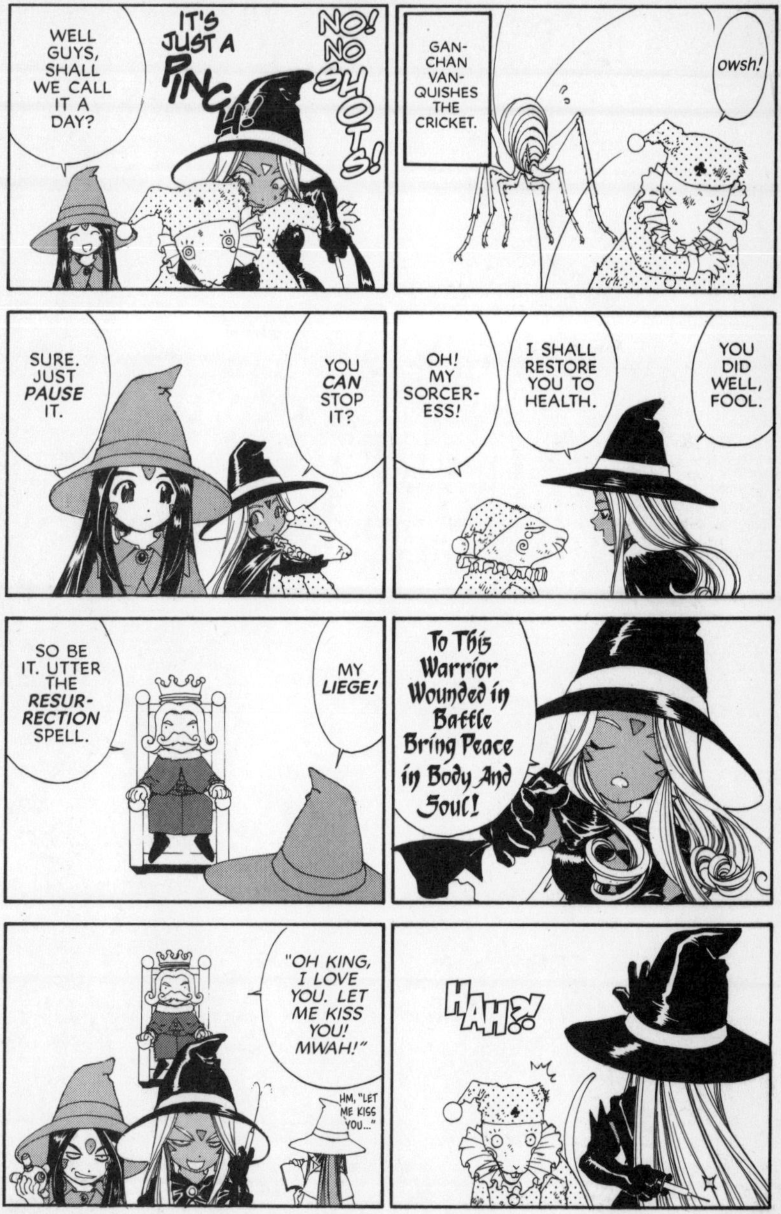
owsh!
GAN-CHAN VANQUISHES THE CRICKET.
NO! NO SHOTS!
IT'S JUST A PINCH!
WELL GUYS, SHALL WE CALL IT A DAY?
YOU DID WELL, FOOL.
I SHALL RESTORE YOU TO HEALTH.
OH! MY SORCERESS!
YOU *CAN* STOP IT?
SURE. JUST *PAUSE* IT.
To This Warrior Wounded in Battle Bring Peace in Body And Soul!
MY *LIEGE!*
SO BE IT. UTTER THE *RESURRECTION* SPELL.
HAH?!
"OH KING, I LOVE YOU. LET ME KISS YOU! MWAH!"
HM, "LET ME KISS YOU..."

EDITOR
Carl Gustav Horn

DESIGNER
Scott Cook

ART DIRECTOR
Lia Ribacchi

PUBLISHER
Mike Richardson

English-language version
produced by Dark Horse Comics

OH MY GODDESS! Vol. 24
©2006 by Kosuke Fujishima. All rights reserved. First published in
Japan in 2002 by Kodansha, Ltd., Tokyo. Publication rights for this English edition arranged through Kodansha, Ltd. This English-language edition
©2006 by Dark Horse Comics, Inc. All other material ©2006 by Dark
Horse Comics, Inc. All rights reserved. No portion of this publication may
be reproduced, in any form or by any means, without the express written
permission of the copyright holders. Names, characters, places, and inci-
dents featured in this publication are either the product of the author's
imagination or are used fictitiously. Any resemblance to actual persons
(living or dead), events, institutions, or locales, without satiric intent, is
coincidental. Dark Horse Manga™ is a trademark of Dark Horse
Comics, Inc. All rights reserved.

Published by Dark Horse Manga
A division of Dark Horse Comics, Inc.
10956 SE Main Street
Milwaukie, OR 97222
www.darkhorse.com

To find a comics shop in your area,
call the Comic Shop Locator Service
toll-free at 1-888-266-4226

First edition: October 2006
ISBN-10: 1-59307-545-6
ISBN-13: 978-1-59307-545-3

1 3 5 7 9 10 8 6 4 2

Printed in Canada

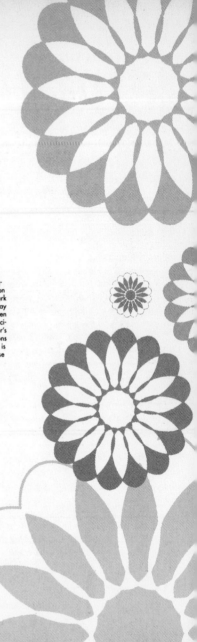

letters to the ENCHANTRESS

10956 SE Main Street, Milwaukie, Oregon 97222
omg@darkhorse.com • www.darkhorse.com

NOTE: Full addresses and e-mail addresses will not be printed, unless you ask! All fan artwork, letters, and e-mails submitted become the property of Dark Horse Comics.

We're going to kick it for you a little different this time, as all the notes for Vol. 24, except the first and the last one (which Lea and I, as otaku, each caught instantly), are from the translator of *Oh My Goddess!*, Dana Lewis. I have no hesitation to say she is one of the very top translators working in the field; moreover her position on the staff of *Newsweek Japan* means she is used to explaining aspects of Japanese life and events to the English-speaking world (and more often, vice-versa). You'll definitely be hearing more of her commentary in the future!

20.3: Vending machines out on a country road at night! It's unthinkable in America, where they'd get robbed or vandalised before you could say "Correct Change Only."

47.2: Mahjong is deep, way deep. Skuld's done good for a beginner, getting her *daisangen* hand with three melds (three-tile sets) of the elements, and Urd's *chinrootoo* of pure terminals isn't half bad. For that matter, Peorth's rare *shooshuushi* with three melds and pair of winds is simply, well, goddess-like. She can sextuple her points if she gets the right last tile. But house rules rule, and if you got to go out to win, you got to go out. *Menzenchin*, Takano? That cheap, low-point closed hand? Tough luck, gals. First call, first win. *Tsumo!* It's kind of hopeless trying to explain all the rules and the very specific hands that the gals get here. They're rare, high-point hands in any case, which Takano breaks with a very simple, basic hand that wins her the game before the goddesses get a chance to draw for the final tiles they need . . . So a chatty footnote like above hints at all that without getting into the arcane specifics...

61.1: In the original exchange, Belldandy starts to say, "I'm a m—" Takano guesses "monstrous" and "Megaton Punch" (Carl butts in here to remark that the same year this story came out, Fujishima's magazine-mate Kenichi Sonoda changed the name of his famous *doujinshi* series from *Chosen Ame* to *Megaton Punch*), whereas Keima guesses "Melandri"—after Marco Melandri, racer on the Team Movistar Honda Motor GP RC211V team—and "megalopa," the larval stage of a crab. Of course, what Bell is trying to say is *megami*, the Japanese word for goddess.

95.3: The exact Japanese proverb she uses here is *ja no michi ha hebi*, "no one knows a snake path better than a snake."

99.2: The toll collectors may hate her, but you have to give Chihiro credit. Toll roads are incredibly expensive in Japan, so expensive that it's often cheaper to take the train or even *fly* than to take a long road

trip. And if you bought those pre-paid *haika* (for "highway card") toll cards, you always wound up with a few hundred yen left on the card. Luckily for Keiichi and company, they did this trip before *haika* were abolished in March 2006. Too many forgeries!

100.4: Originally Keiichi says "Let's go!" in Japanese (*ikou!*) first in Japanese, then he repeats it in English written out phonetically in *katakana*. The use of his somewhat broken-sounding English here was meant to give a sense of Keiichi's over-the-top, forced jolliness to try to please/reassure Belldandy.

117.5: *"One of these Sundays I know I'll die . . ."* These lyrics to the song "Gloomy Sunday" were written by Hungarians Rezsō Seress and László Jávor in 1933. Diamanda Galas covered a version of it on her 1992 album *The Singer*. Urban legend has it that so many listeners committed suicide upon hearing it, that the song was once banned from the radio! The Japanese lyrics Keiichi and the gals endure here are a little different from English translations used by the likes of Billie Holiday. But urban legend aside, Seress did in fact kill himself in Budapest in 1968, jumping to his death after never penning another hit.

139.3: Skuld is thinking all the way back to the events of Vol. 14, *Queen Sayoko* (available in the old flopped edition of *OMG!*), where she misused her angel privileges, and her angel Noble Scarlet is returned to her egg until Skuld matures.

149.4: Mandrake root is traditional in magic, but this is possibly also a joke on Mandarake, the otaku (and *doujinshi*) superstore.

159: Fantastic! It's the return of the Mini-Goddesses! The subtitle for this fractured fairytale was in the original Japanese

Motto Ojamajo Doremi Online, being a combination of the computer RPG game *Ultima Online*, and the sequel to *Ojamajo Doremi*, the anime series currently showing on 4KidsTV under the title *Magical DoReMi*. The English version has been "ethnically cleansed," as I like to put it, meaning most it not all of its Japanese references and names have been changed to American-sounding English ones. The belief, I suppose, is that young audiences wouldn't enjoy a series if it contained a whole bunch of stuff about Japan.

Dear Dark Horse:

Rather than assault you with my commentary right-out, I would first like to thank your company for providing many years of fantastic comic titles. Dark Horse has admirably stayed abreast of non-traditional comics, keeping people like me satiated when looking to escape from heroes in spandex.

It has been a few years since I've been financially able to keep up with the *Oh My Goddess!* graphic novels. Now that I am looking to restart my collection again, I notice on your website that you have volumes 1-20 in an English-reading format, while newer volumes seem to have the Japanese-reading format. Are all of the new volumes going to have this feature? Will you eventually publish a Western format for those who wish to continue to read the comic this way?

While I appreciate being able to read your foreign titles, I find it irksome to read Japanese-format comics, as I am not familiar with, nor do I engage in, reading Japanese-language material. I've heard that this is an attempt to stay "true to the original," but if this is the case, why bother translating the title at all?

Please understand: I am grateful that your company provides American comics-readers with titles that we otherwise would not be able to enjoy. As a longtime comics collector I would rather read comics in the Western format the medium was introduced in, as opposed to re-adjusting to an irregular-reading format.

Thank you for your time,
Olivia Thompson
Allen, TX

First of all, thank you for your elegant letterhead. Not too many people have good taste in stationery these days. The issue you bring up is a very difficult one, and I imagine you're not the only longtime *OMG!* reader who was taken aback when we made the switch with Vol. 21. It is, literally, our new direction—there are no plans to publish any more volumes in the Western format. The change is too radical to be glossed over, but perhaps I can at least offer some explanations—admittedly from my perspective.

Even though my first six years as a manga editor were in the "traditional" format for manga in English (that is, flopping the artwork and packaging them to look like comic books), I have no trouble accepting the argument that manga artwork should not be flopped. Part of it comes from being into the Japanese editions of manga from an early age—so when it did eventually become the U.S. standard as well, not flopping wasn't such a strange idea.

As I've said before, most of the history of manga in English—and most of the history of *Oh My Goddess!* in English—has reached audiences in the form of flopped comic books. The unflopped, graphic-novel–only format is a relatively recent phenomenon when you take the long view. Considering how many people were exposed to great manga and great Japanese creators through that "traditional" format, flopping can

hardly be called wrong. But if you turn it around and see it from the perspective of that creator, it is the unflopped format that cannot be called wrong.

A comics artist simply draws a work to be read a certain way, and the Japanese themselves appreciate this when it comes to *their* editions of *our* comics. For example, the Japanese publisher Jive has done translated editions of Dark Horse's *Hellboy* and *Sin City*—as well as DC's *Batman: The Killing Joke* and Wildstorm's *The League of Extraordinary Gentlemen*—and their editions, although translated into Japanese, are printed left-to-right, just as the art was drawn originally by Mignola, Miller, Gibbons, and O'Neill. And so we now publish Kosuke Fujishima's work right-to-left, just as he drew it.

The unflopped *Oh My Goddess!* is, as you say, an attempt to stay true to the original. And it is never meant to be more than an "attempt," because, as you say again, the true original of *Oh My Goddess!* Vol. 24 is not this book, ISBN 1-59307-545-6, published in the fall of 2006 in North America by Dark Horse Comics, but a book designated ASIN 4063211363, published in the spring of 2002 by Kodansha, Ltd. I'm not trying to be flip—as it were—but just to point out that despite the fact our new editions of *Oh My Goddess!* look more like the Japanese originals, they are, of course, still different in many ways. Staying "true to the original" in this case means "original" in a limited yet important context—namely, presenting the artwork in its original orientation and layout.

Thank you for your gratitude at the titles we publish. There's no getting around the fact this transition is awkward for those who have been reading *Oh My Goddess!* for years. So please know that we are more grateful still that you and everyone else out there buys these graphic novels and reads them. As we will no doubt be over-

reminding people in the days ahead, as of November 2006, *OMG!* will become the longest-running manga series in American history. The larger readership it can reach now in its bookstore format is something Mr. Fujishima's manga inherently deserves, but it would never have gotten to this point without the support of those who read it as a flopped comic book. Please understand that I would never wish this change to be felt as a rebuke to them.

Dear Enchantress,

Greetings. After seeing various media containing Belldandy a while ago, it made me curious about the series, so I looked into it. Two years later, I'm hooked. The storylines are fun and exciting, the art is fantastic, and leaves me wondering, just what IS the number for Heaven? The art has come a long way since the series' inception, and it just keeps getting better. It's a welcomed, often light-hearted respite after growing up with serious series like *Macross*, *Gatchaman*, and recently *GitS SAC* . . . oops, showing my age now . . . lol.

I do have a question regarding the racing board Keiichi used. Is it a real design? If so, what is the manufacturer and model name/number? The only thing I could get translated out of a Japanese AMG Collection book, is that it's called a "racing-gu bodo," has a Tanaka 40cc, air-cooled, 2-stroke, 3.5hp engine, and it's part of the Japan National Championship. The current boards look more like go-karts with skateboard wheels than the sleek design in the manga. Any help would be appreciated.

Per volume 23's goading, I've included a sketch of a "different Goddess in Heaven" for your "Letters to the Enchantress" section. Sticking with the mythologial naming process, I called her Bastet . . . after the Egyptian Goddess of cats, protection, and fertility. I wish in no way possible to mean any disrespect to Fujishima Kosuke-san's

creation. It's quite the opposite. Imitation is definitely the sincerest form of flattery in this case. Bastet's pose was loosely taken off one of the OVA covers, and was drawn during a couple of meetings at work. Enjoy.

Cheers.

Sincerely,
E. Jay Zadina
Detroit, Michigan, USA

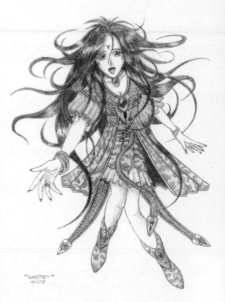
"BASTET"
6/06

You're not going to get away with trying to conceal your age by saying "lol," which no one who grew up with *Macross* (1982) and *Gatchaman* (1972!) should understand (*Gatchaman* was one of the very first gigs of a young Yoshitaka Amano, whose artbooks Dark Horse is proud to publish today). A lot of abbrieviations used on the Internet don't sound cool to me; "lol" puts me in mind of *lolling*, as in the look you have when your tongue hangs slack out of your mouth, and "rofl" makes me think of *rolfing*, as in throwing up, laughing at the carpet, a nod

from Misato, etc. However, I *do* like "o rly," because it takes an old sarcastic expression and uses abbrieviation to make it even more sarcastic—you're letting the other person know you're not sufficiently interested to bother typing all the letters in "really." So it's witty, the way many other bits of net speak aren't.

I really like *Ghost in the Shell: Stand Alone Complex*, but, as an older anime fan myself, it makes me realize one of the present limitations of the field. Namely, how many anime series do you know where all the main characters are old enough to vote? If you're into manga, you can find plenty of stories not only written for, but featuring, an older demographic. When it comes to live-action TV, it's the same. But when you consider anime, you come up short. TV anime hasn't yet developed the age diversification manga has achieved; shows like *GitS:SAC*, *Paranoia Agent*, and *Samurai Champloo* are doing a fine job, but we need more like them.

About the racing board: this is the point where I'm supposed to whip out some amazing erudition and research and tell you all about it, but I'm afraid, in the words of a TV show before my time, "I know nothing!" It's time to activate the gestalt-like hive mind of the "Enchantress" readership and ask for help. I'm man enough to admit when I need it. And as for your lovely drawing of Bastet, I don't think any apologies are necessary! Not only does she have the beneficent goddess expression, you've also stayed true to the series by giving her a wonderful costume design: flowing, ornate, and elegant. Thank you for sending this in!

And more fan art is right up ahead:

Dear Dark Horse Comics,

Hello fellow Oregonians! First, I would like to say thank you for bringing *Oh My Goddess!* to the States. I know I'm taking your time away but ever since I read *Childhood's End* (I happened to see it at the library and checked it out) I fell in love with manga! Of course my parents don't like it and don't think it's art. I saw something in the drawings that move me and no other manga can do what *Oh My Goddess!* does when I read it. Anyway, I made some fan art over the years and I finally have the courage to send them in. It doesn't matter to me if they get to be in the books or not, I just want to share them. I can't wait till the next issue of *Oh My Goddess!*.

A young fan :)

Kaitlyn Swain

P.S. I went to Japan this summer and I couldn't help but look at what's coming next and I feel ashamed. But I didn't read anything and only flipped around! Please forgive me . . . What really shocked me was how cheap manga is! It's only 250 yen!!! At the time it was less than $2.50 per book. Anyway, *Thank You!!!*

Finally, it's okay to print my email address. It's waternymphskuld@yahoo.com

Don't feel bad; I have to use a lot of reference books when I puzzle through the Japanese *OMG!* Again, I'm glad I have Dana Lewis on my side. I don't know why parents would object to *Oh My Goddess!* Is it because of the way Keima and Takano are portrayed?

Well, that's all for now. If you didn't see your letter here, don't despair—we have ones we haven't gotten to yet! But don't let this momentum die down, either; keep on sending in your thoughts in words and pictures!

—CGH

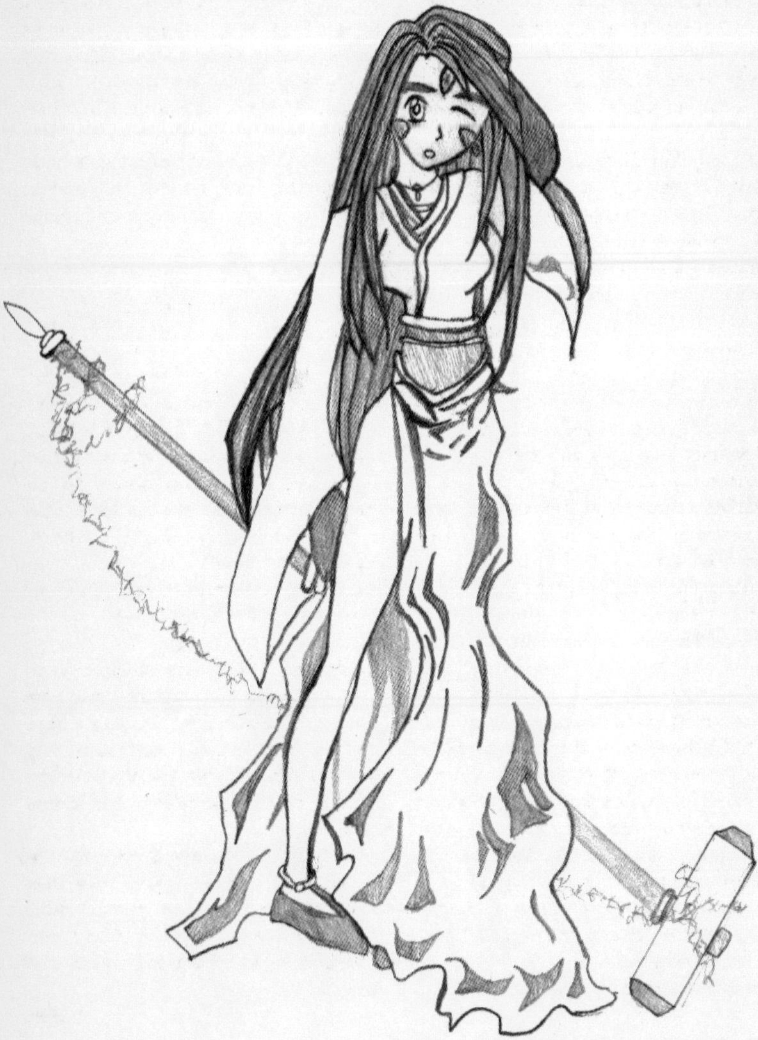
Kaitlyn Swarm
Age 15

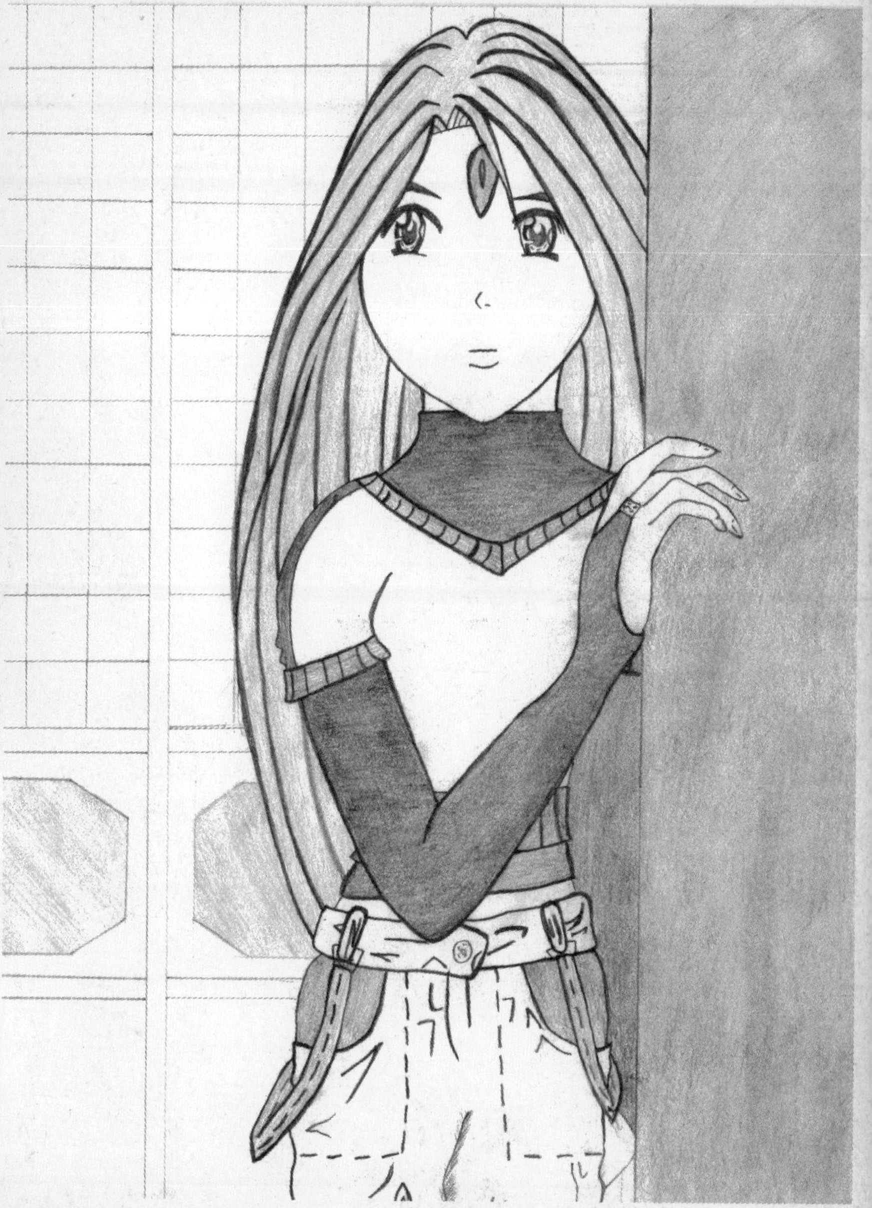

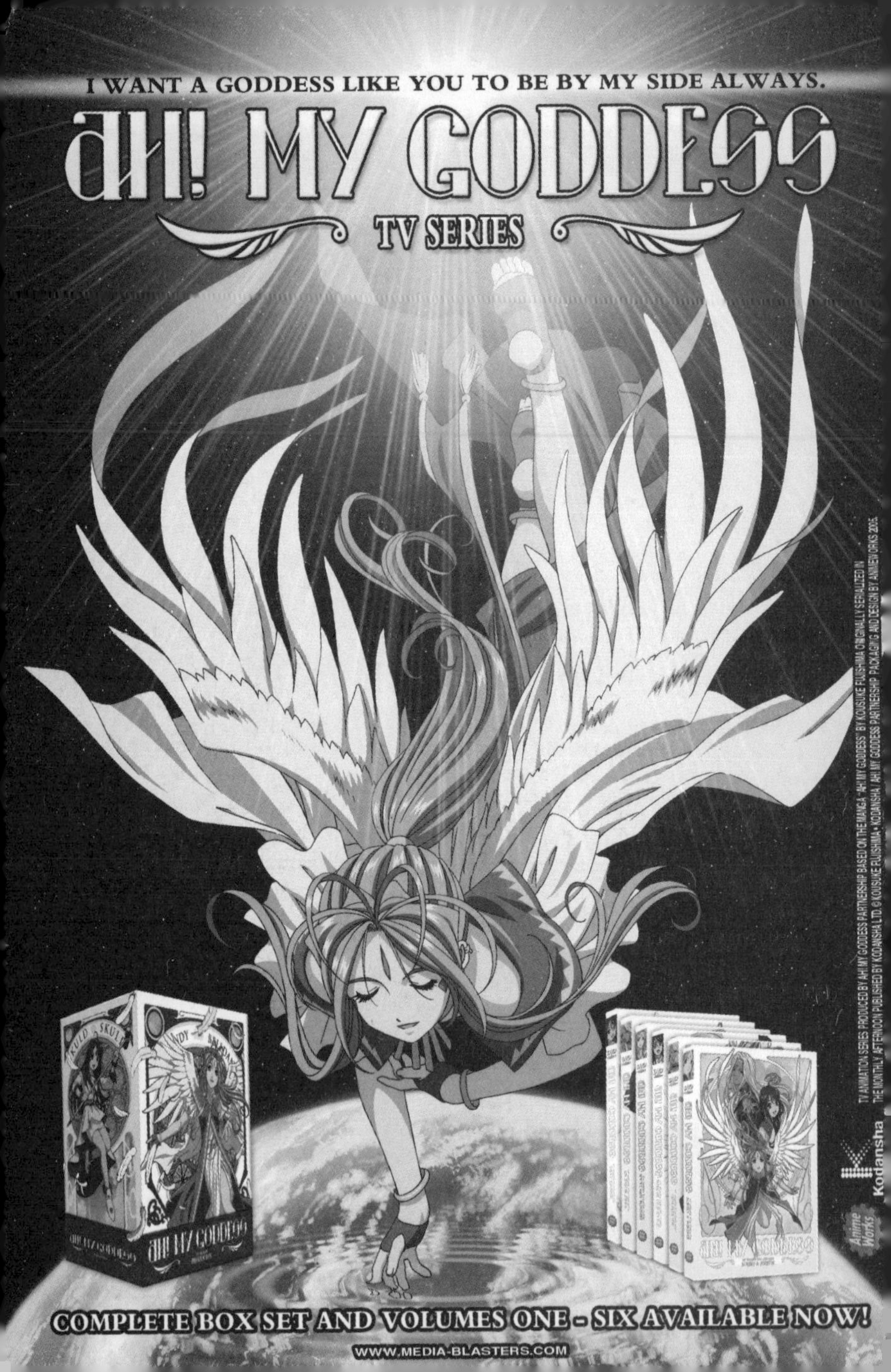

I WANT A GODDESS LIKE YOU TO BE BY MY SIDE ALWAYS.
AH! MY GODDESS
TV SERIES
TV ANIMATION SERIES PRODUCED BY AH! MY GODDESS PARTNERSHIP BASED ON THE MANGA "AH! MY GODDESS" BY KOUSUKE FUJISHIMA ORIGINALLY SERIALIZED IN THE MONTHLY AFTERNOON PUBLISHED BY KODANSHA LTD. © KOUSUKE FUJISHIMA • KODANSHA / AH! MY GODDESS PARTNERSHIP. PACKAGING AND DESIGN BY ANIMEWORKS 2005.
Kodansha
Anime Works
COMPLETE BOX SET AND VOLUMES ONE - SIX AVAILABLE NOW!
WWW.MEDIA-BLASTERS.COM

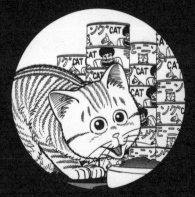

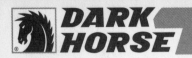
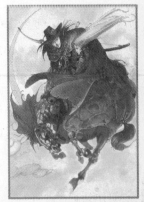
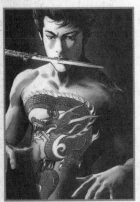
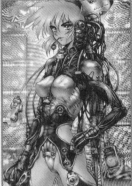
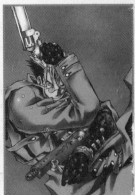

STOP! This is the back of the book!

This manga collection is translated into English, but arranged in right-to-left reading format to maintain the artwork's visual orientation as originally drawn and published in Japan. If you've never read comics this way before, take a look at the diagram below to give yourself an idea of how to go about it. Basically, you'll be starting in the upper right-hand corner, and will read each word balloon and panel moving right-to-left. It may take a little getting used to, but you should get the hang of it very quickly. Have fun! If this is the millionth manga you've read this way, never mind. ^_^

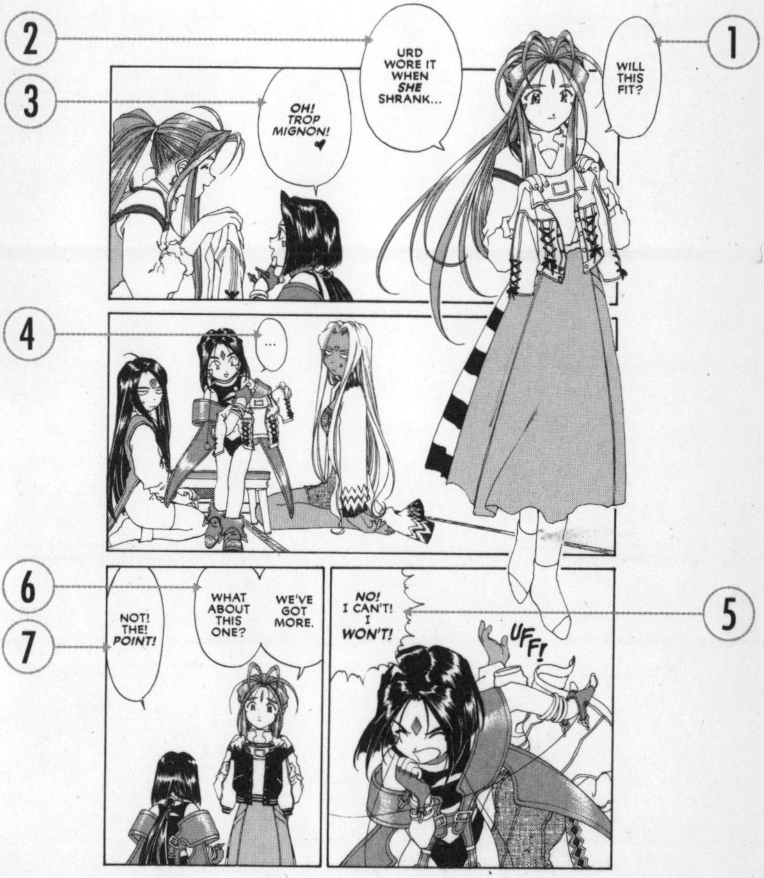
1
WILL THIS FIT?
2
URD WORE IT WHEN *SHE* SHRANK...
3
OH! TROP MIGNON!
4
...
5
NO! I CAN'T! I WON'T!
UFF!
6
WE'VE GOT MORE.
WHAT ABOUT THIS ONE?
7
NOT! THE! *POINT!*